QUEER JEWS

QUEER JEWS

EDITED BY DAVID SHNEER & CARYN AVIV

ROUTLEDGE NEW YORK LONDON

Published in 2002 by
Routledge
29 West 35th Street
New York, NY 10001

Published in Great Britain by
Routledge
11 New Fetter Lane
London EC4P 4EE

Copyright © 2002 by Routledge

Routledge is an imprint of the Taylor & Francis Group.

10 9 8 7 6 5 4 3 2 1

Library of Congress Cataloging-in-Publication Data

Queer Jews / edited by David Shneer and Caryn Aviv.
        p. cm.
    Includes index.
    ISBN 0-415-93166-5 — ISBN 0-415-93167-3 (pbk.)
        1. Jewish Gays—United States. 2. Homosexuality—Religious aspects—
Judaism. I. Shneer, David, 1972– II. Aviv, Caryn, 1969–

HQ75.16.U6 Q44 2002
305.9'0664—dc21

                                                        2002024902

The stone that the builders rejected has become the chief cornerstone.

—PSALMS 118:22

CONTENTS

PART III: INSTITUTIONS

PART IV: CULTURE

ACKNOWLEDGMENTS

CARYN AVIV:

David Shneer, my intellectual comrade and trusted gossipmonger extraordinaire. You made this book happen! Thanks to all the contributors who so thoughtfully and courageously shared their stories. Thank you to my parents and sister: Carol, Chuck, and Amy Abrams, and my extended biological family who have supported and encouraged me to integrate Judaism and queerness. Thanks to the amazing community of Congregation Sha'ar Zahav. To all the people who have listened and challenged: Susan Moser, Jen Petrucione, Andrea Jacobs, Jamil Khoury, Sharmila Rudrappa, Tamar Gershon, Ellie Knepler, Kelly Forsberg, Jill Saberman, Naomi Azriel, TJ Michels, Laura Moss, Judy Wittner, and Lynn Davidman. Finally, thanks to Ilene Kalish and Routledge for publishing this book.

DAVID SHNEER:

Caryn Aviv, whose mind works so much like mine, it's scary. Working on this book with you has been the biggest reward; the contributors whose essays I worked on were talented, motivated, and, for the most part, knew how to keep a deadline. Thank you for teaching me so much. Congregation Sha'ar Zahav's members have helped me see the possibilities of collective action. Thank you to: my biological family, especially Jim, Diane, and Robert Shneer, my chosen family, especially Elizabeth Mizrahi and Monica Vazirani; the Jewish studies community at the University of California, Berkeley; the faculty at University of Denver, especially Nancy Reichman, who supported and encouraged my efforts on this project; Michael Brotherton, my research assistant; Alan Karras, who has been my mentor in so many ways; our editors, Ilene Kalish and Ben McCanna for their fabulous editing, creative suggestions, and encouragement at every stage of the process; and to my husband, Gregg Drinkwater, for inspiring me in so many ways.

Thank you to all the queer Jews who have come before us and made this book possible.

PART I

MIXED BLESSINGS

If I am not for myself, who will be for me?
If I am only for myself, what am I?
If not now, when?   —HILLEL

Can't you see how important it is for us to love openly, without hiding and without guilt?   —LARRY KRAMER

There is no person who does not have his hour, and there is no thing without its place in the sun.   —BEN AZZAI,
               PIRKEI AVOT 4:3

If you are trying to transform a brutalized society into one where people can live in dignity and hope, you begin with the empowering of the most powerless. You build from the ground up.   —ADRIENNE RICH

America, I'm putting my queer shoulder to the wheel.
             —ALLEN GINSBERG

INTRODUCTION

HEEDING ISAIAH'S CALL

David Shneer and Caryn Aviv

WHO KNEW THAT King David and Jonathon were lovers? Or that a queer Jew coined the term *transvestite* and gave birth to the idea of gay rights? Or that the first openly gay Congressional representative was a Jew? Did you know that an official body of Jewish rabbis allowed its clergy to officiate at same-sex weddings way back in 1989? Or that there are over 25 lesbian, gay, bisexual, and transgender (LGBT) synagogues in North America? Did you know that there is a school in San Francisco for children of queer Jews? Peek inside a recent catalog of the clothing brand Abercrombie and Fitch and you will find a lesbian Jewish wedding as a centerpiece. What other minority within a minority is producing such campy erotica as *Kosher Meat* and *Friday the Rabbi Wore Lace*? Queer Jews are everywhere. Or at least so it seems. At the beginning of the twenty-first century, we are witnessing an increasingly visible, flourishing, and assertive queer Jewish culture.

Jews and queers are a vibrant part of American culture.[1] It is no accident that liberal Judaism is at the forefront of advancing queer empowerment and visibility, as the recent decision of the Central Conference of American Rabbis to sanction queer commitment ceremonies demonstrates. *Queer Jews* explores sexual, ethnic, and religious diversity and their interaction with each other. It challenges the very notion of margins and center, sameness and difference, normative and alternative, assimilation and separatism by looking at the experiences of those who complicate these categories. Queer people's demands for inclusion have created an unprecedented, often contentious dialogue about who we are and where we belong within Judaism and civil society. *Queer Jews* makes that conversation public and broadens our understanding of diverse sexualities, identities, families, and politics.

This anthology explores the changes and challenges wrought by queers active in North American and Israeli Jewish communities. How are we transforming culture from the outside in, and from the inside out? What have been the experiences of individual queer Jews who are re-creating our communities and culture to make room for ourselves? How have queer Jews altered the character of established Jewish organizations? What are the stories, struggles, and triumphs of queer Jews seeking to make Jewish communities more inclusive and to create new forms of Jewish life? What remains to be done, and how do queer Jews envision change for a better future?

Despite increasing visibility and influence in Jewish communities and American cultures, only a few major books by and about lesbian and gay Jews have been published in the United States. *Nice Jewish Girls* (1982, 1989) by Evelyn Beck and *Twice Blessed: On Being Lesbian, Gay, and Jewish* (1989) by Andy Rose and Christie Balka explore individual stories of identity and experience. These important works have been critical to the formation of individual identities, organizations, and loosely knit communities, as Rose and Balka contend in their essay here. Influenced by feminism, gay liberation, civil rights, and the anti-war movements of the 1960's and 1970s, these books are a decade old, written in an era when Jewish identity and sexual identity were still seen as opposing one another. Prior to the 1990s, identity politics did not necessarily include bisexuals, transgendered people, and queer youth. Rebecca Alpert's *Like Bread on the Seder Plate: Jewish Lesbians and the Transformation of Tradition* (1997), a more recent contribution, broke new ground by radically engaging Jewish text, tradition, and lesbian experience. Moshe Shokeid's *A Gay Synagogue in New York* (1995) offers a fascinating, sympathetic, and humane portrayal of the complex relationships and communities at Congregation Beth Simchat Torah in New York City. The recently published *Lesbian Rabbis: The First Generation* (2001) offers a timely and important look at how the first cohort of lesbian rabbis is changing the face of Jewish authority, and transforming Judaism from within. The anthology describes in their own words how these courageous women grapple with their own identities and struggles as teachers, spiritual leaders, and role models, as well as how Jewish communities are responding to the increasing visibility of queers in positions of power.

Queer Jews introduces the voices of the "post-Stonewall generation," who have come of age in a visible, empowered, unapologetically queer culture, as well as of older queer Jews who paved the way and struggled to establish institutions and lives of integrity with little community support and few role models. Combining memoir, sociology, historical analysis, and stories from the front lines, this anthology represents a next step—a portrait of change, progress, and the road ahead. *Queer Jews* also documents the internal debates over the price of inclusion and asks difficult questions about sameness and difference—tensions that spark the creative vitality queer Jews bring to Jewish families, institutions, and politics.

These tensions make queer Jews uniquely situated to lead Jewish communities toward change, rather than waiting for those communities to act. Judith Light, an actor and outspoken straight ally of LGBT politics, suggests this is the role of queer communities within American culture more generally. "It is up to you to take charge of the national dialogue and to be *proactive*, not reactive. . . . You are uniquely positioned to create the shift in the wind that fire-fighters pray for and that our world desperately now needs."[2] We take this argument one step further. As Jews, our tradition admonishes us to be a "light unto nations" (Isaiah 42:6, 49:6). In other words, we have a moral responsibility, borne out of our history, to lead cultural change, pursue peace, and seek justice. Thus we are "twice blessed," not just out of pride, but also because of our dual task to lead rather than follow *as Jews and queers*, to change rather than accept the status quo. The authors here demonstrate the variety of ways queer Jews have taken up this charge.

Almost all the essays in this book explore the conflict between the desire to integrate into established Jewish communities, changing them from within, and the comforts of creating and maintaining "separate" spaces for queer Jews. Jonathan Krasner explores questions around separatism and assimilationism by suggesting that, as "queer" and "Jewish" come to inform one another, queer Jews are not as compelled to seek out separate space, but instead create space within established institutions. David Shneer, in his essay on queering Jewish education, shows how one LGBT synagogue is broadening its image away from metaphors of safety and refuge from oppression toward language of progressive leadership within the wider Jewish community, making it an attractive congregation for liberal straight people. Moreover, most LGBT synagogues are affiliated with broader Jewish movements, receive money from general sources of Jewish funding, and are engaged in outreach to diverse populations that include heterosexuals. And more personally, Lesléa Newman struggles with the tension of wanting to be a queer Jewish writer while not having her identity limit how her work is read or how it is marketed. We remain convinced that queer Jews should not be separatists, since as Jews, they always hold a connection to the broader community and historical memory.

Likewise, incremental reform and adaptation, reworking existing social, political, and religious structures, rather than revolutionizing or overturning them, are clearly the preeminent political strategies of this historical moment. The late 1960s marked a transition from an activism that sought equal access to the law, modeling itself on the civil rights movement, to Gay Liberation, which fundamentally criticized basic civil institutions such as marriage and family. Our authors suggest that now those institutions that Gay Liberation rejected have becomes sites of radical social transformation.

Ten years ago, the writers of *Twice Blessed* were still embroiled in trying to reconcile their multiple identities and were less concerned with the "privileges" of heterosexuality, like marriage, family, and other institutions of Jewish culture; now the voices in *Queer Jews* claim those institutions as our entitlements. In 1990, queer Jews were grateful for the honor of being *allowed* to be Reform rabbis; in the new millennium, queer Jews demand nothing less than the *right* to be married by those rabbis.

As radically transformative as this newfound entitlement might seem, there is a noticeable lack of more radical calls for broad structural change that link the concerns of queer Jews to other social justice movements, which so inspired previous anthologies by and about LGBT Jews. As Justin Suran has argued, "sex, identity, and political solidarity were configured not only in relation to established institutions . . . but within the contingent parameters of the surrounding political culture."[3] Gay Liberation used anti-war movements and their tactics to crystallize an oppositional gay identity and gay politics. But these movements no longer have the political salience they once had. Witness the shift from anti-war and anti-authority protests against oppression and disenfranchisement to contemporary gay pride parades, which, although a commemoration of the 1969 Greenwich Village riots at the Stonewall bar, have been accused of losing their connection to political activism, and celebrating the gentrification and commodification of queer culture.[4] This suggests on the one hand a decline in political activism and radical critique that motivated earlier generations, but on the other hand, signals the emergence of wider queer power and queer entitlement, Jewish and non-Jewish alike. While the work to achieve equity and justice is by no means done, and as diverse and fractious as queer communities sometimes are, we have already achieved some critical and tangible social and public policy goals. It is no accident that queer visibility has become so unremarkable that Andrew Sullivan, a conservative gay Catholic writer, had the audacity to publish in the *New York Times* that "the culture wars are officially over."[5] Although we may disagree with his assessment, Sullivan highlights the sense that things *are* shifting and changing in quite profound ways, within the absence of more radical street protests and movements. This book reveals how queer Jews are trying to craft their lives in a post-revolutionary, potentially post–"culture wars" moment.

From all edges of Jewish society, queer Jews are accommodating and adapting to Jewish organizations while pushing them to acknowledge our presence with dignity and respect. The number of groups that have the words lesbian, gay, bisexual, transgendered, queer, or questioning and "Jew" in the title is increasing exponentially.[6] There are more synagogues, gay Jewish *havurot* (community groups), queer Jewish conferences, and other means of creating social spaces for ourselves. Moreover, there are now institutions that cater to a diverse queer Jewish community and reflect generational concerns, including parenting classes, educational and camping programs for queer families. There are now groups for gay Jewish youth, aging queer Jews, same-sex interfaith couples, Jews-by-choice, and more recently queer Orthodox Jews.

Steve Greenberg, an openly gay Orthodox rabbi, seeks to carve a space for himself within Jewish tradition, known as *halacha*, to be gay and Jewish, and in his essay, describes his journey from alienation and fear to pride and redemptive joy with his religious community. Jill Nagle explores her attempts to create affirming, sex-positive queer Jewish spaces and images of God while simultaneously participating in traditional communal venues. Joanne Cohen urges her fellow queers to join mainstream institutions and change them from within as Jewish activists while simultaneously warning of the pitfalls of modeling our relationships on traditional marriage and monogamy. And Eve Sicular brings queerness to the study of Jewish culture by tracing a history of queer motifs in Yiddish film, and examining her own interest in carving out territory for herself within the hallowed halls of Yiddish culture. A notable exception to the transformation-through-integration model comes from Jo Hirschmann and Elizabeth Wilson, two radical organizers who embrace the idea of fundamental social change in their work and remind us that, from the beginning of the gay rights movement, divergent political strategies for effecting change have co-existed. They show how these two political strategies—reform and revolution—inform one another in the constitution of queer Jewish politics. Their essay is one of the few voices in this volume speaking to a broad-based, Marxist-inspired revolutionary platform that hearkens back to the anti-war, anti-imperial activism of the original liberation movements, but does so within a specifically and visibly Jewish framework.

We think the shift from calling ourselves "gay/lesbian" to the more ambiguous, postmodern, and potentially homogenizing "queer" suggests a further reexamination of our collective identities, specifically around issues of class privilege and gender identity. Joan Nestle, in a response to our introduction, argues that as the movement has changed, more margins have been established, with potentially dire consequences. In particular, she decries the class privilege of many middle-class queer Jews, and calls for the return to more radical, less assimilationist, and less particularistic strategies that ignore the links between the struggles of queers and Jews with other oppressed communities around the world.

Queer Jewish politics has now begun to include transgender people who undermine the very notion of masculine and feminine, male and female, sameness and difference. Transgender Jews have particularly complicated relationships with the binary mode of Jewish gender/sexual politics, as Jaron Kanegson's essay about being a nontraditionally gendered Hebrew school teacher reveals. Moreover, transgender people, by their very questioning of established gender/sex constructions, are inherently liberationist in their calls, not to be included in accepted ideas of gender and sex, but to overturn them, as TJ Michels and Ali Cannon discuss in their essay about praying at the Western Wall. The issues and challenges transgender Jews face to make homes for themselves are only just beginning to emerge, and by examining them, we see the special place transgender people have in bringing together the transformation of existing structures and the simultaneous liberation from them.[7]

These trends of expanding the parameters of both Jewish and queer identity seem to be dialectical. The sheer centrifugal forces at work here, the ever more specific identifiers, suggest that queer Jews as an organized group of people are finding differences within themselves. The solidarity wrought by external oppression of a homophobic and heterosexist society is no longer enough to define these groups. We hope the diversity of voices included in this anthology demonstrates that queer Jews define ourselves with increasing multiplicity and innovation. We are also redefining what it means to be Jewish, and what the role of Jewish institutions are and should be.

Established Jewish institutions, rather than queer Jews, are now the ones having to react. Some (but not nearly enough) are taking steps toward actively expanding their scope and programming to include this new constituency. (Of course LGBT Jews have always existed, but only in the past five years have issues specific to queer Jews become part of the agenda for some progressive mainstream Jewish institutions.) In the San Francisco Bay Area especially, queer Jewish issues are "hot" among mainstream Jewish organizations. For example, Jewish Family and Children's Services and the Jewish Federation have each recently introduced a gay and lesbian task force. The Israel Center conducts LGBT outreach efforts that include a "Journey of Pride" Israel–San Francisco travel exchange program. The largest conservative synagogue of San Francisco has a gay and lesbian committee and has recently elected a gay man as president of the congregation. Even the Koret Foundation, a well-known philanthropic foundation, is in on the action, granting the gay and lesbian synagogue of San Francisco a three-year grant to "improve its member services." In the center of American progressivism, the independent organizing of queer Jews is affecting change in mainstream organizations.

In other metropolitan areas, queer Jews themselves are now using mainstream organizations as incubators to develop their own institutions. In Boston, the very mainstream Jewish Federation is a primary funder of a queer education and advocacy program. The Chicago Jewish Federation hired a full-time staff member to develop programming and raise awareness around queer issues. And in Toronto, through the activism of queer Jews, the mainstream Jewish Foundation of UJA-Toronto recently established a Jewish Gay and Lesbian Fund. We envision a time in the not too distant future when every major metropolitan Jewish community will have a queer Jewish resources program to offer programming, education, and technical assistance to actively end homophobia within Jewish communities and affirm the presence and importance of queers.

But are there unanticipated consequences of the growing inclusion and mainstreaming of queers in Jewish organizations? According to Krasner, Temple Israel, the large Reform synagogue of Boston, founded a gay and lesbian *havurah*. But in the past few years, its programming has dropped off, because "queers have become so integrated into the temple that there does not seem to be any 'motivation' to create their own programming." We wonder if separate queer Jewish space might dissolve as other Jewish organizations open their doors to queer Jews. Is this what happens to the original institutions designed as a place of refuge when oppressed groups become integrated?

Although the most visible changes are in communal institutions, the most significant reforms are happening within our personal institutions—our families and intimate relationships. Queer Jews are at the forefront of redefining conceptions of family, relationships, and community, and our reformation project has forced everyone to reexamine what it means to be a family. From the calls for legalized marriage, which are finally being heard in some rabbinic institutions, to bringing children into our families, queer Jews have forced Jews and Americans (and apparently Abercrombie and Fitch) alike to reexamine their "family values." For queer Jews, creating family involves both adopting the dominant social paradigms—a monogamous couple with two kids and a picket fence—and moving beyond the mere assimilation of bourgeois definitions by undermining the assumption that family is determined solely via biology. Queer Jews' calls for integration are *transformative* rather than *assimilationist*.

The construction of queer families means making conscious, deliberate choices all along the life course. Queers have irrevocably changed the meaning and discourse of marriage and reproduction, affecting Jewish communities on multiple levels.[8] Most queers marry, because they *want to*, because they want to express their love publicly to their communities, because they want to bring two lives into one. Most queers do not marry for tax breaks or to make parents happy. For Rabbi Jane Litman, queer marriage transformed the institution from what she saw as an empty ritual into a spiritual practice, which has changed her understanding of commitment and *kavannah* (intention). As Inbal Kashtan remarks, most non-queers who attend queer weddings remark on the intensity, the spirituality, and the "authenticity" of the ceremony, something often lacking at heterosexual ceremonies. At the same time, this drive toward *transformative integration*, for which our authors overwhelmingly advocate, has pushed liberationists, whose voices are not as prevalent in this anthology, to challenge the new hegemony of queer marriage as ideal by reasserting an anti-marriage platform.[9] Joan Nestle suggests that queers are simply adopting social forms already being vacated by the mainstream, while Ruti Kadish is critical of queer Jews' occasionally blind adoption of gender constructs and suggests that perhaps we need a bit more "revolution" in the constitution of a queer Jewish politics and identity.

Who is considered part of a queer family? We have clearly devised creative means to making families that involve reproduction, adoption, extended families, friends, and lovers. To our contributors and many other queers in America today, families include long-term partners, ex-lovers, close friends, friends' children, non-custodial co-parents, "in-laws," and assorted pets. oscar wolfman shows that Jews are redefining the balance between biological relationships and chosen association in defining family, because for non-converts, Jewish identity is derived directly from biological family, while queer identity is derived from non-biological social networks. Looking at queer Canadian Jews that push their biological families to broaden their own self-definitions, wolfman concludes that if biological families force them to choose, queer Jews overwhelmingly pick their chosen family over their biological ones. Thus, both out of necessity as well as choice, the desire for family on one's own terms cannot be doubted.

Although some have argued that queers are merely conforming to models provided by heterosexual society, most of the contributors to this volume see their acts of creating family as nothing less than a critique of the limitations imposed by the heterosexual family model. Marla Brettschneider, for example, provides a detailed investigation into the classist and racist assumptions that shape the adoption world, and how her own dyke family negotiated these institutionalized structures. She argues that class and race inequalities intimately shape the practices and decisions of adoption agencies, as well as the strategies queers use to "work the system" and create the families they want.

Not surprisingly, lesbians are leading the way in remaking Jewish families. Certainly men's biological limitations to reproduce pose a barrier that may hinder bringing children into their families. We also wonder whether differences between "gay male cultures" and "lesbian cultures" might further reinforce the gender gap of queer parenting, although the boundaries between these cultures are often porous, as TJ Michels and Ali Cannon demonstrate. In no way do we want to suggest that biology is destiny for dykes, as many lesbians happily choose child-free lives. But the old joke about dyke second dates (bring the U-haul!) suggests that gender ideologies of maternal nurturing have as much to do with women's centrality in queer Jewish family-making as does their historical Jewish imperative to, as Kadish calls it, "reproduce" the nation.

Jewish women also have created community and culture because of their multiple oppressions, as women and as queers, as Joan Nestle articulates. Lesbian Jews have participated in over 30 years of feminist and lesbian/queer social movements to develop a collective identity based on resistance to dominant power, whether the object of critique is the state, "patriarchy," heterosexism, and/or antisemitism.[10] In this volume, we are witnessing a creative melding of queer, Jewish, feminist practices to renegotiate and reshape patriarchal traditions into ones that honor queer people's own visions of intimacy, family, and community. For example, Hadar Dubowsky describes the emotionally meaningful rituals she developed with her partner and close friends to celebrate her pregnancy and birth.

Although profound change is happening at the levels of community and family construction, and as much as positive representations of queer Jews begin to pervade North American culture, we are disturbed and saddened by the persistent themes of pain, stigma, fear, and alienation that many of our contributors describe. Not everything is as rosy, exciting, and transformative as we would like. The pain of exclusion and isolation from communities continues to exact a huge price for both the individuals themselves and for their communities/families of origin. Sandi Dubowski discusses Jewish communal reactions to his film, *Trembling Before G-d*, a documentary about the pain and ostracism that queer Orthodox people face in their daily lives from their closest community and from the religion that shapes their lives. But it is not just Orthodox queers who face difficult choices every day. Queer Jews of all ages, from budding rabbinic students to radical dykes (and in a few cases, where those are the same thing), continue to struggle with the closet, coming out, coping with fear, and enduring stigmatization despite the increasing acceptance and visibility of queers in American popular cultures. Joanne Cohen weaves a compelling autobiographical narrative about the price of coming out in adolescence, and the pressures many queer Jews face from what she dubs the "*naches* machine," a mechanism that socializes Jews to follow a heteronormative family structure. *Anonymous*[11] writes of the perils navigating the closet through rabbinical school, and the dynamic tension of multiple, but *non-integrated* identities. These painful stories are all the more glaring, because queer Jews seem to have moved from an era of exclusion to one of inclusion. Now that many queer Jews have the option of coming out in all aspects of their lives, and of integrating their multiple identities, those who feel they can't seem all the more excluded, oppressed, and frustrated.

What you won't find in this book is as interesting as what you will. Stories about AIDS, one of the main issues that inspired queer organizing in the 1980s and early 1990s, are little heard in this anthology. In fact, the only place AIDS is found in the volume is in representations of AIDS within American culture. Jyl Lynn Felman writes about the dual Jewish and queer cultural contexts of Mel Brooks' *The Producers* and Tony Kushner's pathbreaking play *Angels in America*, which explores questions of multiple, at times conflicting and at times well integrated, identities through the lens of AIDS. Although we recognize that AIDS is still one of the most deadly diseases, as a cultural marker for queer identity, at least among Jews, it seems to have lost its salience.

WHO ARE WE AND WHY DID WE EDIT THIS BOOK?

Our passion for undertaking this project comes from our own multiple interests as academics and activists, as queers and Jews. We both feel an important connection to and passion for enriching American Jewish culture and politics through our personal and professional lives. The book itself serves as both a cultural text and a further development in a queer Jewish historical memory. It's cliché, but queer Jews are people of the book, and we are acutely aware that the cultural resources that celebrate our lives are so few. These essays acknowledge and pay homage to queer predecessors who were writing their way out of a silent vacuum of images and stories, and who occupy a pivotal space in our collective memory. Writing our own literature, history, poetry, and autobiography has been critical to our survival as queers (just as it has been for wider communities of Jews), and has contributed to queer Jewish communities and the emergence of a reading public. Now queer Jews can go to a bookshelf and find several books of fiction, autobiography, poetry, and other material that can help foster the queer Jewish imagined community and further the development of historical memory. We hope that this book is part of the continuing move to action over reaction, toward self-definition, and to an era when queers, Jews, and queer Jews, who have always been social, cultural, and political leaders, will be able to lead *as queers, as Jews, and as queer Jews,* for we are the ones heeding Isaiah's call.

NOTES

1. We define *queer* broadly to include lesbians, gay men, bisexuals, and transgendered people. We also use the adjective "queer" rather than "same-sex" or "same-gender" when describing commitment ceremonies, relationships, and so on, in order to avoid the dichotomy of sameness and difference.

2. Judith Light, "Light Years Ahead," speech given at the California Alliance for Pride and Equity, February 24, 2001, *Hero 15*, April 2001, pp. 64–5.

3. Justin Suran, "Coming Out Against the War: Antimilitarism and the Politicization of Homosexuality in the Era of Vietnam," *American Quarterly*, 53(3), September 2001, pp. 452–488.

4. The establishment of the "gay pride parade" was in fact *intended* to be apolitical. The goal was gay solidarity and community-building in an era when integrationists and revolutionists could not see eye to eye. In the 1970s, Gay Pride rallies and Gay Freedom Day parades commemorating Stonewall took the place of anti-war demonstrations as the principal venue for public expressions of gay solidarity. Unity over politicized dissent was the goal. See Suran, "Coming Out."

5. Andrew Sullivan, "Life After Wartime," *New York Times Magazine*, March 18, 2001, p. 15. This article specifically refers to the increasing presence of queers on television, in movies, and in other forms of popular culture.

6. Hardly any organization uses the term *queer* in its title, which suggests that the utilitarian use for such a term (to be as all-encompassing as possible) has not yet overridden the negative connotation many people have of the word "queer." Only on the margins of the margins, among radical queer Jewish groups, or within casual community vernacular, is the word "queer" an acceptable identifier. We deliberately chose our title of this anthology to advocate for more visibility and increased acceptance of the word "queer," which reflects the experiences and political leanings of post-Stonewall LGBT people.

7. Several Jews are at the forefront of transgender politics, theory, and culture. Leslie Feinberg, Jack Halberstam, and Kate Bornstein, all writers, activists, and performance artists, are just a few of the many transgender Jews who work tirelessly on behalf of the burgeoning transgender rights movement. Mark Leno, a queer Jew and member of the San Francisco Board of Supervisors, recently proposed the first ordinance to pass in the United States which provides equal access to medical care specific to transgendered people. In Israel, the transgender Jew pop diva, Dana International, was recieved by the Israeli Parliament as a national hero after she became the first transgender person to win the Eurovision music contest in 1998.

8. For example, the *Jewish Bulletin of Northern California* recently covered the roiling debate on same-sex marriages and how many rabbis, particularly in the Conservative movement, craft their personal stances towards officiating these ceremonies. Alexandra J. Wall, "Conservative Rabbis Here Defy Movement's Ban on Gay Nuptials," *Jewish Bulletin of Northern California*, March 30, 2001.

9. There are rabbis at the most left-leaning rabbinic institution, the Reconstructionist Rabbinic College, who question whether queer Jews should struggle for equal access

to marriage or should overturn the institution, a call that echoes the 1960s liberationists debates about rejecting the military rather than aspiring to join it.

10. See *The Tribe of Dina: A Jewish Women's Anthology,* Melanie Kay Kantrowitz and Irena Klepfisz, eds. (Boston: Beacon Press, 1989); *Yours in Struggle: Three Feminist Perspectives on Anti-Semitism and Racism,* Minnie Bruce Pratt, Barbara Smith, and Elly Bulkin, eds. (Ithaca: Firebrand, 1988); *Lesbiot: Israeli Lesbians Talk About Sexuality, Feminism, Judaism, and Their Lives,* Tracey Moore, ed. (New York: Cassell, 1999).

11. This author requested anonymity because he currently attends an institution that forbids out queers from enrolling in its rabbinical school.

REFERENCES

Alpert, Rebecca. *Like Bread on the Seder Plate: Jewish Lesbians and the Transformation of Tradition.* New York: Columbia University Press, 1998.

Alpert, Rebecca, Levi Elwell, Sue, Edelson, Shirley (eds.) *Lesbian Rabbis: The First Generation.* New Brunswick, NJ: Rutgers University Press, 2001.

Balka, Christie and Rose, Andy (eds.) *Twice Blessed: On Being Lesbian, Gay, and Jewish.* Boston: Beacon Press, 1991.

Beck, Evelyn Torton (ed). *Nice Jewish Girls: A Lesbian Anthology.* Boston: Beacon Press, 1989.

Shokeid, Moshe. *A Gay Synagogue in New York.* New York: Columbia University Press, 1995.

CREATING OUR HISTORIES

A LOOK BACK AT *TWICE BLESSED*

Avi Rose and Christie Balka

IN 1986, THE two of us first began to discuss the idea of putting together an anthology about lesbian and gay Jews, and in late 1989, *Twice Blessed: On Being Lesbian or Gay and Jewish* saw its way into print. Neither of us had ever edited or written a book before, and our desire to do so reflected some amount of chutzpah and naïveté. But it also reflected the need we, and many others, experienced at that time: to write our lives into visibility. We knew dozens of articulate lesbian or gay Jews around the country, many of whom regarded themselves as writers and/or activists. But at that time, very few of us had found contexts in which we could write candidly about our lives. We were making things up as we went along and had very little space in which to imagine what Jewish lesbian and gay cultures, religious practices, and politics might look like. *Twice Blessed* promised to give us that space.

Fortunately, some had gone before us. We were particularly inspired and influenced by *Nice Jewish Girls: A Lesbian Anthology* (1982), edited by Evelyn Torton Beck, and by *The Tribe of Dina: Jewish Women's Anthology* (1989), edited by Melanie Kaye/Kantrowitz and Irena Klepfisz. Adrienne Rich,

Harvey Fierstein, Lesléa Newman, and others had begun to write poetry, plays, and stories that reflected lesbian and gay Jewish experience. However, there still were so many experiences not expressed, stories not yet told, and issues unexplored.

For the book that became *Twice Blessed*, we aimed to create something that reflected the authentic lives of lesbian and gay men while remaining accessible to liberal/moderate heterosexual Jews. We envisioned a book that referenced familiar Jewish themes (for example, text, history, family, assimilation) and did not distance people with unfamiliar jargon. Strategically, we did not want to speak only to ourselves. We believed strongly in the importance of reaching beyond comfort and familiarity in order to have a more substantial effect on the Jewish community. We therefore sought to reach people in the liberal center of the Jewish community, to gain new allies in working toward fundamental change in attitudes and policies.

While we wanted to create a book that would challenge people, we also wanted to put together, as a remarkable number of lesbians and gay men expressed to us, "something I can give my parents for Chanukah." As we spoke with individuals and groups of lesbian and gay Jews around the country, people asked us to create something that articulated our strengths and our struggles, our hopes for an inclusive and pluralistic Jewish community. More than anything else, we wanted *Twice Blessed* to be an instrument that would break through the persistent invisibility that so many of us still experienced.

This issue of in/visibility, of speaking what had been previously unspoken or even unspeakable, gave powerful impetus to the book. In speaking up as lesbian and gay Jews, we saw ourselves as drawing from gay liberation and other social change movements of the 1960s and 1970s. These movements validated the importance of women, people of color, and others speaking their truths, rather than remaining hidden amid the dominant culture's assumptions. For some of the book's contributors, speaking out so publicly would clearly have repercussions in their personal and professional lives. We were prepared to accommodate writers who would need to use pseudonyms to protect themselves; ultimately, only two people chose to do so.

We considered many options for the book's title and ultimately chose *Twice Blessed*, suggested with some irony by Rebecca Alpert. The title explicitly affirms a new historical option for lesbian and gay Jews: to be all of who we are and openly claim those identities as a blessing. This option moves us beyond the traditional dilemma of bifurcated selves: to remain closeted within the Jewish community or to leave it altogether. Even today, the title serves as an affirmation that resonates powerfully.

While we actively sought to include a broad range of lesbian and gay Jewish experience and succeeded to some extent, we fell short of full inclusion. Reflecting our own historical era, we did not explicitly include the experiences of bisexual Jews and did not recognize the experiences of self-identified transgendered Jews. *Twice Blessed* came together just as queer theory was emerging in academic and activist circles and before the new wave of queer activism in the 1990s. At the time we edited our book, we understood well that sexual orientation and identity interacts with other identities, including those based on gender, race, class, and physical ability. However, we did not yet understand the extent to which identity is not fixed. We have learned during the past decade that sexual identity—and gender identity— are much more fluid than we had previously imagined. Bisexual and transgendered Jews have played a leading role in these cultural and political explorations, and we are happy to see these perspectives more fully featured in *Queer Jews*.

When *Twice Blessed* came out, it was received with a great deal of warmth and interest. Some of the positive response was predictable. There were well-attended readings at gay and lesbian synagogues and community bookstores, lesbian and gay Jews bought copies to give to families and friends, and we received effusive thanks from progressive rabbis and Jewish communal workers. What was less predictable was the number of Jewish family members who gave the book to their lesbian and gay children or siblings as an expression of love and support. We were heartened by the number of rabbis and other Jewish communal professionals who placed *Twice Blessed* prominently in their offices as a visible sign to congregants and community members that it would be safe to talk about these issues. The book also garnered a number of glowing reviews, though some reviewers were quizzical about why some lesbian and gay Jews were so persistently interested in being part of a community that had rejected us. Notably absent from the response to *Twice Blessed* were invitations from Jewish bookstores or book fairs; there seemed to be little interest.

The most gratifying response, which still happens occasionally, is from lesbian and gay Jews who tell us that the book helped them to feel good about themselves, to come out, and to communicate about issues that had been hard for them to articulate. Some described literally carrying the book around with them for support. Overall our experience was certainly far different from that of the editor and writers of *Nice Jewish Girls*, who in the early 1980s were met with a writ of excommunication from an Orthodox rabbinical council. There was still plenty of hostility and ignorance in the Jewish community, but some of the vehement resistance had already begun to shift.

We did a considerable amount of speaking around the country in the years following the book's publication. While we were usually well-received in person, we both noticed that it was too easy with mainstream Jewish audiences in particular to avoid subjects that were challenging and uncomfortable, and that we had to consciously choose not to do so. Anything about sex itself was difficult to discuss, and it was particularly difficult to engage people in any discussion about bisexuality. We also perceived persistent denial and mistaken assumptions about the existence and need for acceptance of GLBT youth. While people thought that it was fine for us (adults, and someone else's children) to be lesbian and gay, they did not think it could prove to be true for their own adolescent (and younger) children. Many people also implied that it would be tragic for a child to grow to learn that they were not heterosexual. We learned the importance of challenging the assumption that it would be easier for children to be heterosexual. We suggested instead that what is easier for children is to know that our love, value, and support of them does not depend on any particular sexual orientation.

Shortly after *Twice Blessed* was published, several major new developments heralded significant progress in the mainstream Jewish community. In May 1990, the Conservative movement's Rabbinical Assembly passed its first-ever gay-related resolution, which not only condemned anti-gay violence and supported basic lesbian and gay civil rights, but also affirmed that lesbian and gay Jews are welcome in Conservative congregations. This was a milestone resolution for the Conservative movement, which, if not entirely embraced in practice, set an important precedent for change. The following month, the Reform movement's Central Conference of American Rabbis passed its landmark resolution acknowledging the presence of lesbians and gay men in the Reform rabbinate. In 1993, the Federation of Reconstructionist Congregations and Havurot, which had in 1974 enacted a policy supporting lesbian and gay rabbinic ordination, passed a new resolution welcoming lesbians and gay men into its congregations. It also urged those congregations to address heterosexist biases and affirmed the right of Reconstructionist rabbis to perform same-gender commitment ceremonies. These resolutions were all preceded by years of people working tirelessly and courageously behind the scenes.

These policy shifts signaled an important sea change in Jewish institutional life. At that point, most Jews had grown beyond an initial stage of acknowledging the actual existence of lesbian and gay Jews. Even if they "didn't approve" of queer Jews, it had become nearly impossible to deny our growing visibility and presence. The early 1990s resolutions signified that many Jews had also moved further past a secondary stage of "tolerance," characterized by the notion that lesbians and gay men are entitled to basic civil rights and anti-violence protections and have the right to be left alone. Being "left alone" was certainly better than overt persecution, but still implied separateness, marginalization, and isolation. Now, the community was finally moving toward the possibility of inclusion, a far more formidable challenge.

Twice Blessed was in many ways the product of 1980s "identity politics." We believed that, firmly grounded in our own identities and communities, we would be better able to work in coalition with members of other communities, such as lesbians and gay men of color or of other religious denominations. While we still believe in this principle, we have both been frustrated by some of the persistent inwardness we have witnessed during the past decade.

It is very powerful for those of us who are GLBT Jews to find each other and create community, but that is not the absolute end in itself. We can slide into becoming overly comfortable and complacent, never getting around to making connections with others across lines of difference. We understand that especially when you have a history of "otherness" and strong feelings of not belonging, it can be hard to venture back out once you have found a home that affirms all of who you are. Yet true liberation does not lie within a cocoon; it lies in having a strong sense of self and building strong and loving communities from which you can venture out into the world with confidence and spirit. We both hope that GLBT Jews will become increasingly involved in forging coalitions, needed now more than ever when Bush era policies threaten to increase racial and economic inequality while dismantling civil rights protections for queers, women, and people of color.

Our own lives reflect the effort to create community. While still on opposite sides of the country, both of us find ourselves involved in congregations that are not predominantly GLBT, but hold a strong commitment to GLBT inclusion and to the pursuit of social justice in general. Christie's congregation in Philadelphia was founded right around the time that *Twice Blessed* was published, and the book supported a congregation-wide educational process that continues to this day. On Yom Kippur morning in 1999, Adina Abramowitz, one of *Twice Blessed*'s contributors, called allies of lesbian and gay Jews up to the front of the synagogue for an *aliyah*. Christie watched in astonishment as fully one-third of the congregation—nearly 200 people—walked to the front of the room to be honored in this way. While there is no cause for complacency in the face of many battles yet to be fought and won, it is wonderful to experience the matter-of-fact comfort and unreserved embracing of GLBT issues by many heterosexuals. The strength of these relationships and alliances bodes well for the future.

As we were finishing *Twice Blessed* in 1989, we thought long and hard about our visions for the future. We wrote an epilogue to begin to outline an action agenda primarily for the Jewish community, but also for the lesbian and gay community. While the 1990s saw major steps forward in visibility and inclusion in many arenas, the overall agenda still remains largely unfinished. Consider the following excerpts:

> Jewish youth will grow up knowing that heterosexuality is not assumed for them: that they will be supported by parents, educators, and others in growing to know their individual sexual orientations; and that their realizations and choices will be affirmed and celebrated.

> "Jewish family" will be understood to include the full range of Jewish families that actually exist. This new understanding will not be considered as a social problem or as a sign of the demise of the family, but rather as a sign of the diversity and vitality of Jewish family life.

> Communal acknowledgment and support will exist for the large number of ways lesbian and gay Jews will choose to consecrate and celebrate their relationships . . .

> Jewish communities will evolve new traditions of observance and celebration of gay and lesbian experience. . . . The two weeks in the spring during which Parshat Ahare Mot and Parshat Kedoshim are read from the Torah will become focal times of the year to raise awareness regarding gay and lesbian issues.

> Jewish communities and individuals will be willing to undertake a thorough, honest, and ongoing examination of the many ways that homophobia and sexism have affected our perceptions and behavior . . .

> That the lesbian and gay community embrace our full religious, cultural, racial, and ethnic diversity; that our cultural events in particular strive to reflect who we are as a whole . . .

That we (lesbians and gay men) learn from Jewish experience about the crucial importance of preserving and transmitting history. Perhaps we need to set up "Coming Out Schools" and other educational opportunities parallel to Hebrew schools . . .

We have accomplished much during the past decade, and the work to achieve these dreams is ongoing. Many of us have long hoped for a book that would more fully explore new developments in queer Jewish identity, activism, and creativity. We are excited that *Queer Jews* furthers those conversations, stories, and demands for change. We hope that this book will play a strong role in bringing our dreams—and new dreams—to fruition.

HOW A "LIBERATIONIST" FEM UNDERSTANDS BEING A QUEER JEW,

OR HOW TAKING ADVICE FROM A PROPHET, EVEN A JEWISH ONE, IS (UN)TRANSFORMATIVE

Joan Nestle

DAVID AND CARYN asked me to respond to this book's introduction, "Heeding Isaiah's Call." True to their characterization of the "liberationist" generation, I now have the pleasure of reaction. Since I was raised as a secular Jew by a widowed working transgressive mother, I was not exactly clear what Isaiah's call was, and so I searched out my English major's needed copy of the Old Testament and turned to the Book of the man in question. I read my way through the old text, pausing at lines like "obey with a will,/and you shall eat the best that the earth yields/but if you refuse and rebel, locust beans shall be your only food," sundry references to the damned of Sodom and Gomorrah, the misfortunes to be visited upon "the children of foreigners who have poured into the city," and the mincing women of Zion who "shall have their hair stripped from their foreheads." Along with the usual demands for absolute loyalty to the God of the Old Testament were beautiful longings for peace, the protection of orphans and the weak, and other invocations for social justice. As in so many places in the Old Testament, the absurd, the cruel was cheek to cheek with the metaphoric poetry of more humane possibilities. And then I came to the passages that the editors chose as their trope: "I have formed you, and appointed you to be a light to all peoples, a beacon for all nations, to open eyes that are blind, to bring captives out of prison." (Isaiah, 42, 6–7)

Here is where my queerness comes in. I am a 61-year-old woman who came out in the working-class fem-butch bars of Greenwich Village in the late 1950s. I was a freak even before I was queer or I should say that being queer in those days was the same as being a freak. Yes, we lived on the margins, and yes, I learned from other liberation struggles that I too had the right to be fully human in the eyes of the state. But I learned other things on those margins as well: that the pain of historical calamities is widely spread, that the resulting wisdoms are not the possession of any one people, that for me being queer means the opposite of elitism and exceptionalisms. All my historical understandings both as a Jew and as a queer tell me that this labeling of ourselves as "the chosen people" is an unforgivable arrogance. It is an essentialism of the worst kind—ancient words used to separate us from others and even worse, to give us the mantle of a special knowledge that makes us the most fit for the social leadership of others. To be a Jew is to have a history and to be a queer is to have another history, just as to be a woman is to have yet another history. And yes, there is much suffering and oppression in all those histories, but respect to these stories of oppression and resistance is best paid when we refuse to separate them out of the full human story of resistance. We can speak as socially concerned queer Jews without invoking the tribalistic, isolationist language of the Old Testament.

I learned what being a Jew meant when my bookkeeper mother told me of the Triangle Shirtwaist Fire and the coldness of the bosses, when she told me of the wonders of the life of Paul Robeson and why he was considered an enemy of this state. I learned that being a Jew means you use the compassionate lessons of your own history to join in the social struggles of others. Jews and queers are not the only ones in the center of American culture—so are African Americans, for example. Again I invoke the margins where I learned the danger of sweeping generalizations, like the statement by the executive director of the American Jewish Committee, David Harris, who stated, "If the US does not go [to the UN Conference on Racism] nobody in the Jewish community will shed a tear" (*New York Times*, August 28, 2001). These are the kinds of statements that assume so much on the part of so many, and in doing so, erase moments of others' history.

Now I want to say an even harder thing. I do not think, as an old queer

Jew, that calling something transformative makes it so. Perhaps something else is happening. Some queer Jews want to marry, some want to have children, some want to be rabbis—all of this I see as desires, not actions necessarily resulting in progressive social change. Desire itself is a wonderful life force, particularly when a group of people have been told their desires are criminal or a heresy, and these new hard-fought-for freedoms would be wonders enough. But gay Jewish people marrying to form monogamous consuming pairs and have children in all the ways we now can is not in itself a transformative act. It is the fulfillment of desires. A transformative act would be to change the very nature of marriage—for example, a bonding between three people or two couples, or to do away with marriage all together. I also suspect we have won on some of these social battlegrounds because the social institutions we think we are changing are losing their social power in our world. In other words, we are moving into already vacated, or soon to be, social and cultural forms. The voices that now most invoke the sacred values of the family are conservative ones. I realize that one of the pressures of our Jewish history is the oft-stated demand that the Jewish people must replenish the losses of the Holocaust. Again, queer Jews fulfilling this need is a powerful statement, but not one that necessarily changes the emphasis on procreation for religious purposes. My deep fear is that we will not really know who or what is transforming whom. The editors initially had some difficulty getting writings about sex for the anthology. I think about the many Jewish queer voices who are writing erotica. I think about the Jewish queer women involved in sex work, about the turn-of-the-century history of Jewish prostitutes in New York—and again my queer self says when the desires are for greater domesticity, other margins get established.

The loudest voices in the queer movement are located in the center of things. Therefore, conservative voices become more authoritative. Despite Andrew Sullivan's bold (and incorrect) claim that "the cultural wars are over," museums in New York are fighting for their cultural independence under accusations of catering to obscene artists. Abstinence has gained greater popularity in the schools, while sex education courses are under constant attack. A Christian conservative reigns as the nation's attorney general and more recently, an Ohio man was sentenced to seven years in prison for thinking "bad thoughts about children and writing them down in his private journal." (Bob Herbert, *New York Times*, August 4, 2001) In fact, Andrew Sullivan himself is a perfect example of what can happen when a conservative voice constructs a reality from the center of things, which then becomes the generalized view of a people's social position. For Sullivan, who seldom says anything that questions prevailing hierarchies, the pages of the *New York Times Magazine* have opened. Anyone with the experience of the margins deep within herself would know this is how assimilation works, particularly assimilationism based on class respectability. Let us not participate in this closing of our eyes because some of our desires are being met. And if we do, let us be honest about it.

No matter how often some younger, post-Stonewall Jewish queers say we are living in a post-revolutionary time, this queer old woman will not be convinced. I know that all over this world, queers are fighting for human rights, that older Jewish queers, along with others, are desperately concerned with social issues such as health care and decent housing, that funding for queer, atheistic, socialistic artists is at an all time low. Now I look to the struggles for the rights of indigenous peoples, for the fair sharing of the world's resources, for the global recognition of the rights of women to be autonomous citizens of the world. No prophet calls us to these concerns. In my mind's eye, I still see the flaming young women throwing themselves out of the burning factory building, the young Paul Robeson being chased out of Peekskill by bat-wielding bigots, the two young Jewish women, captured freedom fighters from the Warsaw ghetto, facing their deaths, hands intertwined. In their honor, at their insistence, in the name of secular, sexual freedom, I join with all the others of the world, who are demanding that systems of power bend to human needs.

At 61, I still write and publish sex stories that some call pornography, and I still think that the center of things is a very uninteresting place to be, especially for a queer Jew.

PART II
IDENTITY

I had a way of life inside me and I wanted it with a want that was twisting me. —Zora Neale Hurston

[T]hose who had read queer books, had dreamed queer dreams, had committed queer acts, and even been queer in the face of death. . . . People out of the ordinary, people with a vision, have ever been considered queer, yet they have often been the sanest in a crazy world. —Emma Goldman

There were people who were different like me inside. We could see our reflections in the faces of those who sat in this circle. I looked around. It was hard to say who was a woman, who was a man. Their faces radiated a different kind of beauty than I'd grown up seeing celebrated on television or in magazines. It's a beauty one isn't born with, but must fight to construct at great sacrifice.
—Leslie Feinberg

I change myself, I change the world. —Gloria Anzaldúa

Hello, gorgeous. —Barbra Streisand

THE WRITING ON THE WALL

ON BEING A JEWISH WRITER,

A LESBIAN WRITER,

AND A JEWISH LESBIAN WRITER

Lesléa Newman

THE JEWISH WRITER

I'LL BEGIN BY telling a story. Years ago I taught creative writing to a group of high school girls who had come from all over the country to Mt. Holyoke College to brush up on their math (creative writing was an afternoon "fun" activity, along with arts and crafts, and sports). The first night of orientation, a speaker was brought in to lead us in some "touchy-feely" exercises that would explore the notion of diversity. For many students, this was their first experience away from home, their first time sharing a dorm room with a stranger, their first time interacting closely with people of different races, ethnic and economic groups.

"So," our fearless leader smiled, "we are all different, yet we have many things in common. I'd like to divide you up as follows: people who like strawberry ice cream go to the left side of the room; people who like chocolate chip, go to the right." The room divided itself along fairly even lines. Our leader beamed. "Now," she said, "those of you with inny bellybuttons go the left side of the room; outies go to the right." There was some giggling and lifting of T-shirts as the room reshuffled itself: some people stayed right where they were, others made a beeline for the other side of the room. Our instructor pointed this out to us, then said for our final grouping that people of color were to go to one side of the room and white people were to go to the other.

The atmosphere of the room changed immediately. No one giggled now. Students and faculty moved along sober lines, some to the right side of the room, others to the left. A small group of people gathered in the middle of the room. I was among this group. We were a little nervous, a little embarrassed, and a little proud. Our facilitator was more than a little puzzled. "And who might you be?" she asked with a forced smile. No one spoke for a minute. Then a voice emerged that I recognized as mine. "We are the Jews," I heard myself say over the fierce pounding of my heart.

I remembered this experience years later, after attending an afternoon panel in New York City about being a writer and a Jew. Of course there were as many opinions on the subject as there were panelists and audience members in the room. One man who sat on the panel announced that he was a Jew, but staunchly denied that he was white. Another panelist, a Jewish woman formerly married to a black man snorted: "I dare you to walk into a roomful of black people and make that statement." An audience member who identified as "someone who is not Jewish" asked the panel why everyone had to put themselves into a "neat little identity box," for weren't we all basically the same? And yet another panelist raised the question, what is Jewish literature? Writing done by any Jew, whether it has Jewish content or not? Or any writing with Jewish content, whether or not it is written by a Jew? And of course, it could be argued that the above questions are really moot until we backtrack and tackle that age-old dilemma: Who is a Jew? Several of the panelists had been cast out of the fold for various reasons (marrying out of the faith or race, choosing a spouse of the same gender), but as one panelist said, "You can become a Jew, but you can never unbecome one." And of course she underlined her statement by giving the example of Nazi Germany. If they came to take the Jews away, she—an out Jewish lesbian—would be rounded up right beside the very people who denounced her.

The panel was a typical Jewish event in that it raised more questions than it answered (plus there was coffee and cake). I left with my head spinning, wondering where, and indeed if, I fit in. I certainly feel like a Jewish writer. When in doubt, it is easy to reassure myself by browsing the titles of my own short stories and poems, "One Shabbos Evening," "The Babka Sisters," "Bashert." So by birth and subject matter, I am a Jewish writer. Nonetheless, the event exposed my own insecurities about whether or not I am "Jewish enough" to claim the title "Jewish writer." I grew up as a "holiday Jew." We celebrated Chanukah and Passover and observed Rosh Hashanah and Yom Kippur. I did not have a Bat Mitzvah. I cannot read Hebrew. I do not light Shabbos candles. Yet being Jewish is at the very core of my being. When my spouse and I had a commitment ceremony, I insisted that it be officiated by a rabbi. I needed to stand under a *huppa*, and it was vital to me that my spouse break a glass. (All right, I'll admit it: I even had to have the musicians play "Sunrise, Sunset.") And one of the ongoing dilemmas in my relationship is where our final resting place will be. I have a palpable desire to be buried in a Jewish cemetery, where my beloved is not allowed. And I cannot bear the thought of spending eternity in her family plot, where my headstone would be the only one with Hebrew letters for miles and miles around.

The rabbi in the local temple (which I attend at most once a year) affectionately calls me a "nostalgic Jew." I long for connection to Jewish culture, yet I reject much of the patriarchal aspects of my religion as vehemently as it rejects me. But does eating hammentaschen, listening to Klezmer music, and writing stories with characters in them named Zelda and Irving give me the right to claim a Jewish voice? What about a writer I know whose father is a German Jew and whose mother is Irish Catholic, and who grew up in Boise, Idaho, where there was no Jewish culture? Can he claim a Jewish voice? Then there's another writer I know who was raised to believe she was Catholic (her house had the biggest Christmas tree on the block). When she was 17, her grandfather died and at the funeral, which was conducted all in Hebrew, she found out she was Jewish. Can she claim a Jewish voice? How about the Jewish writer who was born a Southern Baptist, converted when she got married, and shucked her identity when she got divorced. Can one "unbecome" Jewish? Then there's the Jewish writer who writes children's Christmas stories. Can we all have such different experiences and all still be considered Jewish writers?

Even though I consider myself a Jewish writer, all of my questions aside, I have rarely been acknowledged as part of the Jewish literary canon, which is odd since I claim both Jewish heritage and Jewish themes in my work. I attribute my exclusion from the Jewish canon to a second label I claim: I am a lesbian.

THE LESBIAN WRITER

"How do you feel about being described as 'one of America's most respected lesbian writers?'" a reporter recently asked me. I told her I felt flattered and proud. She paused before asking what she really wanted to know. "But wouldn't you rather be known simply as one of America's most respected writers?" The label "lesbian writer" has been a mixed blessing since it was bestowed upon me 15 years ago with the publication of my first novel, *Good Enough to Eat*, the story of a Jewish woman struggling with food, body image, and sexuality who eventually embraces her attraction to women. The benefit of owning the label "lesbian writer" is that it makes it easy for me to find a particular audience and for a particular audience to find me.

The disadvantage of being pegged a lesbian author is that it limits my audience to a subset of the general reading population. I think that my work appeals to a broad audience (lesbians, feminists, Jews, gay men, academics, allies to the gay community, liberals, and so on.). However, publishers and booksellers see my work being of interest to only a small niche of people who fall into the same group as myself (Jewish lesbians). Where I see ever-expanding markets because of my many labels, the publishing world only see a small segment of the reading population.

Ironically, an editor for a mainstream New York press told me that his heterosexual authors were extremely jealous of his gay and lesbian authors, because they have a defined audience. He likened publishing a novel without a targeted market to "throwing a rose petal into the Grand Canyon." It instantly disappears. Gay and lesbian books are like the tortoise, not the hare. They do not make a big splash and then vanish like the average mainstream book, whose shelf life, it is said, is somewhere between milk and yogurt. Gay and lesbian books stay in print for years. They get reviewed in dozens of gay and lesbian publications. Slow and steady wins the race. Our books persevere.

Perhaps. But I am still not sure whether being named a lesbian writer has been a blessing or a curse. Carrying that label means, more often than not, my books are relegated to the gay and lesbian section of any given bookstore, which in and of itself is a blessing and a curse—a blessing because readers looking for a lesbian book will know exactly where to find it; a curse because consumers browsing the general fiction section in search of a wonderful read will not have the good fortune to stumble upon a lesbian book.

More to the point, what is a lesbian book anyway? Is it any book with a lesbian character and/or lesbian content? If this were the case, Wally Lamb's novels, *She's Come Undone* and *I Know This Much Is True*, would have been labeled lesbian books and probably would not have been chosen for Oprah's book club. Is a lesbian book any book written by a lesbian? If that were true, Dorothy Allison's *Bastard Out of Carolina* would have been labeled a lesbian book and probably would not have been a National Book Award Finalist. (That same year, there was an enormous controversy over the fact that *Bastard Out of Carolina* was not chosen as a finalist for the Lambda Literary Awards, which recognize gay and lesbian literature.)

It seems to me that the criterion for lesbian literature is based upon the sexual orientation of the author of a book and the book's content, similar to the way that I would define Jewish literature. But even if I define it that way, my audience does not. I wrote a children's book entitled *Matzo Ball Moon*, which is a Passover story about a young girl and her mother, father, grandmother, and brother. It's a Jewish children's book and has no lesbian content whatsoever (unless of course you count the fact that my name is on the cover). Yet despite this heterosexual family constellation, a publication called *The Lesbian Review of Books* chose to review the book favorably and at length (in fact, the review contained many more words than the book itself). I can only conclude that the book was chosen for review because I am an out lesbian writer.

The publishing industry uses a double standard when it tries to define these labels. Several years ago, a prominent mainstream publication ran an interview with Jane Hamilton discussing her novel titled *The Short History of a Prince* about a gay man. The headline of the interview read "Jane Hamilton: A Kinship with Society's Outcasts." Recently this same publication ran a review of my latest book, *Girls Will Be Girls*, a book of short stories about lesbians. The reviewer stated, "With the amount of lesbian 'in' references, the author writes for a specific audience." When heterosexual writers employ gay characters, they are considered inclusive and liberal; when lesbians write about lesbian characters, we are accused of being narrow-minded and unable or unwilling to write to a "universal audience" about "universal themes." To borrow a phrase from Maya Angelou who said, "I speak to the black experience, but I am always talking about the human condition," I speak out of the specific experience of being a lesbian about the universal experience of being human.

Yet, just like my insecurities over my self-proclaimed identity as a Jewish writer, I remain firmly ambivalent about the label "lesbian writer." First, there is the ever-nagging insecurity, am I "lesbian" enough. I am a high femme, and nine times out of ten, because I wear makeup and skirts, it is assumed, by straight people and queers alike, that I am heterosexual. I didn't come out until I was 27, and I do have a heterosexual past. And if I didn't have my own issues about my many labels, in response to *Matzo Ball Moon*, I received what I call my one and only anti-fan letter from two lesbians and their daughter who were horrified that I'd written a book about a heterosexual family. They ended their letter with a plea: "Please don't stop writing books like *Heather Has Two Mommies*." Lesbian trumps Jewish even if there are no lesbians in the story.

Sometimes I ask myself if I still have some internalized homophobia I have yet to work out. In other words, am I ashamed to belong to a club so proud to have me as a member? Am I simply being ungrateful? After all, there are many, many writers who have yet to be published at all and who would gladly change places with me in a heartbeat. I know I have been extremely lucky. I have also worked very, very hard and like most writers, I want and feel I deserve as wide an audience as possible. The elusive crossover book continues to evade most lesbian writers, especially those of us who insist upon writing openly and honestly about our lives. The books that do cross over into the mainstream have the lesbian content wrung out of them until what's usually left is the proverbial great aunt who lives with "a friend" far, far away from the central characters and action.

THE JEWISH LESBIAN WRITER

It is interesting to me that I am usually labeled "lesbian writer Lesléa Newman" but rarely labeled "Jewish writer Lesléa Newman" (and rarer still labeled "Jewish lesbian writer Lesléa Newman"). Yet much of my work is written in what I consider my native language, "Yinglish," or English sprinkled with Yiddish words and phrases and written in Yiddish syntax and sentence structure. In fact, three of my books contain so many Yiddish words and phrases, I had to include a Yiddish glossary for the "Yiddish-impaired" reader. Yet when I go into a bookstore to look for my novels and short story collections, I don't find them in the general fiction section along with other Jewish fiction writers such as Cynthia Ozick and Grace Paley. My books are banished to the lesbian and gay section, along with other Jewish and Gentile gay and lesbian writers. This bothers me, not because I am ashamed of being a lesbian. I am as proud of being a lesbian as I am of being a Jew.

What upsets me is that only readers who have already made up their minds that they want to read a book about or by a lesbian or gay man will come across my titles, as opposed to readers who are merely browsing the fiction section in search of a good read (note: I have never seen a Jewish fiction section in a mainstream bookstore). If my heterosexual colleagues are trying to make their mark in the vastness of the Grand Canyon, I sometimes feel like publishers and booksellers have put me in a tiny corner of the world, where only those looking for me will find me. This is the readers' loss as well as mine. Identity politics is a mixed blessing. It is empowering for people to find gay and lesbian sections and Jewish nonfiction sections in their local independent or chain bookstores. And it means that part of my audience knows exactly where to find me. But a fiction browser, or even a person looking for Jewish books, won't find me.

Ultimately, I'm first and foremost a writer, one who creates stories from experience and imagination. Some books, like *Matzo Ball Moon*, come directly from my experience of having a Jewish childhood. (Did I also have a lesbian childhood? That's another essay.)

Other books, like *Heather Has Two Mommies*, come from the experience of living in a lesbian community among many two-mommy households. Is *Heather Has Two Mommies* a Jewish book? There's nothing in the book that says the characters are Jewish, but there's nothing in the book that says they aren't Jewish, either. And the book's author is certainly Jewish.

So what's a Jewish lesbian writer to do? Keep writing as openly and honestly as she can about whatever she pleases. And wait for the day when books are judged solely by what lies between their covers, not by what labels their authors claim or are given, and certainly not by what their authors do between other covers, which is really nobody's business but their own.

A GAY ORTHODOX RABBI

Steve Greenberg

I AM A gay Orthodox rabbi. I resisted this identity for a long time. Throughout the years when I struggled with it, many would counsel me to reject one or the other of these inert elements. An Orthodox friend urged me not to barter my soul for sexual freedom. Gay friends told me to get out of the Orthodox world, which they saw as intractable, cruel, and oppressive. Sometimes I wondered if I was fooling myself to think that with enough effort, oxygen and hydrogen might be squeezed into water. Thankfully, there were moments when a glimmer of possibility shone through, when I could begin to see how the Torah might be read differently, how Talmudic passages could add up in other than damning ways. It took me five years to do the research for a book that argues just this, that gay Orthodox Jews are neither wanton sinners nor obsessive compulsives for seeking both the intimate love of partner and the love of God. The intellectual and religious justification was just the last act of the story. The two journeys, religious and sexual, while not simultaneous, are intertwined over a period of almost twenty years. Becoming a gay Orthodox rabbi has taken more than half my life.

The Orthodox story is easier to plot. I adopted traditional Jewish observance in my teens. An Orthodox rabbi had introduced me to the vertical and horizontal Jewish worlds. What I call the vertical world is the world of intellect and meaning. Studying Talmud felt like a feast of the mind with scholars of six different centuries invited to share in the conversation. The horizontal world was the world shaped by the people of the little Orthodox community that welcomed me in. Overcoming my parents' resistance, I excitedly escaped Columbus, Ohio, to attend Yeshiva University in New York City.

Becoming Orthodox was a spiritual and intellectual conversion accomplished over two years. Despite the conflict between my gay life and my Orthodox Jewish life trajectories, most of the important coming-out episodes of my life were within the embrace of my newfound Orthodox community. The stories below come together, to mark a set of passages. The genesis of my gay identity begins with a childhood seder.

PASSOVER 1966

In my youth, we attended the seders of my mother's elder cousin, a survivor of Bergen-Belsen whom we affectionately called Uncle Al. Al had a gentle high-pitched voice peppered with a raspy Yiddish accent. His singsong chant of the Haggadah was done without much attention to the written text. He had learned the Haggadah *baal-pe*, by heart, sometime after a number was burned into his skin. In the camps where forgetfulness was blessing, only those things burned into memory or onto flesh remained. Aunt Charlotte had married my Uncle Al after a divorce. She and Uncle Al raised her two children, but had none of their own.

Those seders were of course occasions of great excitement for us children. Lots of unusual relatives that we saw only on Pesach, joined to my family by this single cousin of my mother, sat around an endless table, anxious and ready for the festivities to begin. Aunt Charlotte shuttled back and forth from the dining room to the huge kitchen, which, by seder time, was bursting with incredible quantities of unbelievably delicious glatt kosher food. While the kitchen always seemed ready to explode, the dining room was always more patient. Not so attentive, but respectful, guests were annually washed in the eerie angelic drone of Uncle Al's recitation of the haggadah, as if in Bergen-Belsen with his eyes closed.

An unspoken honor was given to this hardened man with a high-pitched voice. Never was a word uttered to anyone about what happened to him during the war. Charlotte protected him from the nightmares and migraines he would experience if he dared to talk about those times. Surrounded by his wife's family, there was a quiet sadness about him. While the noise and activity rose and fell throughout the seder, Al held court at two seders, separated by his weighted brow and joined by his high-pitched *galitsianer* Yiddish singsong.

Every year, Aunt Charlotte's sister brought her two kids. Jackie and Terry were late teens during my early adolescence and they were both stunningly beautiful. Only years later in recounting the occasions of those seders did my mother bring back the memory of those two beautiful youths.

On a visit home to Columbus, Ohio, we sat around and reminisced about those wonderful seders. At some point in the stories, my mother interjected that Marc, my younger brother by three years, could not keep his eyes off of Jackie. She had remembered with a glint, a motherly smile, that her son of nine or ten years had an obvious crush on Jackie, the teenage beauty. What she did not notice, and what I did not remember until that very moment, was that I was transfixed every year by Terry. The conscious memories of Uncle Al and Aunt Charlotte, the smells, the tastes, the sounds of Uncle Al's high-pitched chanting had all along protected a dangerous and exciting secret. I looked forward to those seders every year, in no small measure, to feast my eyes on Terry's dark eyes, his fluid manner, his dimpled smile. No one at the table could have noticed how I spent half the night staring at him. Terry's specific presence in my mind was covered by the absence of a category in which to place him. Instead, the erotics of his presence simply mixed in with everything like a fragrant spice.

A few years later, the arrival of the hormonal hurricane left me completely dumbfounded. Just when my body should have fulfilled social expectations, it began to transgress them. I had no physical response to girls. When other boys became enraptured by girls, I found my rapture in learning Torah. I was thrilled by the sprawling rabbinic arguments, the imaginative plays on words, and the demand for meaning everywhere. *Negiah*, the prohibition to embrace, kiss, or even touch girls until marriage, was my saving grace. The premarital sexual restraint of the tradition was a perfect mask, not only to the world, but to myself.

My years in yeshiva were spectacular, in some measure because they were so intensely fueled by a totally denied sexuality. There were many *bachurim* (students) in the yeshiva whose intense and passionate learning was energized with repressed sexual energy. For me, the environment deflected sexual energy and generated it as well. The male spirit and energy I felt in yeshiva was both nourishing and frustrating. I do not know if I was alone among my companions or not. From those early years, I remember no signs by which I could have clearly read my gayness or anyone else's. I only know that I was plagued with stomach aches almost every morning. — *A wise man*

In 1976, beset with an increased awareness of my attraction to a fellow yeshiva student, I visited a sage, Rav Eliashuv, who lives in one of the most secluded right-wing Orthodox communities in Jerusalem. He was old and in failing health, but still taking visitors who daily waited in an anteroom for hours for the privilege of speaking with him for a few minutes. Speaking in Hebrew, I told him what, at the time, I felt was the truth: "Master, I am attracted to both men and women. What shall I do?" He responded, "My dear one, my friend, then you have twice the power of love. Use it carefully." I was stunned. I sat in silence for a moment, waiting for more. "Is that all?" I asked. He smiled and said, "That is all. There is nothing more to say."

Rav Eliashuv's words calmed me, permitting me to forget temporarily the awful tensions that would eventually overtake me. His trust and support buoyed me above my fears. I thought that as a bisexual I could have a wider and richer emotional life and perhaps even a deeper spiritual life than is common—and still marry and have a family.

For a long while I felt a self-acceptance that carried me confidently into rabbinical school. I began rabbinical training with great excitement and a sense of promise. At the center of my motivations were those powerful rabbinic traditions that had bowled me over in my early adolescence. I wanted more than anything else to learn and to teach Torah in its full depth and breadth. I finished rabbinical school, still dating women and carefully avoiding any physical expression, and took my first jobs as a rabbi. There were many failed relationships with wonderful women who could not understand why things just didn't work out.

Ten years after the encounter with Rabbi Eliashuv, in 1986, I was living in New York City and finally trying to make sense of my life. I decided to enter the Gay and Lesbian Community Center on Thirteenth Street in Manhattan. I had passed it many times without going in. I wondered if I should take my kippah off or not. Eventually I went inside, head uncovered. There was a meeting of Act Up inside, boisterous and blatant. I sat at the back wondering if I belonged here. I wandered to the bulletin board later and stumbled across a young man, perhaps in his late twenties, in a streimel and long black coat, white knickers, and earlocks. I was in shock: "What is a Satmar Hasid doing here?"

↳ *from Hadi Hasidic group,*

Barely able to open my mouth, not knowing quite what to say, I asked him, "Are you . . . ?" He replied, "Yeah, I am gay." At that moment, a million thoughts flooded my mind. What an amazing capacity to wander into this place, looking like he does. What does he do? Has he had sex with a man? How does he manage the tremendous oppositions. I reached into my pocket to show him the kippah I had tucked away when I entered the center. It dawned on me suddenly that in the Gay and Lesbian Community Center I had become a closeted Orthodox Jew. Facing him in his Hasidic garb I grasped the irony of this "coming-out" encounter.

He agreed to speak with me for a few minutes. We went down the street to a diner for a cold drink, but he would not even drink the water. I asked him about his life. He said that he lived in two worlds. I asked if they ever touched each other. He said that recently he had trimmed his beard a quarter of an inch and let his bangs grow a bit as well. His ten-year-old daughter caught the meaning perfectly. Seeing him at some point in this hairstyle changed so slightly, she said, "Iz tati gevein a shegitz?" ("Is daddy becoming a Gentile?") I left Shmuel that afternoon amazed at the capacity of such a young man to live in two minds, two languages, two worlds so deftly.

Nine months later I was walking one warm Sunday afternoon in Soho and I stopped into the Center to munch on a muffin that I had just bought. There is a courtyard in back of the Center that is used by folks on sunny days as a place to bring a bagged lunch, to meet people, to hang out with a cup of coffee, or to read the paper. By this point in my coming-out process, I had decided that my kippah was not coming off. I made a blessing and began munching on my snack when I spotted a guy dressed in bicycle shorts, tank top, earrings, and a Caesar haircut. The rest of the crowd was dull in comparison to this guy, despite his gay-clone look, and for some reason, he seemed familiar to me. On my way out, I said hello, and he smiled back. I said, "Do I know you?" He answered, "Yes, Steve, its Shmuel."

"Shmuel?!" He explained that he had divorced his wife and had moved in with his Hispanic lover. He was learning a new trade having been blackballed from the diamond district. He dresses up just a bit to visit his kids. He does not keep kosher, nor is he Sabbath observant any longer. I asked him if he still believed that God gave the Torah at Sinai and that all Jews were duty-bound to fulfill it. He said, without hesitation, "Yes, but I simply cannot do it."

Shmuel preferred two independent pure worlds, even before he left his Jewish world for the gay world. Shmuel leaves the tradition unadulterated, if abandoned. In order to stay inside, I have had to tamper with the mold. For

Shmuel, Jewish life is as sharply defined as gay life. Each has its customs of dress and rules of belonging. They are two pure and incommensurate worlds. My struggle became clearer to me at that moment with Shmuel. I understood that I was suited better to ambiguity rather than to pure belonging. Shmuel forced me to admit to myself that purity is part of the problem in the first place, that for me, the interpenetration of worlds is desirable.

However, if Shmuel was split in one way, I soon became split in another. If gay experience is part of God's creation, why, I began to ask, was it so reviled by God's law?

In the years of my painfully slow coming out, I was fitfully able to face myself as a gay man, but it was becoming much harder to face God. While I had begun to feel more at ease about myself, I began to feel terribly out of place in synagogue. The worst was Yom Kippur.

Every Yom Kippur gay Jews who attend services are faced with a dilemma. The dilemma is lost on those who show up for Kol Nidre in the evening and Neila the following evening. Only those who essentially spend the whole day in synagogue confront this pain. In the afternoon service of Yom Kippur, the service of least attendance during the whole 24-hour-long marathon of prayer, the portion from Leviticus delineating the sexual prohibitions is read: "And with a male you shall not lie the lyings of a woman, it is an abomination."

I cringed to hear my shame read aloud on the Day of Atonement. The emotions accompanying the reading have changed through the years. At first, what I felt was guilt and contrition. Later, I felt a deep sadness for being caught up in gay desire and I would petition heaven for understanding. At other times, I would sob in my corner seat of the shul, acknowledging the pain of those verses upon my body and spirit. I have tried to connect myself with Jews of countless ages; listening in shul, their deepest feelings of love and desire turned abhorrent, ugly, and sinful. Finally, listening has become, in addition to all else I might feel, a protest.

During this entire period, I never missed the afternoon service on Yom Kippur. Never did I leave the synagogue for this gut-wrenching reading. It never dawned upon me to walk out. Over the years, I developed a sort of personal custom to stand up during the reading. I have always spent Yom Kippur in the seriously prayerful Orthodox environments. No one ever noticed me wrapped in my Kittel (a white cotton robe worn all day on Yom Kippur and in which pious Jews are buried when they die) with my tallit over my head, standing up for a single portion of a Torah reading, and crying.

Finally on Yom Kippur 1996, I took my submission/protest one step further. I decided that it was not enough to stand up. I wanted to have the *aliyah* (to be called up to the Torah) for the reading of those very verses. I arranged with the *shamos* (a sexton) that I would have the proper *aliyah*, and when it was time, I went up the bima in the center of the shul. My heart was pounding as I climbed the steps to the table, where the scroll is read. I felt as if I was standing on top of a mountain in a thunderstorm. My head was swirling as I looked out at the congregation seated around me. The men standing on each side of me at the podium were intent on their jobs, oblivious to me. Before me was the scroll.

It is hard to express the feeling of standing before an open Torah scroll. The Torah scroll possesses the highest level of sanctity of any object in a synagogue. If dropped, the whole congregation must fast. To stand there before the scroll as it is rolled open is both intensely intimate and public. I have studied this scroll for years. On Simchat Torah, I have danced with it. I kiss it weekly as it passes through the congregation on Shabbat. The plaintive and magisterial melody of the reading on Yom Kippur is both ominous and comforting.

I said the blessing, the scroll is rolled open, and I am exposed. I hold on to the handles of the scroll for balance. I am surprised. The words are poetry. The uncovering of nakedness repeats as the language of sexual abuse. Thou shalt not uncover the nakedness of thy father's wife, or thy sister, or thy daughter-in-law, or aunt. I am aware of the power of this text on the Day of Atonement for all those who have been sexually abused. A day of healing cannot avoid enumerating the myriad ways that the intimacy of families can be turned into violence.

And then it comes. The horrible verse. To my surprise, when it is read, I no longer feel pain or even danger. I feel strangely empowered. By exposing myself to this verse, it has become exposed to me.

I finished the final blessing and the *shamos*, as is customary, begins to say the *mi sheberach*, a publicly spoken and somewhat self-styled blessing of healing that those who have *aliyot* are allowed to construct spontaneously: "He who blessed our ancestors . . . shall bless." And then one can fill in the blank and add whomever, one's own family members by name, the rabbi, the officers of the congregation, someone who needs assistance, anyone. The *shamos* begins the *mi sheberach* and waits for my cue. I say, "mishpachti (my family), the rabbi, officers of the synagogue, and their families . . . the whole congregation"—and pausing—"*v'kol holei AIDS b'tocheinu*" and all those suffering from AIDS among us." The *shamos* froze. He rephrased my blessing, saying "and all those ill among us." I stopped him. No. This time I say it sharply and slowly: *"V'kol holei AIDS b'tocheinu."* He repeats my blessing word for word wanting to be finished with this already.

Standing amid the congregation, I felt the eyes of many upon me, but I was not looking at them. Gazing at the scroll, for the first time that I can remember, I felt it looking back at me.

In March of 1998, I came out of the closet in the Israeli paper *Maariv* as the first gay Orthodox rabbi. I formally came out to support a new gay and lesbian community center in the holy city, the Jerusalem Open House, which I had helped to found. While the timing was orchestrated by my desire to propel the Open House, I really came out because a switch had flipped in my mind. The closet, which had been the protector of my dignity, had become the armor of my shame. I was finally ready to defend the wholeness of my life, to stand up for the integrity and legitimacy of being who I am—a gay Orthodox rabbi.

JEWISH DYKE BABY-MAKING

Hadar Dubowsky

I REMEMBER WHEN the lesbian midwife told me that she just wanted to "make sure" I understood the consequences of circumcision. She handed me an article discussing circumcision as mutilation and violation. I had already told her that as Jews we would be circumcising our son at home with a *mohel*. She didn't understand how a pair of hip young feminist attachment-parenting lesbian moms could choose to inflict such a "barbaric" procedure on our son.

It wasn't the first difficult choice I've faced on this journey of becoming a parent. Nor was it the first time the values of my friends and dyke feminist community have clashed with my Jewish values. It began even before he was born.

Choosing to have a child was not a difficult decision. I always knew I wanted to be a mother and give birth. But choosing the sperm—that was an entirely different matter. We chose donor #169 very carefully, with much thought and deliberation. We started with downloading information about potential sperm donors off the sperm bank web site.

In choosing our donors, all of our hidden values and expectations came to the forefront. My butch girlfriend Terry grew up in a working-class Catholic family in Baltimore and wanted a donor that would reflect her background— alcoholic, working class, athletic, transgender. "Hey, where are all the alcoholic donors?" she asked, sifting through the profile sheets of perfectly polished college students. "How come all these guys have high SAT scores? Where are the transgender factory workers?!"

My sister Sara, a student at MIT, was scientific in her approach. "It's all about genetics, not environment," she stated. "Look! This one speaks four languages! They say that language acquisition is genetically determined!"

"I will not have anyone over 180 pounds!" asserted Terry. "I want my kid to be genetically predisposed to be athletic! At least that's part of my heritage!"

Secretly, I was looking for a donor who was Jewish, dark, and smart.

"Hey! Here's one!" I cried out. "He's studying education and government and has hazel eyes!"

"Yes, but look," my sister said, leaning over my shoulder. "Under interesting features, it says 'brow.' What do you think that means? He probably has one big eyebrow!" Sara laughed, took out a pen and drew a doodle of a cartoon man with one huge eyebrow.

"C'mon, Sara!" I exclaimed. "It's not funny! We're running out of Jewish donors!"

"Why does it matter if the donor is Jewish?" she asked.

It hadn't mattered to me at first. Originally, we were planning to go with a live donor, and none of the friends we asked were Jewish. But when that fell through, and now that we were picking off the page rather than from our friends, I wanted to have Jewish sperm. I wanted the kid to feel like she or he was a hundred percent Jewish.

Likewise, a few years earlier I had asked Terry to convert. I wanted to raise a Jewish child and I didn't want him or her thinking, "Well, my other mommy isn't Jewish so I'm not really Jewish." Although Terry was raised Catholic and Christian, she no longer identified as such and was politically active in speaking against the Christian Right. We still did some rituals from her childhood like make sugar cookies at Christmas but we both agreed to have a Jewish home. She was fine with converting; she knew that in our society, if you're not specifically something other than Christian (Jewish, Muslim, Hindu), you are automatically seen as Christian. Terry is so anti-Christian that being Jewish was a great alternative.

My sister's question was not that unusual. In addition to questioning my choice of Jewish sperm, some friends questioned my decision to become pregnant at all. My friend Linda, an African-American lesbian who worked as a volunteer with black children with AIDS, got angry when she heard I was trying to get pregnant. She thought the lesbian birthing-boom was racist, selfish, and bourgeois. "You know how many black babies there are who need homes! And here you are, another white lesbian, spending thousands of dollars to have a white child!" she challenged me.

For me, I think wanting to bear a child was connected to being Jewish. In some ways Denise was right: there were many children out there who needed to be adopted. I had gotten on the New Mexico State Foster Care web site to read their bios and learn about that process. But I knew I wanted to bear a child before we adopted, if we chose that route. My Jewish body and soul were yearning to bear a Jewish child. My grandmother is a Holocaust survivor and many of my family members died in the camps. While others worried about overpopulation, I had been raised with fear that the Jewish people would be wiped out. I learned that, after such loss, it was almost imperative that Jews procreate. For me, part of that meant using Jewish sperm.

"Here's one!" said Terry and as she held out his profile, we hushed. A light seemed to appear from the page. "He's 6 feet, 170 pounds, and plays soccer," she said softly, in a near whisper.

"He has brown wavy hair, straight A's, and studies economics!" said Sara, smiling.

"He's Jewish, from Brazil, and has olive-toned skin," I said with a sigh. It seemed like we had found our perfect sperm machine. "It's love—love at first sight!" I sighed.

Once we had chosen the sperm, the next step was inseminating. The doctors and nurses at the fertility clinic had no idea what to do with us. We'd arrive for inseminations with candles and incense, Adrienne Rich poetry, and Hebrew prayers. They weren't used to my clit ring, or Terry's butchness, or my request to masturbate before they injected the sperm (to give them more mucus to swim in, of course).

"What would it mean to bear and raise children in the fullness of our power to care for them, provide for them, in dignity and pride?" Terry and I read Adrienne Rich's words together after the insemination as we waited for the sperm to swim as far as they could go. The examination room was dark, lit only by our fertility candle. Terry rubbed my belly and read in Hebrew: *"Y'hi ratzon milfanayich Yah Rachameima."* ("May it be your will before you, Yah, Womb-Mother.") Terry entered me, following the sperm on their path, blessing them with her energy. "Swim spermies, swim," she whispered.

One of the hardest parts of the insemination process was waiting each month to see if I was pregnant, not knowing, wishing, praying, hoping. We spent thousands of dollars on the process, using money I inherited when my grandmother died. My grandmother was a strong tough Jewish woman, who taught in the Brooklyn public schools until she was 76 years old. When her husband died at age 45, she never remarried. Perhaps, if she had lived at another time, she might have been a lesbian. Instead, she was a homophobe. One of the classic Grandma Miriam lines I remember was in response to hearing about a gay man: "That's not a man, that's a *feygelah*. Neither fish nor fowl, man nor woman!"

Nevertheless, I used her money to buy vials of sperm, each one promising the chance for a child. Month after month, my periods came and went, and I grew impatient. I found myself becoming obsessed with rituals: if I just stand upside down for 20 minutes afterward, if I just say "*Modah Ani*" each morning, if I just eat a good breakfast, or if I just think good thoughts during the insemination, it will all turn out okay.

While waiting, I found a renewed interest in praying. I prayed to God, Adonai, Shechina, my ancestors. Living in New Mexico, I also prayed to Saint Anthony, the Catholic saint, finder of lost items. It couldn't hurt, I thought to myself.

As time passed, I began to get jealous of mothers I saw with their babies. "I bet she doesn't even want that baby!" I growled to myself when I saw an unkempt wailing toddler in the supermarket.

My jealousy escalated to ridiculous proportions. One day, in the lettuce section of Price Club, I waited behind a teenage mother with her infant. "Excuse me!" I snarled as I passed her by with my empty cart. In her cart, her baby sat in the front seat, gurgling and drooling on her *Pat the Bunny* book. Her cart was full of diapers and baby wipes. I was intensely jealous.

"Please return my patience to me," I prayed to Saint Anthony that night.

I looked to Jewish texts and found Hannah the biblical figure we read about every Rosh Hashana who had difficulty conceiving. She went to the Temple to pray and was so upset that her prayers were slurred by her sobs, but the priest thought that she was drunk and chastised her. Now, knowing how she feels, I think that she was drunk, drunk on sorrow. "Oh Lord of Hosts," Hannah prayed, "if you will look upon the suffering of your handmaiden and will remember me and not forget your handmaiden, and if you will grant your handmaiden a human seed, I will dedicate him to the Lord all the days of his life and no razor will ever touch his head!"

Okay, so there are some feminist issues around Hannah, but I was desperate for some kind of role model, some kind of context to frame my experience. When I finally became pregnant after a year and a half of trying, like our matriarch Sarah, I laughed. I couldn't believe it. I called Terry at work, telling her, "I might have some good news." Four home pregnancy tests later, I was still in shock.

My parents were ecstatic when I got pregnant. Any previous disappointment they had in my lifestyle seemed to melt away as they focused on their future grandchild. Most of their friends were already grandparents, and they had been waiting for their turn. With a gay and single older brother and an unmarried straight younger sister, I was their best hope. In their eyes, it would have been worse if I had spent my life single and childless, rather than as a lesbian bringing forth the next generation. When my mother found out I was pregnant, she went to the attic and pulled out old baby clothes. "I need to know if it's a boy or a girl so I'll know whether to send your brother's baby clothes or yours and your sister's," she told me.

I think that being pregnant was the first time I won my father's approval. He never celebrated my art, my writing, my karate, my lesbian relationships, my activism, or my women's studies degree—all great sources of pride for me. He was glad when I got my teaching degree because he thought it would give me more stability than working at a Jewish feminist magazine and it would provide for me, given that I wouldn't have "a man to take care of me." I don't think that he read a single article I wrote for *Lilith* magazine over the two years I worked there.

Childbearing gave him something to be proud of about me. Instead of being the radical feminist lesbian daughter with the shaved head and piercings, he could picture me as the Jewish daughter/mother/wife he had always wanted me to become. Of course I still had my piercings, my politics, my butch girlfriend, and my attitude, but nevertheless, now he wanted to connect. He wanted to be involved, give suggestions of names, talk about vacations with his first grandchild, and check on the pregnancy. Suddenly, I, by way of my fetus, mattered.

My queer friends varied in their feelings about my new "breederdom." My best friend, Riqi, cried when I told her I was pregnant. We had been best friends since we were 18, had gone to Israel together, lived on kibbutz together, slept together, fought, made up, fell in love, fell out of love, and built a beautiful friendship like the two passionate Jewish dykes that we are. She committed herself to being there with me every step of the way, even from afar, and planned to fly out for the birth.

Those who had been with me through the activist years, the non-monogamy years, and the dyke drama years were unsure about the whole thing. My dear old friend David, a radical faerie rabbi living in Vermont, was disappointed. "I can't believe you're becoming a breeder. Can't you lesbians just resist those biological urges and peer pressure?" he complained. "Don't expect me to babysit!"

"I'm a lesbian so I don't have to deal with kids," insisted Donna, calling me from her big job on Wall Street. "I don't know why you are doing that to your body. It seems like a foreign invasion to me. Aren't you worried about stretch marks?"

"You better still have time for me," my friend Ann demanded. "You're still going to be able to go out to the bar and have fun, right?" She insisted. I shook my head yes, trying to hold back the urge to vomit from the weeks of "morning sickness."

"Sure, nothing's going to change," I lied. I knew that my life was in for a bigger change than I could ever imagine. I hoped that in time, my friends would adjust and be happy for me.

Of course there were also friends who were completely supportive and there for me from the very beginning. Elissa took me shopping for bigger clothes and stood patiently by while I vomited every half and hour or so. My old straight Habonim camp friends emailed me suggestions for herbal nausea remedies and stories of their birthings.

My friends created for me two beautiful pregnancy rituals. During the first ritual, a group of lesbians got together and hennaed my pregnant belly. Lying naked before them, they each took a turn coming over and drawing designs on my belly and breasts with the warm, brown liquid. After about an hour, we were all naked rubbing the henna on each others' breasts, bellies, arms, and thighs. Nothing like a group of dykes to make motherhood into a sexually liberating experience.

My non-Jewish friends wanted to throw me a baby shower but, following with the superstitions of my *yiddishkeit* tradition, I felt it would be bad luck. They couldn't understand why I didn't want a shower. I tried to explain to them about Jewish superstition, but they insisted. "You need the presents," Kathy pointed out. I agreed to a shower as long as it had a ritual component.

The morning of the shower, Riqi, Terry, and I supplied colored yarn, fabric pens, blank onesies, and little plastic babies. Using balloons for the head and body, Riqi and I had made a piñata that looked like me pregnant. When our friends broke it, out fell plastic babies and candy. "There's something twisted about that," said Kathy, not knowing whether to be amused or appalled.

We did our own lesbian shower games: Pin the Fetus on the Lesbian, Try to Guess—Butch or Femme, and measuring my growing belly. But it was the Mothering Circle that really made it a lesbian gathering.

Everyone cried at the Mothering Circle, a combination of pagan ritual, group therapy, and feminist consciousness raising. As we passed a ball of colored yarn, each woman told a story of a mother, her mother or being a mother and a blessing for the two mothers-to-be. Karen cried as she talked about her distant mother, Kathy talked about her protective mother, and Jami talked about her lesbian mothers. Terry talked about her dead mother, and I talked about Terry and I becoming mothers together. "I couldn't imagine this journey with anyone but you," I told her. We all wept. We ended the day with me lying naked (again!) while my closest friends covered me with wet gauze to make a body cast of my pregnant breasts and belly.

When it came to my friends who had also been trying to get pregnant, there was bittersweetness, longing, and envy. One lesbian couple had been trying to get pregnant for three years and had just miscarried. I had a hard time telling them. Some gay male friends expressed jealousy. There was something that felt weird to me—here were all these gay men dying of AIDS and then all these lesbians reproducing. Sometimes it felt downright creepy at parties to go from discussing new medications with the hope of merely maintaining life to discussing sperm and spending money to create life.

Being pregnant was a magical mystical experience. Everything was out of my control: my vomiting, my bladder, my lack of energy, my emotions. When I went to San Francisco Gay Pride and a store tried to deprive me from using their restroom, I gave the manager an earful. Riqi made a sticker for me that read: "Beautiful Pregnant Jewish Dyke." It probably should have read: "Beware: Loud Raging Pregnant Jewish Dyke." Luckily I made it through the pregnancy without doing too much permanent damage.

We didn't know the baby would be a boy but we started contemplating the circumcision issue early on. We were going to raise the child as Jewish and we wanted to be thoughtful in each of our decisions that would affect his/her life. Because circumcision would have a permanent effect, we wanted to think it through carefully. We asked everyone for their opinions, trying to sift through the information and arrive at a decision that felt right for us.

I remember the conversation I had with my friend Ken. We met when we both lived in Brooklyn, through radical faerie pagan events, queer activism, and neighborhood potlucks. He's tall, sweet, spiritual, and would call himself a feminist. "On my penis I have a red mark," he told me in all seriousness. "I'm sure it's from my circumcision. I've had to do a lot of healing around that spot, mourning the loss of my foreskin."

For a while, I was anti-circumcision. It seemed barbaric. It is removing flesh. It is not consensual. It is permanent. "If the Jewish people have a ritual that is wrong, is it my duty to follow it?" I questioned.

Most of my friends having babies in New Mexico were choosing not to circumcise. I thought about assimilation and how dangerous circumcision was at times in history when Jews were persecuted. "Sometimes it is important to follow the rituals of your people even if those around you can't understand. Assimilation is a powerful force," a Navajo friend reminded me.

In Vermont, I asked David if he misses his foreskin. "Honey", he drawled. "giving head to an uncut penis is nasty. It collects crusties! You'll be doing your son a sexual favor by getting him circumcised."

"Too much information!" I retorted.

My biological family was split as well. My brother, a gay man living in the Castro, thought circumcision is cruel and had no intention of ever attending a *bris*. My sister wasn't sure what to think. My parents expected a *bris* and asked me throughout the pregnancy if I had the *mohel* lined up.

My grandparents never dreamed that there wouldn't be a *bris* if it was a boy. For my grandparents, it was non-issue. They planned to bring bagels and rugelach from New Jersey. "You can't get the real thing out there in New Mexico. It's like a third world country!" they told me.

"*Oy, vey,*" I thought to myself. "There may not even be a *bris*."

In Judaism, this gender division begins so early, just days after birth. I wish that I could hide my child's gender from the world for the first few years so s/he could grow up without the pressures of gender socialization, like that old story from *Ms.* magazine, "Baby X." But right away everyone wants to know if it is a boy or a girl so they can plan accordingly. Toward the end of my pregnancy, my mother asked me over and over for a due date. "We need to have a date so if it is a boy we come right away and still use our frequent flyer miles," she pressured.

"Please return my patience to me," I prayed again to Saint Anthony.

As a feminist, I was troubled by the gender disparity in the whole circumcision issue. For a boy, *brit milah*, the act of circumcision, ties him to a covenant with God. For girls, there is no parallel physical act. Does this mean that girls don't have a covenant with God?

I asked my rabbi, and she said something about women's role as healers. An old article from the 1970s I found talked about menstruation as women's bloodshedding. Another article defined the covenant of women and girls as the moon cycles and *Rosh Chodesh*. In the book *The Weave of Women*, the baby girl's hymen is pricked with a pin in a ritual they call hymenectomy. I was still troubled by the pain, by the gender disparity, and by the idea of two mothers subjecting our son to something we have never experienced.

"Look at it this way," David said, trying to be funny. "It is the ultimate lesbian feminist act—symbolic castration to punish your son for being part of the patriarchy." I didn't laugh.

I looked to more Jewish feminist resources and found writing about baby naming ceremonies to have for girls in place of a *bris*. They have lots of different names: *brit bat, brit hanayrot, simchat bat*. Some of the other ritual acts to mark the covenant between a girl and God I found included lighting a candle, giving her a Hebrew name, blessing her, wrapping her in *tallit*, placing her on Elijah's chair, anointing her with oil, and giving her *Tzadakah*.

All of these ritual acts seem wonderful, loving, and nonviolent. Couldn't we just do those for our son? Is that enough? Does he need to have a piece of his flesh removed? Why are girls brought in with kindness and tenderness while boys are subject to pain? Won't that influence the way he views the world?

Does it matter if he is the only Jewish boy in his summer camp that is not circumcised? How can two radical dyke moms place value on fitting in? Does it matter that it's not consensual? Don't parents often make permanent choices for their children that are nonconsensual? What about a ritual that marks a boy as belonging to a people? If it were a Native American ritual, would the white midwife and white attachment-parenting friends be so opposed? Is it okay to physically alter your child in the name of tradition, community, and culture?

We decided that whether it was a boy or a girl, we would have a baby-naming ceremony on the eighth day. It felt right to me to plan something gender neutral. It didn't solve the circumcision question but at least it made me feel like I was doing something in a feminist way. I was glad that the ritual would not focus around cutting flesh. We decided that if we chose to circumcise, it would be at home with close friends and family in the morning before the naming. The naming ritual would not have any mention of circumcision. In my mind, I started selecting poems, songs, and blessings for the naming. Adrienne Rich's poetry, "Free to Be You and Me" and florescent gel pens made their way into the ritual.

My labor was hard and long. I sweated, grunted, and squatted for 24 hours drug free before having Pitocin, an epidural, a cesarean, and, finally a baby at hour 30. I was so tired and drugged out that when Terry told me, with tears of joy running down her cheeks, that it was a healthy boy, I was too over-whelmed to cry or speak.

Within the next few hours, the relatives were called and flights were booked. We needed to call the rabbi and decide whether to call the *mohel*. Still drugged, hooked up to IVs and a catheter, and exhausted, I slurred out to Terry, "Yes, I want him to be circumcised." Looking back, I'm still not sure where the decision came from. Was it Jewish guilt? Fear of disappointing my family? Perhaps it was just plain exhaustion.

When the time came for the *mohel* to do her job, I was still torn and emo-tionally ambivalent. I was glad that my father and grandfather were present to be with my son as he joined the tribe of Jewish men in this male ritual. It still felt strange to hand him over to the "men," a group that had hurt me over the years by their exclusion of me as a woman and a lesbian. Terry didn't know where to go. Should she be with the men in the living room or in the kitchen with the women? "I feel like a bat," she whispered to me. "Neither fish nor fowl, man nor woman."

In the end, she chose to be with Rafael. Riqi did too, and they both gave him wine as the *mohel* made her cut. I was in the living room with my grand-mother, sister, and mother. I couldn't look. I needed to be around my matri-archs, taking my place in that female Jewish role of emotional observer. I know that there are feminist issues with that whole division, but right then, I just needed the comfort of my tribe of women. I still wasn't sure if I had made the right decision. "Forgive me, my son," I thought as he cried from the pain.

That night we had the naming ceremony, or *Brit Shem*, for our son, Rafael Ma'ayan. The room was filled with our friends, neighbors, family, and com-munity. We blessed him, sang, danced, and ate. Named after the angel of heal-ing, I hoped that Rafael would bring forth healing and justice to the world. Looking around the room at the loving faces surrounding me, I felt at peace.

That evening both Rafael and I had purple scars on delicate parts of our bodies. My scar, which cut across my abdomen, ached. His scar across his penis was swollen. My scar marked where he came to life. His scar marked where he joined the Jewish people. Neither of the scars sat well with me. I hadn't chosen mine and I still wasn't convinced the cesarean was really necessary. He didn't choose his, and I still wasn't sure it was the right thing to do. My feminist value of the right to control one's own body felt compromised by my Jewish value of tradition.

Six months after his birth, I got a new tattoo near the birthing scar. This time I was choosing to be marked, rather than being marked because a male doctor chose it for me. I chose an open hand, a *hamsa*, for the design. Inside the purple hand is a blue circle, signifying my womb. Inside that is a red heart, symbolizing my son. Motherhood has been a journey of opening my heart. The open hand, the open womb, and the heart remind me to keep my heart open, to trust others, and to be forgiving of others and myself.

I love my new tattoo. I love my son and I love watching him grow and emerge more as an independent being each day. I love watching my butch lover dress him up in khakis and a blue shirt so they can match for Shabbat services. I love dressing him up in purple pjs and nursing him to sleep. I love the way we struggle to hold onto our own truths, visions, and dreams as we move between our communities, embracing some values, reflecting on others, and leaving some behind. I hope that Rafael, in turn, learns to navigate this complex world in a way that makes him feel worthy, giving, healing, and whole.

A YOUNG MAN FROM CHELM

OR A NONTRADITIONALLY GENDERED

HEBREW SCHOOL TEACHER TELLS ALL

Jaron Kanegson

ON MY FINAL day as a religious school teacher at a Reform Jewish congregation in the San Francisco Bay Area, I was stacking up my last workbook and gathering my coat when Shira, the school principal, cocked her head and smiled slightly. "You know," she said, "when you came in for your interview last fall, Rabbi Silverstein saw you waiting on the bench in the lobby."

She paused. I pictured myself sitting on the shiny hard wood, and remembered the button-down blue shirt I'd had laundered and starched, the dress shoes I'd shined, and the sharp crease in my favorite and only pair of black wool dress pants. I'd left my tie at home for fear of overkill, but my lover had still thought I looked handsome, nearly wrinkling my outfit with her good luck hug and kiss.

Shira shook her head a little. "You know what he asked me?"

"Umm, no." I didn't know, although I could imagine that he might have said all sorts of things: that the parents wouldn't like me; that the kids would be afraid of me; that the other teachers would think I was a freak; or that he didn't like me, was afraid of me, and thought I was a freak.

"He asked me," she said with a grimace, "if you were a new Bar Mitzvah student!"

BOY-DYKE-FAG, HEBREW SCHOOL TEACHER

Two years ago, I took a part-time position teaching at a Reform Jewish religious school. Many of my friends thought I was flat out nuts, though most refrained from telling me so directly. Some of them even said, "Hey, cool, great." But I noticed that even those who'd been raised Orthodox, or who seemed much more devout and/or secure in their Jewish identity than I was, hadn't set foot in a "Hebrew school" classroom for years and had certainly never considered taking such a job. While I did eventually learn that one or two of my older Jewish friends had hidden pasts as Hebrew school teachers, such an endeavor seemed oddly unthinkable among my contemporaries.

The issue, however, may not have been that my friends weren't open to becoming Jewish religious school teachers, but that they didn't see the profession open to them. Their doubts about me taking such a position stemmed largely from the fact that I am a visibly queer, nontraditionally gendered/transgender-identified person. Moreover, when I applied to teach Hebrew school for the first time, I was already the executive director of a fledgling community-based organization by and for transgender, transsexual, intersex, genderqueer, and questioning youth.

MY GENDER IDENTITY

Born into an apparently indisputably female body, I've never felt completely comfortable being seen as a girl or a woman. What exactly this means about me in a culture that I am well aware consistently devalues girls, women, and anything considered female or feminine is something I've pondered for years. With my build, hairstyle, and predilection for clothing our culture considers masculine, I'm frequently seen as male, often as a gay or teenage boy, and called "he."

I've become accustomed to this situation; in many ways, I prefer it. Yet, I do have a "female" body, as do the people with whom I generally tend to become romantically involved. Since I've chosen so far not to alter my body with hormones or surgery, living as a woman, as well as my experience being raised as a girl, are also essential parts of my gender experience. Additionally, although male-appearing, I am not traditionally butch/masculine, but instead come across as effeminately male, even boyish. This has led me at times to identify with the term *boy dyke*. My particular attraction to butch women and to FTMs (female to male transgender people) also puts me outside the butch/femme paradigm. In conjunction with my feminine brand of masculinity, my primary attraction to similarly gendered people has also led me to describe myself as a "faggy butch," a "pansy butch," and a "(boy) dyke fag." Generally, I simply put myself under the umbrella term of *transgender*.

Just as I identify with both the dyke and the FTM communities, I also use both pronouns. Although life would be simpler if I could avoid pronouns altogether, this is difficult to achieve. Because the world we live in is entrenched in a two-gender system, people have frequently tried to pin me down on which pronoun I *really* want to be called. In reality, I might be most comfortable with a third non-gendered pronoun. Since that's not yet a realistic option, the pronoun I'm most comfortable with often depends upon where I am or whom I'm with. This is because the words *he* and *she* are not static terms, but have shifting connotations depending on the situation.

In a gathering of female-to-male transgender people, for example, I'm most comfortable being called "he." At an FTM meeting, "he" means male-(or partially male-) identified people, explicitly including people who have been born with, or still have, a woman's body. Therefore, "he" fits me relatively closely. And, in those situations, "she" generally means the broad category of woman, pictured as long-haired, feminine, heterosexual, and so on—none of which applies to me.

In a group of butch dykes, however, I usually prefer to be referred to as "she." That's because, in such a group, "she" includes a wide variety of gender expressions by female-bodied people, including very masculine gender expressions. "He," on the other hand, is generally describing heterosexual men, born in male bodies, and raised with male privilege as boys/men. In that case, "she" most closely describes my experience, while "he" alienates and separates me from those around me, however alike we might be.

Overall, I've learned to let go of trying to control what gender people see me as, or what pronoun they call me. As long as I appear ambiguous, different people are going to see me in different ways. A constant lack of surety as to how people are expecting me to act—like a straight teenage boy? a gay young man? a dyke of 30? a straight woman with short hair?—is the main drawback. Our culture has no place for people who aren't easily categorized. Because people become extremely uncomfortable if they think they've made a "mistake" about which gender someone is, and because many spaces are divided into male-only and female-only, I often find decisions about which bathroom to use, which verb forms to use in gendered languages such as Hebrew, or even where to pray (if I were to enter an Orthodox synagogue, which I've never dared to do) fraught with unnecessary stress and even danger.

MY JEWISH IDENTITY

On the surface, it's not difficult to explain why I do call myself Jewish. Yet, my current ambivalence toward Judaism did not arise when I first, in my late teens, questioned my sexual orientation and then my gender identity, nor did it suddenly appear when I began, also as a teenager, to identify as a feminist. Instead, it's been with me ever since I can remember, reflecting both a deep religious divide in my family, and feelings of exclusion I ascribe to the experience of growing up as a girl in a patriarchal religion. Since I first understood I was a Jew, my Jewish identity has been shadowed by doubt and alienation.

My father's family of origin was strongly Ashekenazi-Jewishly identified. His father, renowned for his toughness, spent five years as a Russian soldier during World War I, one on the front lines and four as a prisoner of war, part of which he spent working in coal mines. After the war, he rejoined his wife, met his four-year-old son for the first time, then was shot through the testicle in a pogrom. The three of them and a second son left Poland in the 1920s to come to the United States because, as Jews, they were in danger in Poland. Nearly the entire rest of their families, including parents, brothers, sisters, cousins, aunts, uncles, and neighbors, later disappeared during the Holocaust.

My father and his sister, a second American-born family, grew up in the Bronx during the Depression era, when it was a predominantly Jewish and Italian immigrant neighborhood. His mother was a homemaker who kept a kosher house. His father was self-employed as a deliveryman, carrying crates of seltzer, deliveries of coal, and chunks of ice up and down long flights of stairs all day. Although my father's parents fought with each other bitterly, and my grandmother was known to go after her children with a rolling pin if they made her angry, neither of them ever openly discussed the relatives they'd lost.

My mother's family, while also Polish, was devoutly Catholic. All of her grandparents immigrated to the United States for economic reasons. She spoke Polish the first four years of her life, and grew up in the Polish Catholic neighborhoods of Buffalo, where her mother was a homemaker and her father worked 60 hours a week as a butcher in a grocery store he owned with his brothers. She attended an all-girls Catholic high school, and then a Catholic women's college. When she was 11, her family changed their last name from Davidowicz to David to avoid anti-Polish discrimination.

Interestingly, I've been told Davidowicz is a Jewish surname, and my mother's father told my father he had Jewish ancestors. Still, when my parents married and my mother agreed at my father's insistence to convert to Judaism and raise their children as Jewish, her family was not overjoyed. Although most of her relatives accepted her decision, distant cousins still living in Poland, with whom she'd corresponded and visited, ended their relationship. Although I'm not sure she'd agree, I always felt that deep in her heart she was still Catholic. Mourning the loss of Christmas, Easter, and other holidays that had been large family celebrations when she was growing up, my mother often bitterly attacked Judaism and Jews when my father insisted that, as a Jewish family, we could not celebrate Christian holidays.

The glaring contradictions between my parents' original two religions (Jesus is Lord, Jesus is a dead guy; Jews are the chosen people, Jews killed Jesus, and so on) also made it difficult for me to believe in either one. When my parents ultimately divorced after 20 years of marriage, I felt their differences lay in part with the intolerance that each of their original religions preached against the other. Then, less than a year after their separation, when our family and extended family was struggling to adjust to the change, the rabbi pointedly chose to speak on the day of my younger brother's Bar Mitzvah about the evils of divorce. Since I felt very strongly that my parents' marriage was emotionally dead and over long before they separated, and since the rabbi's speech was very painful for my family to sit through, this experience further convinced me of the limitations of organized religion in general and of Judaism in particular.

The not uncommon rule my parents set when I was growing up was that if my brother and I wanted to have a Bar/Bat Mitzvah when we turned 13, we had to attend Hebrew school. I went, but I hated it. Many parents required their children to attend, but didn't care how they behaved. Few of my close friends went to Hebrew school, and those who did were scattered among a few different congregations. Initially excited about learning Hebrew, I hated sitting through disruption after disruption and was often so bored I'd bite my fingers to keep from falling asleep in class. By fifth grade, most of the other girls spent breaks putting makeup on and reading teen magazines, and I felt completely isolated.

At that time, a major theme in Conservative Judaism seemed to be that it was important to hold onto one's Jewish identity in order to keep Hitler from achieving a posthumous victory in eliminating the Jews. We watched reels of concentration camp liberation footage, filled with stacks of naked starved bodies and discarded eyeglasses. I was horrified, but simultaneously confused. Children are considered Jewish if their mothers are Jewish, and my mother was an often unenthusiastic convert. Though the Nazis would have considered me Jewish, I wasn't sure what I thought. When, seeking reassurance, I asked my fifth grade Hebrew school teacher if she thought I was Jewish, she peered at me a bit doubtfully over her glasses and said, "What do you think?"

In a perverse way, I took comfort from the fact that the Nazis would have considered me Jewish. But, as I grew older, I realized I didn't want to base my identity on standards created by Hitler. I didn't know what else besides heredity to base my Judaism on, however. If being Jewish was about religion, I didn't think I qualified, since I wasn't even sure if God existed. If I wasn't really Jewish, I wondered, why should I ally myself with such a persecuted group? After my Bat Mitzvah, about which I felt very conflicted, my Jewish education ended.

When I began college at Dartmouth, which I later left for UC-Berkeley, I went to one seder at which the chicken dinner was still half-frozen, and to one Hillel Shabbat service in which the words "honor the patriarchy" were part of the service. A staunch feminist and women's studies major, honoring the patriarchy was pretty close to the last thing I wanted to do. Additionally, difficulties in my relationship with my father meant that I didn't see him nor any of my Jewish relatives for several years. Finally, by 18 or 19, I came out as a dyke. For the next several years, although I took one Hebrew class when I first moved to Berkeley and was delighted to find that my teacher was a charismatic Jewish gay man, paganism was the only type of spirituality that held any real meaning for me.

Now I'm able to appreciate Judaism's environmental slant, its links to the rhythms of the earth, and its long history. I see many parallels between paganism and aspects of Judaism. Nonetheless, it took me nearly ten years after leaving home to begin reconnecting with a Jewish identity. This happened in fits and starts. One ex-girlfriend of mine, herself a light-skinned Mexican-American and Spanish-American woman, considered me a woman of color because I was Jewish. I didn't share her view, mostly because of my white skin privilege. But, her attitude led me to carefully think through whether being Jewish might be at least in part a racial or ethnic identity, and therefore not one I could simply dismiss.

BECOMING A HEBREW SCHOOL TEACHER

After beginning to reexplore my Jewish identity, I saw an ad in a nonprofit employment newsletter about part-time positions teaching in Bay Area Jewish religious schools. Since I enjoyed teaching, I decided to look into it, went on a few interviews, and ended up with two job offers. I decided to give teaching Hebrew school a try.

My first day teaching was a Sunday morning. After the morning prayer service, when all the teachers and students were together, I walked into a classroom full of 20 reluctant sixth graders. I had just begun taking attendance when Sam, whom I later discovered to be a very hyperactive but creative and sweet young man, interrupted me. "Are you a boy or a girl?" he demanded.

I didn't know what to say. I guess I'd naïvely been hoping that the students would simply see me as male (or, if not, simply as female). I had neglected to take into account that I'd missed the very first day of school, due to a trip scheduled before I was hired. Though the substitute teacher had probably talked about me as "she," my students seemed to think I looked more like a "he." "Well," I replied, "let's discuss that after I finish taking attendance and know all of your names." Afraid I'd be fired my first day if I was too honest, I wanted a chance for discussion, to ask students how they saw me and why, and why it was important to them. A few students giggled and muttered.

By the time I had finished taking attendance and had each student introduce herself, another student, Mara, told me her father was coming early to pick her up and expected her to meet him out front. New school safety rules meant that was not allowed. I asked the teacher next door to look in on my class while I walked Mara to the office. I could hear Sam arguing with the other kids as I left the room.

"That was rude!"

"I was just asking!"

"You shouldn't have said that!"

"Why not?"

As soon as I walked back into the classroom, Sam shouted, "We figured it out!"

"Figured what out?"

"My question before, we figured it out. So never mind."

Perhaps foolishly, I let the topic drop. I'd been warned before I began teaching that it would be "best" not to come out to the students or talk about my personal life, so I felt worried about saying the wrong thing. Not until that evening did it occur to me that I didn't know what, exactly, the students had "figured out" my gender was.

The following Wednesday evening, I returned to teach two high-school level classes on Jewish folktales and gender and Judaism. My first-day enthusiasm was tempered by Stacey (the head of the high school education program), Deborah (the head of the elementary education program), and Shira each taking me aside as they came in to discuss phone calls they'd received. Parents had called (not to complain, they each emphasized) to find out if I was male or female, why their children weren't able to tell, and why I hadn't told the children immediately if I was a man or a woman. They each had the same question: What happened? I explained the series of Sunday's events to each of them. "Well, don't worry," Deborah said. "I told the parent who called me directly that you're a woman with short hair. And I'd like you to let your class know right at the beginning that you're a woman."

"Could I have a short discussion with the students? I'd like to talk about what gender they thought I was, and discuss why it matters to them."

Shira looked pained. "I'd really rather you didn't," she said. "Keep it to 30 seconds."

I did as she asked, and over time the students seemed to relax somewhat about my appearance, although a number of their parents gave me what appeared to be distinctly disapproving looks any time I encountered them. With the high school students, I didn't seem to have any overt problems with gender confusion. I did have a student or two drop my class at the beginning of each semester because, I was told, their parents were conservative and didn't want me as a teacher. I also never came out to most of my students in any way, which felt very odd, given my extensive work with queer identity-based organizations.

Although I made it through the entire school year, I felt so unwelcome and anxious during the hours I was on campus that I had nightmares about teaching there almost every week, not to mention mounting gloom every time a teaching day approached. And, because I felt I had to hide so much of myself from my students, I had a very difficult time connecting with any of them in the manner essential to being a truly compelling and effective teacher.

GENDER AND JUDAISM

Although I taught at that school for just one year, I did learn something important. Preparing for the class I taught on gender and Judaism was an eye-opening experience. Surprisingly, a familiar and deep-seated feeling of confusion I'd been carrying for over 15 years after completing my Jewish education finally lifted.

During the year I had my Bat Mitzvah, I went through a special evening "confirmation" class with the other B'nai Mitzvah students, after which I graduated. I remember feeling absolutely convinced by the end of it that I had somehow misunderstood something important. In class, we learned about being a Jewish adult, and discussed sexuality, responsibilities, and Judaism. But I felt deeply confused. Every time we covered a new topic, such as the importance of keeping various *mitzvot*, the rules applied only to Jewish men. It seemed to me as if our teacher, the male rabbi who headed the religious school I attended, was simply trying to break it to us gently that all Jewish women are supposed to do is raise Jewish children and keep a kosher home.

I also noticed that while some of the young men in my class were asked to help out with Saturday morning prayer services, none of the young women were. Even though I won the only award for student excellence when I graduated, I'd never been invited to help with services, and decided it was because I was lacking in some way. It was true that I usually did not attend services, so I thought that might be the reason. But, when boys became Bar Mitzvah in my congregation, they read directly from the Torah. Girls read only from the Haftarah.

It was a Conservative congregation, not an Orthodox one, and I can no longer remember if we learned about the *mikveh* (ritual bath) or the rules of *niddah* (sexual purity). Few people I knew kept a kosher home, so that responsibility did not seem very important to me. By the time I ended my Jewish education at the age of 13, I simply couldn't believe that so much of what was integral to Judaism did not apply to Jewish women. In what I can only guess must have been a self-protective twist of (il)logic, I decided that I must have skipped too many classes, and somehow ended up ignorant of what it really meant to be Jewish. This feeling was the basis of much of my insecurity about becoming a Hebrew school teacher.

The more I prepared for my class on gender and Judaism, however, the more I realized I'd never misunderstood at all. Traditional Judaism treats men and women extremely differently, to the point where, in my opinion, women might not even be considered Jews at all, but simply sidekicks to or caretakers of the only *real* Jews, Jewish men. I'd also always held the belief that to really be Jewish, one would have to follow its dictates in their purest form, Orthodoxy. Not being Orthodox was part of why I felt I wasn't *really* Jewish, and some small part of me always thought that perhaps one day, when I fully embraced Judaism, I would be Orthodox. The more I read, however, the angrier and sadder I became. I admitted to myself for the first time that Orthodox Judaism, traditional Judaism, will simply never have a place for me. Not only as a queer person, not only as a nontraditionally gendered person, but simply as a female-bodied person who believes women and men do not belong in fundamentally different roles.

I worried when teaching that class about gender and Judaism, which I did for two semesters, that it was my job to help my students, who were mostly female, learn about Judaism in a positive light. I did my best to convey to my students, who were understandably also often angry about limitations placed on the role of women in Judaism, the differences between the realities of traditional Judaism and modern-day and Reform Judaism. I also encouraged them to recognize that we all have the right to help Judaism grow and change into a tradition with room for us all.

In time, it became a relief to have realized that I probably never really had deeply misunderstood traditional Judaism. I began to make peace with the fact that I will never be an Orthodox, nor even a Conservative, Jew. Instead, I began to look for ways I could appreciate and belong to an alternative Jewish tradition. I decided that Reform Judaism is "real" Judaism, perhaps a version in which I can take part. I also began to appreciate, partly through my study of Jewish folktales, that Jews are not simply members of a religion, but also part of a diverse culture, an ethnicity, a tradition, and a people. With all of those elements in mind, I began to seek a place for myself in Judaism.

JEWISH TRANS/GENDER IDENTITY

As I discussed earlier, my gender experience has been about more than simply being born in a female body. Since virtually every culture across time and place has had some members who, either physically or emotionally, do not fit standard gender roles, I began to search for Jewish examples. I have to admit that, despite much looking, I haven't found a lot of discussion about nontraditionally gendered Jewish people. But, there are a few exceptions.

Rabbi David Seidenberg, for example, whom I met at a recent Shalom Center retreat, has found seven different genders/gender categories listed in the Talmud. Created before surgical or hormonal intervention was possible, these nonetheless include, in addition to "standard" male and female, five additional categories that can be roughly described as follows: *andro-*

geenos, which describes people who have at least some sexual characteristics of both male and female; *tumtum*, who have no clear characteristics of either sex; *aloneet*, a biological female with no secondary sex characteristics; *sarees chamah*, a male who "naturally" has no secondary sex characteristics; and *sarees adam*, a male who lacks secondary sex characteristics due to castration or other intervention. Although it is difficult to make these terms fit most modern day transgender people (none of these would respectfully describe a post-surgical transsexual woman, for example), Rabbi Seidenberg postulated that a modern-day pre-transition or non-transitioning FTM could describe himself as *sarees chamah*, a male who naturally lacks testosterone. More importantly, he stated during our conversation, the Talmud's recognition of these seven gender categories means that Judaism acknowledges that individuals fall into more gender categories than simply "woman" and "man."

Leo Rosten also defines the word *timtum* in *The Joys of Yiddish* as an androgynous person. He writes, "In the *Mishnah*, a *timtum* is a person whose sex is not determinable, because clothing covers the genital area" (p. 400). Unfortunately, he describes the word as also having a negative connotation, referring to an incompetent person. Micah Rebel Prince, in his trans Jew 'zine *TimTum*, redefines the word with a more positive slant as "A sexy, smart, creative, productive Jewish genderqueer" (p. 1). While perhaps technically incorrect, at least until now, I like his definition best.

Rabbi Jane Litman pointed out to me that, for the non-Talmudic scholar, one of the only other places nontraditionally gendered people can be at least posited in Judaism is in relation to contradicting elements of the creation story at the beginning of Genesis. First it says "God created Adam . . . male and female he created them" (Gen 1:27). Later comes a description of Eve's creation from Adam's rib, or, depending on the translation, from his side. The most popular rabbinic explanation for this retelling of human creation, popular for good reason with feminists, seems to be speculation that Eve was not the first woman created. Rather, Adam's first partner was Lillith, who was created simultaneously and who refused to lie beneath him. When Adam protested, Lillith chose to become a demon instead of compromising, even with the punishment of one hundred of her demon children dying every day. Countless folktales portray Lillith as both a powerful seductress, and a killer of pregnant women and newborn babies. Yet Lillith, the rebellious, dominant, "bad" first woman who refused to submit to a man has been a far more interesting model for many women than Eve.

Another explanation for the discrepancies in Genesis, as explained in the Midrash, is that the first human was, as some translations imply, literally "male *and* female." This first human was said to be male on the front and female on the back. Thus, when God liberated Eve from Adam's side, s/he was simply separating the already created first human into two. This interpretation is fascinating for two reasons. First of all, as feminist scholars have pointed out, this version clearly describes Eve as equal to, indeed one half of, Adam. Secondly, as Talmudic scholars have postulated, it means the first human was, like God, both male and female. Indeed, they have gone so far as to label the first person a "hermaphrodite" (an archaic and impolite term used to describe intersex people).

This interpretation is pivotal, both because it acknowledges the possibility of more than two genders, and also because it acknowledges the place of intersex people in Jewish tradition. If intersex children were understood as holy, as reflections of the first human being ever created, perhaps Western doctors would stop genitally mutilating intersex children at birth and in surgeries throughout childhood in an effort to make them look "normal." As I have learned more about the terrible treatment physically intersexed children receive at the hands of the medical establishment, I have become convinced it is wrong to surgically alter the genitals of a person too young to give permission. I believe Jewish people should find ways to honor and celebrate the births of all our children without any form of childhood circumcision/genital mutilation.

DRAGGED INTO THE STORY: JEWISH FOLK TALES

Of all the images of Jewish people, I look most like a Bar Mitzvah boy, or perhaps, except for my lack of *payes* (side locks), a yeshiva student. Many people, friends and lovers included, have noticed this resemblance. Perhaps because I fit this image, people who see me as male or boyish often know right away that I am Jewish. Those who meet me in dyke environments, or read me as female, more often have no idea. Aside from Yentl, whom I do not resemble, there are few popular images of female Jews who look like me.

Despite that fact, rediscovering Jewish folktales has helped me to feel more of a connection with my Jewish heritage. My favorite Jewish folktale of all time, a Chelm tale, follows:

> A young man from Chelm, who was studying to be a Sage, was very
> troubled. He decided to go to the Chief Sage and ask him for advice.

"I have a question for you," he said. "I'm getting a little older now, and I'm very worried. Can you tell me why it is that no hair is growing on my chin? It couldn't be heredity, could it? After all, you know my father has a nice, thick beard."

The Chief Sage stroked his own bearded chin as he sank deep into thought. Suddenly, his face lit up. "I know!" he exclaimed. "You must take after your mother!"

"That's it! My mother has no beard either!" the youth cried in admiration and relief. "How wise you are!"

One reason I enjoy Jewish folktales in general is that they often revolve around the theme of misplaced, contested, and inconstant identities. This Chelm tale is no exception, and I believe it's one of very few instances where the possibility of nontraditional gender identities is acknowledged by mainstream Jewish culture.

This story also in some ways aptly describes my own experience of gender. Like the protagonist, I take after my mother physically. Her height, breasts, narrow hips, and smooth chin are all mine too. Yet, at times this seems baffling, because I often feel intensely that it is a male person, or at least not a woman, who inhabits my body. Even strangers often see me as a man, even in the women's restroom. So, I usually just use the men's room. In many ways, I am that young man who, mysteriously, lacks a beard.

Since the tale provides no real answer to the question of why the young man lacks a beard, the non-Chelmite can entertain all sorts of possible explanations. This Chelm story is one of my favorite ones to share, and most queer people I've shown it to have been both surprised and delighted. Though less subtle than most, I have found that this story is only one of many Jewish stories that can be read as having a queer, or even a transgender or intersex, subtext.

TEACHING AT SHA'AR ZAHAV

Despite gradually feeling more kinship with my Jewish identity and even teaching an adult class on Jewish folktales at the Harvey Milk Institute in San Francisco, after my first experience teaching Hebrew school, I never thought I would consider doing it ever, ever again. When I received a phone call one evening from David Shneer, Sha'ar Zahav's then education director, asking me if I had any interest in teaching second grade, my stomach squeezed in panic.

He was too charming to hang up on, however, so we had a long conversation. That night I woke up sweating from a nightmare about, once again, standing in front of a classroom of Hebrew school students. Perhaps as a result, my now ex-lover found the idea of me teaching Hebrew school *again* a rather dubious one. I didn't dare tell any of my friends I was even considering it.

Nonetheless, I decided to visit during the next religious school session to check it out. In truth I was not unfamiliar with Sha'ar Zahav, a largely queer, feminist Reform congregation in San Francisco. I'd attended some High Holiday services there, and many of my friends, including transgender friends, regularly went (and still go) to services there. This, in fact, was part of what made me gradually realize there might be a part of the Jewish community to which I could actually belong.

When I walked in the next Saturday morning, there were children everywhere. Infants and toddlers were there with their parents for family education, and kids ranging in age from six to thirteen showed off their day's work during closing circle. Parents seemed to come in sets of one to four, in all genders, and there was a more racially diverse group of children than I'd ever seen in a synagogue before. Everyone looked happy to be there; the children laughed and chatted and seemed to actually be having fun (something I never would have imagined).

After some thought, and with great trepidation, I took the job. By the end of the school year, I had shocked myself, both by admitting that I'd enjoyed teaching there very much, and by agreeing to return the next year. Many of the problems I had encountered at the first place I taught simply did not exist at Sha'ar Zahav. Not only did I feel encouraged to discuss my gender identity and presentation with my students if I wished, but the parents, rather than scowling, actually seemed to like me. I very much enjoyed the 12 students in my class, and was fortunate to have a high school student who helped out, as well as a transgender-identified friend in the process of converting to Judaism at Sha'ar Zahav who volunteered in my classroom.

While it was fun and exciting to share folktales, Jewish history, and writing Hebrew in script with my students, I also appreciated that both the congregation and religious school seemed to encourage the radical exploration of Judaism. In fact, the subsequent head of the religious school *required* the teachers to talk to our students on Passover about the feminist tradition of putting an orange on the Seder plate, to remind us of how women have long been excluded from full participation as Jews. Of course, I was only too happy to oblige.

In less than one school year, teaching at Sha'ar Zahav had a major impact on my life. In the past several months, I've come to feel that whether Judaism is an ethnicity, a religion, a community, or a culture, and whether or not I believe in God, embrace Orthodoxy, or generally dislike organized religion, I can allow Judaism to be part of my life. Getting to know all of the queer and straight families there also helped me to realize something I've never really believed since I came out as queer nearly 12 years ago; despite being a dyke/queer/transgender person, I can choose to be a parent.

Partly as a result, my now ex-partner of several years and I began seriously exploring having children. Although not everyone wants to be a parent, through that process I came to the realization that I do want to have children, and one way or another, I probably will. Before our relationship ended, my former partner and I decided that we would raise our children as Jewish. Raised in a vaguely Christian atheist family in the Midwest, and not generally comfortable with organized religion, she nonetheless felt welcome at Sha'ar Zahav, a major factor influencing that decision. Now that I am single, I have temporarily put my plans to become a parent on hold. I now know, however, that having children is one of my life goals for the near future and that when I do so, Sha'ar Zahav is one place I will find support.

I am grateful for the existence of Sha'ar Zahav and other congregations like it. I also believe, however, that something more than queer friendly synagogues needs to be created before people like myself will feel fully welcome in the larger Jewish community. I, for one, am still waiting not only for the women's Torah Jewish feminists have long declared to be in need of creation, but also for the queer person's Torah, and the transgender and intersex person's Torah. While I'm certainly proud of many aspects of my Jewish heritage, I still find myself deeply ambivalent. As long as countless people both like and unlike myself are largely invisible, ignored, and shut out by much of Jewish tradition and most of the Jewish community, my connection to Jewish culture and identity remains tempered by feelings of alienation.

QUEER NAKED SEDER

AND OTHER NEWISH JEWISH TRADITIONS

Jill Nagle

queer \'kwir\ *adj* [origin unknown] (1508) **1 : a** WORTHLESS, COUNTERFEIT
<~ money> **b :** QUESTIONABLE, SUSPICIOUS **2 a :** differing in some way from
what is usual or normal **b:** (1) ECCENTRIC, UNCONVENTIONAL (2) mildly
insane : TOUCHED **c :** absorbed or interested to an extreme or unreasonable
degree : OBSESSED **d :** HOMOSEXUAL—usu. used disparagingly **3:** not quite
well *syn* see STRANGE—**queer•ish** \ish\ *adj*—**queer•ly** *adv* ˆ— **queer•ness** *n*

na•ked \'na-ked, 'nek-ed/ *adj* **1:** not covered by clothing: NUDE **2:** exposed or
raw **3 a :** scantily supplied or furnished **b :** lacking embellishment:
UNADORNED **4 :** UNARMED, DEFENSELESS *syn* see BARE

se•der \'sa-d r\ n, often cap [Heb *sedher* order] 1865 : a Jewish home or community service including a ceremonial dinner held on the first or subsequent
evenings of the Passover in commemoration of the Exodus from Egypt

I CAME INTO Judaism ass-backwards. That is to say, I joined a group called Queer Minyan in the fall of 1993 because of the friends who spearheaded it. Rich and Alina had initially converged around creating Queer Minyan because they were tired of feeling excluded from Aquarian Minyan, the local New Age–flavored straight-dominated Jewish Renewal synagogue. The leaders had made well-intentioned efforts to "reach out" and "include" queer Jews, but the overall feel of the place was still hopelessly heterocentric.

So we sat around, about nine of us, in Rich's living room, discussing what the group would entail. God, Alina decreed, would be called *Shekhinah*, one of many names for God, this one referring to the feminine element of God. No one argued. Centuries of *Adonai*, "Lord," had certainly paved the way for a tiny group of queer, feminist, and feminist-agreeable Jews to adopt *Shekhinah* as their source. Prior to this group meeting, I had overheard discussions of *Shekhinah* versus *Adonai*, and really didn't give a flying hamantaschen, because I didn't know enough to feel part of the discussion. With the onset of Queer Minyan, the name of God began to matter to me.

Then came the question of belonging. Some of us wanted an open group, others wanted "queer Jews only." Those in favor of an open group couldn't conceive of any Jewish group excluding others. Those wanting a closed group spoke of feeling some shame around not being good enough—in other words knowledgeable enough—Jews. Most of us were raised in assimilated households, and knew very little about Jewish liturgy, custom, or law. We wanted a place to question, to grapple with God, liturgy, and what it meant to be Jewish without feeling "on display" in front of non-Jews who might be surprised at our ignorance. This discussion was complicated by Mitchell, the only non-Jewish fixture of Queer Minyan, and for that matter of nearly every other queer Jewish chavurah in the Bay Area. Mitchell, the honorary Jew, the matzoh queen, the mensch. Who knew he was born Irish Catholic?

We began (and to this day continue to hold) services on the third Friday of the month with a version of the traditional chant, *"Hi-nei mah-tov u-mah nayim, shevet achim gam yah-chad."* "How good it is for brothers to gather together", which goes *"Hi-nei mah-tov u-mah nayim, shevet aqueer gam yah-chad"* "How good it is for queers to gather together." We took turns leading services, calling upon God as *Shekhinah*, *Yah* (one), *Ruach* (breath), and only very occasionally *Adonai*. At one point, a man expressed wanting to reclaim positive images of a male deity through *Adonai*, but the conversation didn't get very far. I still think it is an important one, though. It softened me toward accepting *Adonai* as a name of God, at least when used by gay men in a queer, feminist *minyan*.

Around this time, I had also begun exploring group sex, SM, polyamory, and various facets of the sex trade. In fact, I had come out to the San Francisco Bay Area with the express intent of "becoming a slut." Until this point, I had known myself only in monogamous, or painfully nonmonogamous, relationships. I was confused and leery about serious partnership; curious and hungry for new kinds of sex and relating.

In retrospect, spirituality and sexuality seemed a logical and timely coupling. In many senses, that union had already begun; some of the sex parties I attended in the Bay Area began with a pagan ritual, calling in the four directions, welcoming the goddess, a deity who declared, "All acts of love and pleasure are my rituals." With that, we would begin the carnal sacraments. Another piece of this was that, at first unconsciously, I began choosing Jews nearly exclusively to lust after and to love wildly.

This wasn't always so. As a very young adult, I regarded other Jews as a clannish group to which I wasn't allowed to belong because I didn't know enough. Yet at the same time, it was only the other Jewish kids at my elementary school (about four, total) who twice a week got carted away from school to a "gifted" program chock full of . . . other Jews. But these Jews all seemed to have more stability, money, and panache than my faded, dysfunctional K-mart–clad family, so I failed to make the grade on the class level as well. Whatever a Jew was supposed to be, I was convinced I simply didn't cut it—and so resented other Jews, internalizing and reproducing the stereotypes about "them." But deep down I still felt Jewish, even through all that. At least we were all smart, or so it seemed.

Though I grew slowly in my awareness, it wasn't until 1990, as an adult in my mid-twenties that I began to grow my Jewishness on another level entirely. I had begun working for a social service agency that served newly immigrated Soviet Jews. Almost the entire staff was Jewish, half of whom were Russian born and had thick accents. In both my Russian- and U.S.-born colleagues, I saw my mother, my aunts, my grandmothers, my cousins, and yes, myself. I realized that those parts of me I felt were excessive and needed to be reigned in—the opinionated, raucous, sensual, sexual, argumentative parts—were not personal failings to fit into WASP culture, but were integral to my Jewish culture. I fell into new levels of self-love, which extended to my attractions as well.

By the time I arrived in San Francisco in 1992, I had a Jewish girlfriend,

Dawn, who lived in Boston with her Catholic girlfriend in an open relation-ship. I sought out Dawn for her reputation as a slut, and she also turned out to be a knowledgeable Jew, to boot, complete with Orthodox schooling. At the very beginning of our relationship, before I moved to the Bay Area, Dawn and I had had a threesome with another Jewish woman that wound up with us all in a delightful pile singing Hebrew songs from Jewish summer camp. That, you could say, was a proto-Jewish sex ritual, though I hadn't such a name for it at the time. Once I moved out to the Bay Area, Dawn and I stumbled into another threesome with a different woman. It was Shabbat. It was also the eve of a Christian holiday that takes place in December, whose name I often forget.

We wound up in the home of Chance, a very cute clerk at Good Vibrations who invited us to her home to watch porn videos. For 24 hours, Chance, Dawn, and I fucked, watched porn videos, ate, and fucked some more, not necessarily in that order. We noted more than once that it was a *mitzvah,* or good deed, to have sex on Shabbat, and what good Jews we were, and how fortuitous that we three Jewish women should all wind up in each others arms (and legs) on Christmas (Oh yeah, that's it!) Eve. Dawn returned to Boston, and Chance and I dated for a few months and then morphed into friends. She remains one of my best buddies to this day.

So, by the time I got to Queer Minyan, I was ripe for a Queer Jewish spir-itual practice. With its pagan- and Buddhist-influenced rituals, Hebrew songs, *nigguns* (wordless melodies), chants, and deeply personal, meditative moments, Queer Minyan became a place that I would come to call my spiri-tual home. A year or two into it, I was even inspired to lead services, some-thing I never would have imagined just two years prior. Since Queer Minyan only met once a month, I began exploring other Jewish venues as well.

I went to a Jewish renewel synagogue in San Francisco and listened to a prominent male rabbi give what was and still is probably the most politically interwoven sermon I have ever heard. I appreciated all the connections he made to the real world, but two hours of one man talking, got old very fast. Where was the diversity of leadership, chorus of voices, and consciousness around theistic nomenclature that had paved the way for my deep union with Jewish tradition? It turned out my Queer Minyan initiation was anything but traditional.

I quickly realized that the lay-led, queer, and woman-centered Judaism of Queer Minyan had ruined me for the rest of the (sexist) Jewish Renewal movement, *for it had convinced me beyond a shadow of a doubt that I was created in the image of God!* I reeled at the idea of an ancillary "women's study group," and balked at the occasional magnanimous reference to "outreach" and "inclusiveness" of "gays and lesbians." Who was this man to invite me into a place that is made of Me? And why doesn't he hand over the microphone from time to time, so we hear holy voices other than his? We mostly knew what he was going to say anyway. Who thinks his voice is more important than ours? Him? Not me. God? Not bloody likely.

Though the rabbi sometimes used "she" when referring to *Adonai*, it felt pasted onto a male-centered program, not reflective of a woman-centered outlook. He invited us to use the language that worked for us and not get "hung up" on that which didn't. "The God you don't believe in doesn't exist!" he enjoined. But I preferred the Queer Minyan tradition, in which we had special meetings to argue about processes, policies, and liturgy, and the program evolved accordingly. Often we even stopped and argued during the service about what should happen next, or how something was phrased. In other words, the liturgy reflected multiple visions, not just that of one person, which in most cases of religious leadership, including this one, equals one man.

Even larger than just my own and my queer Jewish compadres' issues, however, I believe a woman-centered Judaism offers a great deal to all Jewish spiritual seekers. For one thing, it takes the burden off the men to do everything and be all powerful. Secondly, it transforms in everyone's eyes the notion of what power—and what the image of God—looks like, sounds like, leads like. This transformation opens up places of possibility inside us and for connecting with others. Most of the world's religious spokespeople are men. Judaism could model what egalitarian spiritual leadership looks like. This looms especially large now, post-September 11, 2001. The more women come to the forefront in every arena, the more opportunities to balance the havoc men have spearheaded.

In one form letter, I was asked what the synagogue could do better. Well, here it is: Encourage women to lead. Pick a name for God not laden with such patriarchal history—there are only about 80 or so Jewish names for God from which to choose—like *Ruach* (breath), *Yah* (one), or *Shekhinah*. Much of the deepest transformation throughout the ages has begun with renaming.

Still, even in my lay-led queer feminist righteousness, I missed being part of a larger, more heterogeneous Jewish Renewal community. I didn't want to be forever locked into a queer Jewish ghetto. So, with a mixture of hope and despair, I stuck my toe out every so often. It became a dance; weaving in and out of communities that nurtured me in various ways.

At Keneset HaLev, a wonderful "community of the heart," I found a more lighthearted, embodied version of the same thing: one man, one voice, with "inclusion" of others from time to time. In fact, it was even worse in moments.

One such moment was when the *maggid* (lay teacher) invited a man about to be married up to read a passage from the bible about how women should stay at home and spin wool. I was outraged. I nudged my friend. It turned out she was *used* to such sexism in her liturgy. Apparently most, if not all, women and queer men who grew up Jewish had resigned themselves to making internal adjustments when their spiritual leaders insulted and marginalized them with their liturgy. I was even more convinced: *My spirituality is that and only that which raises me up as the image of God.* Everything else is poison to my spirit, often promulgated by kind hearted, well-intentioned brothers, but poison to my spirit nonetheless. Though ass-backwards, I had no doubt I was on exactly the right track. Women encouraged me to speak out. Here it is, sisters!

I in no way intend to single out criticism of these leaders for practices that are commonplace across Jewish tradition. This is simply where I found myself, and so it becomes part of my story. I wanted to believe it would be different, that a man at the turn of the Christian era millennium who took on the enormous responsibility and authority for a group of spiritual seekers would naturally find the most egalitarian way possible to lead worship. Obviously, it wasn't so. For the record, I cherish and respect both these men as part of my spiritual community, and would go to their synagogues again. I mostly love what I find there, and what I don't love, I embrace as the blessing of the principled struggle of a diverse community. And, I invite them to change things for the better.

Now on a mission, I gathered information. *Shaddai*, I discovered, was the only name of God that also signified a body part: breast. When it was my turn to facilitate Queer Minyan again, I led everyone in prayers thanking the holy nurturer, *Shaddai*, for the light, the bread, and the wine. Here was the pagan goddess invoked in those early sex parties that was now making her way into synagogue! Here was worship centered around my holy fucking female body! *Now* we were talking, the goddess and me! The goddess *was* me; I, her. The sensations I felt stroking my own hungry breasts were and are beautiful, holy, and pure.

My paths of sexual and spiritual exploration had begun to converge. I had also begun a very intense relationship with Adam. I now had a boyfriend and a girlfriend, both Jewish, both long distance, both in open primary relationships, and with a scarily long list of other attributes in common. Adam and I began exploring a level and quality of energy with each other that neither of us had ever experienced. During our relationship, he began to believe in God, because, he said, it was the only way he could explain what happened when we made love.

While Adam and I wrote reams of ecstatic poetry about the other, took Tantra to new Hebraic heights, and welcomed goddess into our bed, Dawn and I threw sex parties, engineered threesomes, and slutted it up in public. I was well into my official slut apprenticeship with Dawn, and had dubbed her my "mentor in brazen hussiness."

One of the few times during those two years when I wound up with both Adam and Dawn was at a queer studies conference. I had seen Adam, and we were taking many minutes to make our first physical contact, doing a very subtle dance of breath, eyes, and hands, noticing all the tiny changes in our feelings as we reconnected after so many weeks. Suddenly, I heard, "Oh my God!" from across the room. Dawn had spotted me and was climbing as fast as she could over the backs of the chairs in the auditorium to run toward me, oblivious to Adam's and my quiet ritual. I looked at Adam as if to say "Oops! I think we're gonna get cut short." Moments later, Dawn almost knocked me over with a big bear hug, which I returned, shrugging with one hand as I looked back at Adam.

The program was beginning, so we got settled fast. Sitting between the two of them, I literally did not know who to be. But here "I" was, between the two flesh pillars of my life, who flanked me with their contradictions and their uncanny symmetries. They paralleled the seemingly disparate rituals: the clothed and the naked offerings to the goddess (sometimes Shabbat on a Friday and sex party on a Saturday of the same weekend) that studded my nights like stars, inches apart to our eyes, but light years from each other.

Or were they?

One Pesach, I received an invitation to a Queer Naked Seder, held at what was known to some as the Radical Faerie House, where lots of queer sex parties were held. Radical faeries are a loose-knit association of queer men who see themselves as outside the mainstream gay community, particularly its more commercial representations. They are more likely to have tribal-style body modifications, and names like Dandelion, Clover, and Pussy Willow.

The house itself is three stories, with a dungeon in the lower level, and a kitchen usually full with food during parties, living room, deck, giant hot tub, and waterfall on the second level. There is a plush, open living room full of pillows and intricate geometric stained-glass lamps. There are more dick images—in marble, plexiglass, oil paint, latex, plastic, and, yes, wood—than one set of eyes can usually take in in a single evening, especially when the room is filled with live dicks (they can be so distracting!). The Radical Faerie House sits innocently next to a large, imposing church.

The Queer Naked Seder, Downy and Seth's idea, began on the top floor and worked its way down to the dungeon. By that time we had divided into Egyptians and Jews, and the Egyptians were using the SM equipment to enslave the Jews, reenacting the Pesach story. Having been cast as Miriam (I was one of only a handful of women there), I led the naked Jews out of the dungeon with my tambourine, up onto the deck, and through the parted waters of the giant hot tub. For 40 years, we wandered the desert staircase, until we reached the top deck of Jerusalem—all in God's glorious skin and nothing else. We made our way back to the large living room and continued with the more traditional elements of Pesach ritual: the bitter herbs, the maror, the hardboiled eggs dipped in salt water.

When our common Jewish story was once again honored for that season, the Queer Naked Sederites commenced the rituals more common to that room: stroking, licking, fucking, and sucking using the safer sex supplies kindly provided by the gracious host. Boys will be boys, after all, and what else would one expect of naked boy-loving boys? Besides, we have little or no evidence to suggest that this latter component of the ritual was not, in fact, in keeping with the earliest historical traditions.

Meanwhile, I had begun hosting sex parties of my own with my best friend Dana. (I had met her at one of my first sex parties. It turned out she too had been hauled away to that very same smart kids school in Miami. It also turned out our moms had gone to Miami Beach High School together in the 1950s, and known each other.) "Have your worlds collided enough yet?" Shaddai asked me playfully. "Nah," I responded in earnest prayer. "I'm just beginning."

I had realized that I found the climate of most sex parties decidedly non-erotic. I had also realized that I got very hot and bothered after many performances with erotic content I had attended, and resented not being able to fuck the audience right then and there. Thus, Sluts on Stage was born.

Dana, another woman, and I hosted a series of sex parties preceded by erotic performance. One spring party, a woman dressed in Easter Bunny ears and cracked raw eggs on her naked body. This same woman, at another party, set herself on fire. Another time, I sang a version of the e. e. cummings poem that begins, "I like my body when it is with your body it is so quite new a thing . . ." set to music and played by a guitarist friend. People danced, stripped, read erotic stories, and shared fantasies and their barely clothed bodies. Then and only then, we oozed into the corporeal portion of the program. Because I was so busy hosting, I never really experienced the organic melding of Eros into sex that was my raison d'être for the party itself, but other people seemed to enjoy themselves.

I began to notice that *play parties*, the term by which San Francisco's sex-radical community referred to these postmodern orgies, provided something not available in other areas of life: sex-optional space. Most spaces in our lives are sex-prohibitive; it would be a serious transgression of social norms to have sex in most restaurants, movie theaters, or outdoor events. Or else they are sex-mandatory: Two people naked in a bedroom. Turned on, one might be insulted if the other suddenly started tapping their Palm Pilot.

But here were rooms full of people, some cuddling lazily in puppy piles, others fucking madly, over time forming intricate histories of knowing each others' sounds, predilections, and hot buttons. Moments created themselves out of these circumstances, moments with sweetness and humor unique to the situation. For example, at one Sluts on Stage party, Dawn had been getting it on for quite some time with a lovely young woman. When they stopped for a bit of air, their conversation revealed that a) it was the lass's first sex party, and b) she also was Jewish. They sang a *shehekhiyanu*, a blessing for when something is done for the first time, or for the first time that year. I loved hearing the familiar Hebrew ringing out from among the piles of bodies strewn along the floor. By the end of the prayer, several other Jews had joined in the melody, much like Gentiles when they sing "Happy Birthday."

At another party, I lay cuddling with Chance, years after we had stopped fucking. A couple of other people were lying near us. We kept our voices low out of consideration for the other more active players, standard sex-party etiquette. To our left, one woman fucked another doggy style with a dildo in a harness. To our right, a man fucked his partner in the same position. We noticed the stereo fuckers with amusement—their rhythms as they matched and syncopated and became disjointed once again, their expressions, and the beautiful symmetry of it all.

Finally, both the tops noticed each other, took in the whole scene, and burst out laughing. Chance and I and our little gallery of observers laughed too. Then both groggy but gleeful bottoms shyly stuck their heads up and looked around. My heart leapt with joy. Where else could such sacred choreography be witnessed, such joy and comfort in our bodies be nurtured? I began to see the power of sex-optional space as holy unto itself.

Around this time, Adam and Dawn both moved to the Bay Area, then slipped out of my life shortly thereafter—out of my romantic life, anyway. Devastated, for the first time in my life, I leapt immediately into another relationship, crowding the space I would in the past have used to grieve deeply. I met Flash: big, bad, butch, Jewish, tattooed, pierced, funky-haired, and absolutely fearless. I had throbbed for her for years, beginning with one of her own erotic performances, before she finally noticed me. In fact it was that performance, in which she mime-fisted a man and woman in parallel scenarios, that turned me on so much it clinched my decision to combine performance with sex party.

When December rolled around again, it was now three years since Chance, Dawn, and I had ushered in Shabbat and Christmas with pornography and hors d'oeuvres in that tribadistic trio. Carrying on the tradition, Flash and I decided to host a Jew Girl Schtup-Fest, a sex party for Jewish women who might otherwise feel bored, alienated, or horny on December 24. My growing cadre of Jew girl buddies, ex-lovers, and crushes all showed up with dreydls on, and a splendid time was had by all.

The following spring, now the third-year incarnation of the Queer Naked Seder, I was asked to lead the service itself. Downy, Seth, and I converged to create a new liturgy based on this departure from tradition that was itself becoming a tradition. Taking a Seder that Adam had put together a couple of years before, I replaced nearly all of God's names with *Shaddai*, "as it is by, through and for experiencing and naming the pleasures of our bodies that we arrive at this place," I wrote in the Seder. The cover featured *Shaddai* in Hebrew letters fashioned of blooming vulvas and squirting phalluses, as well as the dictionary definitions above of "queer," "naked," and "Seder."

The following is an excerpt from the introduction, which (to the best of my memory) I wrote:

> In the name of respecting all sentient beings, tonight we have instead a
> *blood orange*, symbolizing the historical power of blood, and in particu-
> lar, women's cycle of life-giving bleeding. The orange also sits on the

seder plate in honor of Jewish women leaders. Susannah Heschel, daughter of the big *macher* Abraham Heschel, reportedly asked a council of conservative rabbis about the possibility of women becoming rabbis. She was told,

"A woman has as much chance of becoming a rabbi as an orange has of winding up on the seder plate."

It is said that "Whoever enlarges upon the telling of the Exodus from Egypt, those persons are praiseworthy." Tonight, we find and subvert instances of enslavement mentality (such as the orange) in our own communities, creating little Exodi as we go along. We also ask and answer questions, sharing stories from our own lives and multiple traditions.

Many of us have dropped Judaism as a religion because of its lack of ability to help us make sense of our (post)modern lives, one of the basic functions of religion. We have turned to other spiritual traditions or material practices for order, solace, and meaning. Rather than robotically repeat traditional words we learned growing up, and save our "true" spirituality for when we are alone, or with non-Jews, we reclaim *community* as the very foundation of Judaism. We honor the material world of the present, and our wonderful bodies as holy in themselves, and we resurrect traditions of early Judaism, retelling stories that speak to our hearts, our souls, our bodies, and our inquiring minds.

What we are doing tonight may look and seem like a radical departure from the traditional Judaism many of you know. It may feel strange— like a perversion, of sorts, of an honored tradition. In fact, we are in many cases doing something even *more* traditional, by resurrecting the earth-based roots of Judaism, aspects that our modern material world has long ago let fall by the wayside.

Just as we don't know what forms enslavement and liberation will take 20 or 100 years from now, and what their versions of Pesach will look like, so our great-grandparents could probably not have predicted a Seder exactly like this taking place right now. We may trust ourselves to figure out what is needed in each historical moment to continually move our consciousness out of slavery, to enlarge upon the telling of the Exodus in ways responsive to the times in which we live. Let us explain to you, dear ancestors: We conduct tonight's ritual naked, or nearly naked, to enact the breaking free of the slavery of shame, anti-eroticism, and siege upon our queer, kinky, perverted, and otherwise deemed unacceptable bodies. We claim the sacredness of our body, and all its consensual activities. We embrace body and spirit as one, and so *daven* (pray) unclothed. Our naked bodies are the offerings, the sacraments, and the vessels for our holiness. With our "counterfeit" embodiedness, we reject the hegemony that renders them so. Our queer naked bodies are incarnations of *Shaddai*, the Embodied Spirit.

We were all a bit nervous that year because Downy's parents had accepted his invitation to attend the Queer Naked Seder. I was still getting used to people my age getting into hot tubs naked with their parents. I projected a sort of fragility onto them: Could they handle the overt sexuality? Would this or that make them uncomfortable? They were fine; it was my friends and I who were nervous. But here was a bit of the heterogeneity I had been missing —here was the Queer Jewish ghetto sliding into the suburbs, property values fluctuating like mad, and I was *schvitzing* like the Red Sea.

I survived the Queer Naked Seder. I'm still not sure if Downy's mom was flirting with me. But I couldn't handle the possibility of having sex with two members of the same family (the year before, I had had a sweet interlude with Downy, her lovely son), especially if one was the offspring of the other, let alone the whole family being in the same room. So I just didn't let myself go there.

By now, other Queer Minyanites were infected with the Holy Fuck Bug. A handful of we fag-identified women managed to make our way into theretofore all-male sex enclaves, and create some sacred moments in the face of fags newly familiar with the female form, not to mention some hot homo sex of our own. I hosted a couple of Mitzvah Shabbats, basically a Shabbat ritual in which we thanked *Shaddai* for the light, bread, and wine, and then moved into erotic space (in other words, had a "play party"), the mitzvah part of the Shabbat. Around this time, Alina, one of the founders of Queer Minyan, created and hosted a bleeding ritual, honoring her menstruation. Somewhat skeptical, I went.

The process of sharing our stories about bleeding, eating red, red fruits and juices, and blessing and honoring bleeding *yonis* (Sanskrit for "vulva," and a popular alternative to "pussy" or "cunt" in many New Age and pagan circles) surprised me by its effects. For a while, anyway, the vaguely uneasy sense I had had in my body was transformed. I felt a new comfort and relaxation.

This vaguely uneasy sense of being a stranger to, for example, the permutations of my own pussy, led me to conclude at different points that I might feel happier in a man's body, insofar as hormones might let me approximate that, and my aching identification with (alternative) fag culture, bodies, and sex. But the blood ritual quieted my angst, and helped me feel more at ease in my beautiful female body. Thank you, Alina, and the rest of you who were there.

Now, the worlds had mixed, indeed. Everywhere I went, I saw people I knew from somewhere else. Sometimes it was (is) a little unnerving to see someone in a social or spiritual setting, fully clothed, who was naked, blindfolded, and screaming in bliss when last you met.

More and more, I found my spirituality began and ended with my body—that is, many of the most important messages of my life begin with a sensation or feeling in my body. Western culture separates the life of the mind from the world of the body. The spirituality I am drawn to weaves them together once more. Many facets of alternative medicine embrace and explore the mind-body connection, but in no arena have I felt the opportunity for direct, embodied worship in community more than in the Sacred Sex Party, the various combinations of Jewish and pagan rituals preceding sex-optional space. Even those parties without express rituals at the beginning very often create a container of intention (and also have many of the same guests) to fashion a climate that holds sex as sacred, and others in the space as worthy of the greatest respect.

These days, though I go to the occasional sex party, I have not hosted a sex ritual in a long time. I don't feel the same drive. I have also found a shul that, while not perfect, meets my needs for community and for uplifting of the spirit, for song, dance, strong women, big bad butch dykes (yes, one leads a Torah service!), and, yes, love. My world is multiple and paradoxical, but I no longer feel fragmented and torn.

I feel like a kaleidescope.

EPILOGUE

After writing a first draft of this essay, I went to the Jewish renewal synagogue that has been my spiritual home most recently, and, I expect, for the foreseeable future. The male rabbi who usually leads services was away. The women who usually flank him on the stage and speak only occasionally led the service instead. Congregants I spoke with afterward really enjoyed the variety and diversity—I know I did. I believe it's time in this arena, as well, to make more room for women. I, and others who want this, need to speak up to encourage this.

Ironically, at one point, one of the women addressed the question of separation: "Our great sense of separation," she said, "owed to our bodies." Living as spiritual beings in bodies separates us from one another. I wanted to shout out how it didn't have to be that way, how it isn't that way everywhere, how bodies coming together (though we don't usually *daven* that way in synagogue) can be the most holy of acts.

WHOSE SIDE ARE YOU ON?

TRANSGENDER AT THE WESTERN WALL

TJ Michels and Ali Cannon

Blessed are you, Adonai our God, Ruler of the Universe, for having created me according to Thy will.   —MORNING BRACHAH

THE WESTERN WALL in the Old City of Jerusalem, where the First and Second Temples once stood, unequivocally represents Judaism's holiest site.

It is a site where the religious wrap *tefillin* and fulfill their *mitzvot*, where secular tourists stuff prayers into its weed-filled cracks, and where the diaspora focuses its collective emotional attention, even thousands of miles away.

But it is a site where males and females do not mix, where 13-year-old boys vibrantly rejoice in reading the Torah for the first time, where girls the same age are expected to contain their prayers to near whisper, where women have been heckled and had eggs, chairs, and feces hurled at them by men incensed they dare to don *tallisim* and conduct Torah services in public religious space.

And it is a site where two queer Jews, a transgender man, and a transgender butch, independently faced life-altering experiences—exhilarating and painful respectively—as they descended upon it, where two people traversed the confines of gender and blurred the boundaries the *mechitzah* seeks to maintain.

It is a site where they each problematized their gender, or gender problematized them, and where they prayed, most significantly, as Jews.

▼

We first met after TJ, an editor at a Jewish newspaper, interviewed Ali for a story on his involvement in a queer Jewish performance ensemble. In the course of the conversation, we learned we both had transformative experiences at the Western Wall: Ali spoke of the poems he wrote, about passing on the men's side of the Wall. TJ had struggled to pen an article on visiting the men's side—after being refused entry on the women's side.

TJ later agreed to write on the juxtaposition of gender and religious identity using the Kotel incident as a launching pad for this essay. She invited Ali to collaborate, evolving into this dialogue.[1]

Our goal is twofold: To posit the compelling, but often contentious, butch/female-to-male transgender discussion—what Gayle Rubin first coined as "frontier fears," later inspiring Judith Halberstam and Jacob Hale's "butch/FTM border wars"—in a Jewish context.[2] We feel it both necessary and urgent to explore where and how we connect and diverge vis à vis our respective locations, but seek to avoid replicating the combativeness of earlier community debates. The few works to elaborate on the various nuances of masculine gender identifications primarily originating within lesbian communities are seminal. However, we know of few that specifically address regulatory notions of Jewish masculinity.[3]

Secondly, we wish to carve a space for transgendered people within Jewish tradition, and vice versa, by paying particular attention to how our queer sexualities and trans locations challenge and intersect with our spiritual and cultural identities. Combining subjective and analytic discourses, it is our hope to demonstrate that with the same indefatigability that has preserved the Western Wall and the continuity of our people, so too, will our struggles transform our traditions and communities.

TJ: We're beginning this dialogue at an interesting cultural juncture: when transgender is just starting to click in the queer world and queer is beginning to register in the Jewish world. Using our respective experiences at the Wall —this holy site fraught with symbolism and metaphors—we're two transgender Jews talking about being and living as transgender Jews. I'm hoping we can illuminate areas of overlap as well as departure. Both of us participate at the same synagogue and are heavily invested in various dyke and trans communities, but we currently occupy different locations on the gender/sexual continuum. I have not transitioned in the "typical" sense: hormonally and/or surgically. I guess transgender butch or boy are the most intelligible ways within queer culture to describe myself, for now.

Ali: While "transition" has historically been used by psychiatrists and surgeons to describe the moment in which one makes a medical intervention in the gendering of their body—sex reassignment surgery—I think that the modern transgender movement is challenging the narrow assumption of those definitions. In the six months since I made the big decision to start testosterone, I have not been viewed as a woman, except for once or twice over the phone because my voice is still changing. But I began my transition more than two years ago, when I first started living as a man.

I'm really interested in exploring, as a trangender man, our experiences in terms of how we differently identify along the butch-trans spectrum. I think it's important for both of us to tell our specific stories to engage Judaism in a new type of conversation about what we mean when we say gender and gender identity.

TJ: And how Israel played a role in our identity formation specifically.

Ali: Right. I'll start by describing my experience in Israel in 1999.

As background, I should mention that I came out as a lesbian in 1982, two years before I "came out" as a Jew, as was true for many of the dykes of the "nice Jewish girls" generation.[4] As Evelyn Torton Beck argued, many of us didn't have the tools to overcome internalized anti-Semitism until we first chipped away at our internalized homophobia.

But I've spent much of the past 17 years claiming a strong Jewish identity that was not part of my childhood. And taking my first trip to Israel was definitely a spiritual journey for me.

By the time my girlfriend Jessica—who's now my wife—and I were preparing for our trip that summer, my sense of self was shifting. I was, in a very limited way, starting to identify as transgendered. I didn't know exactly what that meant for me but I knew that it meant something.

After we got the tickets to go to Israel, I still had to apply for a passport. I filled out the application, checked the female box—I had not legally changed my gender from female to male—and submitted the form along with my female birth certificate and my head shot. And my passport came back from the federal government with an "M" on it! In the words of Irena Klepfisz, an important mentor of mine, this was *bashert* to happen to me; it was something I had to pay attention to on many levels. Essentially I went to Israel with a passport that said I was male, so I practiced going into men's bathrooms and prepared myself to live as a man for some period of my stay.

TJ: That's amazing. You realize, Ali, that you may very well be the first FTM to be recognized as legally male, according to a federal document, long before getting the restroom thing down pat? I almost feel compelled to say a *shehechiyanu!* Can you talk a bit about how a religious site became the catalyst for a queer epiphany?

Ali: Going to the Wall was a specific site of gender identity formation and resistance for me as a Jew and as a nascently identified transgender person. Israel is a more markedly gendered place. There are gender police at every religious site. Throughout the trip, we'd gone to various religious sites, and I never was given the modest clothing for the women to wear. And I don't have a flat chest! *No one* ever noticed that I had breasts, which is weird for me because as a butch, and now as a transgendered man, I'm very conscious of the fact that I have breasts. So to claim my male identity at that holy place was to affirm my right to seek the deepest sense of myself as a Jewish man in the making.

Of course, walking down that path to the Wall, I knew that I was crossing the great binary divide of Jewish law and regulated social religious space; as a born woman, I was also aware that I was not "supposed" to be there.

This excerpt from one of the poems I wrote about going to the Wall expresses some of what I am talking about:

> in the day light
> I wrap the large cream tallis
> With dark blue stripes
> to honor the heavens
> around my body
> the most sacred aloneness
> that Judaism allows
>
> bowing at the Kotel, rocking back and forth
> like a million Jewish men before me
> I write prayers for the transgendered
> Ask that the Jewish people
> become less binary
> less misogynist

but this is too technical
I am here at the Wall
and this is where I belong

a man in a black coat comes up to me asking for money
without tzedaka I am not worth his time

I leave this holy site of men
still a man on these streets
not even my passport betrays me[5]

TJ: It sounds like the way you experienced Israel and the Wall was something of a metaphoric Bar Mitzvah, both a Jewish rite of passage and "becoming a man."

Ali: By the time I went to the Wall, there were a lot of questions coming up. It was both "This is rite of a passage," and "Is this really a rite of passage?"

It's important to note here that my close friends who lived in Jerusalem thought I was going to the men's side of the Wall as a butch dare, to see if I could pull off passing as a man. But Nicole and Ruti didn't know that I was experiencing Israel as a man instead of a dyke. I had mentioned, nonchalantly, that my passport had an "M" on it, but that was it. So, they didn't really get it, because I didn't talk about it—because I was afraid to talk about it.

I knew that going to the Wall was a rite of passage for me as a Jew and as the man I was becoming, but it was somewhat private. The issue for me centered on how much of my trans identity I was claiming. I knew that I wanted to go to the men's side. Even in my young trans identity I wasn't interested in going to the women's side. However, had I been in a different place in my identity, I would have wanted to go to the women's side. I had hardly ever been in communities with men. Yet I was able to take our lesbian friends' three-year-old son up to the Wall, aware that as a man, I was responsible for sharing this experience with him within the prescribed boundary of male space and generational time.

I even went back to the Wall to pray again—still not out to my close friends—and so the journey was also mediated by that fact. Regardless, that act of going to the Wall and living as a man for three weeks in Israel catapulted me into a sense of urgency; I had to seek out the FTM community when I came back to the States. I had to reconcile that rite of passage because I had claimed something most sacred about myself as a man before those ancient stones. I was left to come to terms with my trans identity for the year and a half following that important trip to Israel.

What was your experience of going to the Wall, TJ? How did that impact your sense of gender identity and your identity as a Jew?

TJ: To give you some background, my agenda for going to the Western Wall was simple: to pray to God. And that was huge; powerful enough for me to "forget" that what, or who, I would pray *as* could very well come into play.

Before this trip, I had returned to Judaism after several lapsed years—not surprisingly, the period of time between my Bat Mitzvah and coming out as a dyke. Whereas I never felt the need to "come out" as a Jew—I enjoyed both (ostensibly) egalitarian Reform and Conservative environments growing up—I had only recently acknowledged my belief in God. This dramatically tilted my identity from passive to active: I was shifting from the cultural Jew who "felt" Jewish to a more observant Jew who has a felt need to engage with Judaism and God.

I'm sure I viewed it as a rite of passage; gone were the days of shul day-dreaming during the Amidah. I had it in my head that I would come to know the *kavanah* of prayer and that God is somehow "closer" there. I wouldn't say that today, but at the time, I suppose some sort of Zionist socialization had seeped its way in.

Complicating matters, though, was I didn't have this warm, fuzzy "Jew among Jews" feeling in Israel as I had anticipated. I could almost taste the bitter division between the religious and the secular. It's a dichotomy that's foreign to most American Jews, because our communities in the United States are so pluralistic.

Ali: This clearly was a spiritual journey for you, then. You weren't checking out the gay scene?

TJ: Somewhat in Tel Aviv, but the Old City is a whole other animal. I was with my sister, Mindy, and her partner, Melissa. We're a trio of queers. Given that we were in the Middle East, none of us particularly wished to stand out, but with my baggy shorts, T-shirt, and shaved head peering from underneath a baseball cap, I guess I didn't do the best job of camouflaging myself.

To get to the Wall, we entered through the Dung gate instead of the Jewish quarter tunnel, meaning we had to go through a set of metal detectors and security turnstiles marked women's or men's entrance. Without much thought, I followed my sisters. As long as I don't bind my breasts, which I generally don't, I operate under the assumption that my sex will be read as unambiguously female; my gender pegged as some version of dyke. And when I do pass—I owe it all to the military cut and hairy legs—it tends to be momentary, with considerable embarrassment on the part of the other. Since I had forgotten to pack long pants in my knapsack, I was a bit nervous the groundskeepers would make me put on one of those horrendous skirts to cover my bare calves. Luckily, nobody stopped me, and I figured I was in the clear.

As we stepped onto the plaza, I could feel myself getting intensely emotional with a good hundred feet before the stone itself. I told my sisters to go on ahead. I needed to be alone.

I began to slowly make my way, until a uniformed officer stopped me in my tracks. I didn't speak enough Hebrew to know what he was saying, but he was very, very agitated. Damn, I thought, all this fuss because he can see the few inches of skin between my knees and my workboots. I could see a box of those raggedy *shmatas* out of the corner of my eye so I pointed over to them, to indicate I would put one of them on, however humiliating. But that didn't seem to change his mind, which confused the hell out of me. By now, he was yelling and gesticulating wildly. My heart was racing; I felt completely intimidated and at a loss for what his problem was. Finally, he pointed to the other side of the plaza.

In other words, this soldier—or was he literally the gender police?—figured he was on to me; he suspected I was a guy trying to sneak into the women's side.

Ali: That must have felt entirely disorienting.

TJ: It knocked the wind out of me. I assumed I'd be viewed with suspicion for rejecting femininity, but I hadn't expected to pass per se. You and I both have probably garnered considerable skill in the gender attribution game. I know that when I'm read as male, I replay every detail in my head: What kind of space was I in, what was I wearing, who was I with, my demeanor and disposition? Alternatively, when I perform gender in unconvincing ways, I mentally analyze the endless particulars that may seem absurd to non-trans folks. By virtue of being non-normatively gendered, I believe many of us become acutely aware of—that's code for "obsessed with"—how we are being perceived. That said, in a foreign land I don't have the context to assess people's perceptions of gender.

Ali: Which at home allows us to perform gender in ways meaningful to our culture. Neither of us had a point of reference to expect we would be treated as men as readily as we were. I may have been forced into thinking about it in advance of the trip. Because of the passport issue, I feared for my safety if I *didn't* pass. But I was shocked that it took absolutely no effort—and it sounds as if you were operating under the assumption that Israel was an inappropriate place to make the effort.

TJ: It didn't occur to me to attempt the men's side from the get-go, not that it felt "right" to go to the women's side. The divider itself is incredibly problematic on multiple levels. As Jewish feminists have noted, the *mechitzah* doesn't just separate women and men: It keeps the women *away* from men. But from a transgender critique, the *mechitzah* functions much like the binary gender system that says there are two, and only two genders, which must be congruent with one's sex, in other words, genitals.

Not to mention that in Israel, especially the Old City, I was almost entirely in "Jew mode," the first time in my adult life that queerness ever took a backseat. By way of some epistemic inheritance, I "just knew" this holy, historical setting coursed through my bloodstream by birthright or some such *meshugas*.

Though I have constructed my Jewish identity in consciously chosen ways as an adult, being a Jew is the one constant that has at least *felt* essential to my existence; inexplicably, it is who I am. But the hegemonic power of the Orthodox had forced me to take pause in Israel. How did I know myself to be a Jew when these black-hatted sorts were the "real" thing?

This impression already had me emotionally overcome before this male soldier, whose language I don't share, began to verbally attack me. Fearing for my safety, I backed away from him, to advance toward the men's side.

But paralysis stopped me dead. In my mind, I was devoid of any option. Even if I walked over to the men's side, someone would surely notice my breasts, yell at me or kick me out, or worse. I had no access to the women's side *or* the men's side—and no recognizable gender. Long before Israel, I had stopped identifying as a woman, but here I couldn't even "count" as one. Being considered among the men, in this context, made just as little sense.

So in that moment, I phenomenologically vanished. I had absolutely no identity to reasonably cling to, my body was rendered meaningless. What I had once clung to as a fundamental truth—I am a Jew—not only had been called into question, but became a casualty, too, as my gender ceased to be intelligible.

In the past few years, hanging out in the margins had somehow, paradoxically, become this comfortable place for me to loiter. But no amount of gender anxiety has before prevented me from passing, as *possessing* a gender. It must be horrifying for people who are absolutely gender ambiguous or at an awkward stage of transitioning. Most people don't know how to interact with transgender people because our culture remains so preoccupied with trying to figure out if you're a man or a woman. This was that kind of debasement—I just was utterly indiscernible. There was no space for me.

Ali: What you're saying about feeling debased, your body rendered meaningless, seems to be at the core of something incredibly painful. What's different about my experience is that I was starting to recognize that I no longer could be in that margin of having my gender be ambiguous; I just couldn't survive from there. So what ended up being your next move?

TJ: I had to pull myself together because I was intent on *davening*. From behind my sunglasses, tears were streaming. I made my way to the men's side. There was all this commotion and jubilation. Men were dancing around the Torah and Bnai Mitzvah. Admittedly, it was quite spectacular to be that close to it all. And in their preoccupation, no one noticed me. But as I neared the actual Wall, I took a glance to my right, toward the *mechitzah* that separated the men from the women. I could see all these women struggling to look over it: It was their sons and grandsons and nephews that had just read from the Torah, who were being elevated in chairs by their elder patriarchs. The women could only experience these celebrations from behind the divider.

And there were Mindy and Melissa, pining to catch a look, to snap a photo. I stood there, facing them perpendicularly. It was chilling. My sisters, my first feminist dyke mentors, were being kept from what should have been accessible to all. Guilt-ridden, I felt a wave of unwanted privilege, and it made me incredibly uncomfortable. I tend to feel at most ease being among men—well, within fag space—but not as a means to acquire privilege. Passing had always been such a thrill, a validation. But this? I didn't want it.

It took being in Jerusalem, on the men's side of the Wall, for me to realize that years of gender dysphoria—all the things that I wanted to reject about my own body—had at times lodged itself as femme phobia, or even a form of sexism. I resented having feminine characteristics attributed to me, to have the "fact" of my sex feel at odds with my gender. Given that so few people can read the fiction of it all, I've had moments of anger that I've projected onto those who embody femininity.

So here came another epiphany, which I transformed into a choice: either be the oppressor or be the oppressed, which really isn't a choice at all. I had to get over to the women's side where I "belonged," and I had to get past that guard.

I headed back over and sure enough, he got in my face. Mysteriously, he spoke to me in English this time. I still remember the timbre of his voice, his manner of questioning me in a slow deliberate grunt. "Are . . . you . . . a *woman?*" And I paused because it's almost never something I answer affirmatively. I had to say yes. He took a step back, looked me up and down, and had this "you're despicable" look on his face. With a deep breath, I headed up to where the women were gathered, and it is on that side of the Wall that I prayed. Sobbing, I asked God to guide me, with patience, to become a better Jew.

Ali: As transgender people, our bodies hang in the balance—to be found out, scrutinized, made unwhole by outsiders' perception of us. You had so much taken away from you by that gender-policing guard. He challenged your right to define your gender on your own terms.

But I am curious to hear you say more about how being on the men's side made you feel like being on the side of the oppressor. This speaks to me about the issues of transitioning and the accusation of "betraying" women.

TJ: That reaction does seem a bit extreme now, but mind you at the time, my agency and autonomy had been challenged by that guard, flooding me with a sense that I had turned my back on feminism the moment I came out as trans. And I'm willing to concede this emotion; this guilt comes despite the arsenal of logical defenses many of us built up against those who accuse us of betraying "the sisterhood." Like you said earlier, you were afraid at first to share with Nicole and Ruti that you were experiencing, not to mention enjoying, Israel as a man. These kinds of fears, I think, are almost presupposed when you're socialized in the lesbian-feminist world.

There were few environments for me to confront that until I went to Israel and witnessed firsthand how pervasively patriarchal Judaism can be.

But I think you're touching on something crucial here. Within the queer world, we hear a lot about, and fall prey to, the anxieties surrounding that fuzzy, discursive overlap between lesbian, butch, boydyke, transgender, FTM, and so on. So often the people who challenge and "cross" gender boundaries by transitioning have been, and still are accused of, betraying the lesbian community. And in Jewish lesbian communities, the issues become even more complicated. Jewish feminists have long complained about how sexist Judaism's customs can be, and have constructed an entire body of knowledge and ritual to reclaim an egalitarian Judaism. The notion that someone born female would want to become party to male privilege raises suspicions and hostility, unfortunately, but I think this is misguided. Your experience testifies to that. Appropriating masculinity via a trans trajectory—and all the discrimination that comes with that—is not necessarily synonymous with appropriating the misogyny of paradigmatic men.

Ali: The whole notion of betrayal to me is an avoidance of looking at the complex notions of gender that transgender folk call into play. Betraying women, betraying feminism, for being transgender, for wanting to be seen as a man, for feeling like a man, for living as a man—these are big things that disrupt certain boundaries feminist theory has constructed in the hopes of creating justice for women. I feel like most people who conform to conventional gender categories are not walking around in their bodies the way you and I are walking around in our bodies. Normatively gendered people can't theorize about who we are from their own personal experience, and therefore, what right do folks have to accuse us of betrayal? There's a dangerous tendency among non-trans academics (in other words, most of academia) to theorize *us*, and that is part of the silencing of our voices, bodies, and self-identifications.[6] Of course, that's happening in the Jewish lesbian community too.

A recent example of this occurred the night you attended Chutzpah: A Queer Jewish Show, where I read my poems about the Wall at Luna Sea, a women's theater and performance space. The annual show originated as a Jewish dyke ensemble, but expanded to include FTMs and bi women.

A well-known Jewish lesbian writer shared the stage with me. She read a poem named something to the effect of "Butch Resisting the Pressure to Change Genders." The content of the poem—which included the line "is this what we fought for?"—was even more hurtful than the title suggests. One FTM walked out. Another, a friend of mine who formerly identified as butch, was in tears. This writer refused to engage in a dialogue about her piece in a talk-back with the audience. Later, I was accosted by one woman who asked me what right I had, as a man, to be performing.

As a newly out transgender man, it was difficult to be up against that betrayal, on stage, in a primarily Jewish lesbian context. I'm proud to say that the theater, the cast, and most of the audience supported and celebrated trans inclusion in this location. However, that I was exposed to this hostility is not necessarily an anomaly.

TJ: I think one of feminism's failures is its desperation to maintain this seamless category of "women." The first thing we learn as we become budding radicals is that biological sex and gender are not the same thing. Imagine if we—that is, all women and genderqueers—let this feminist mantra really take us somewhere, instead of locking the door because it appears it might hit us on the way out.

For one thing, many of us who no longer identify *as* women nonetheless identify *with* women.[7] Our consciousness, histories, and life experiences involve considerable investment among queer, dyke, and women's communities. Hence, many FTMs and transgender butches' self-constructions still embody or pay historical debt to dyke nomenclature.[8]

Ali: I will always feel connected to the life I lived as a lesbian. My former self informs who I am in so many ways: the way I make love, the centrality of lesbians in my life, the anti-oppression models I've learned and still adhere to. I can't imagine a time in my life in the future when I wouldn't still make proud reference to my former dyke identity. That will always be something I am walking around with and that lends itself to much of my consciousness as a feminist transgender man who opposes gender-based discrimination of any kind.

TJ: Gender oppression, to me, is this culture saying there's two, and only two, things you can be. If you're not a man, you're a woman, period. Sure, there's more room to deviate presentation nowadays, but at times it feels like it's merely some androgynous vortex—Gap-mentality consumerism—that has sucked us all in. I'm much more interested in broadening our gender imaginations, not merely blending what's already in front of us, nor calling for a third gender, which really only winds up reinforcing the hegemonic two.[9] And at the same time, not feel forced to abandon the tradition and rituals, in our case Judaism, that contribute such richness and spiritual meaning to our lives.

Ali: I think we learned from our respective visits to the Wall and this discussion that we can begin to carve a space for transgender people within our culture. My wife and I did exactly that by having a huge Jewish wedding.

A lesbian Reform rabbi married us—a transgender man and a bisexual woman. Jessica and I were married under a *chuppah* created by our family and friends. We circled one another seven times, exchanged rings, and recited the

Hebrew declaration of commitment: "Behold you are sanctified to me with this ring in keeping with the traditions of Moses, Miriam, and Israel before our God and this community."[10]

We felt it was a radical act to use the same words Jewish brides and grooms have been saying for centuries, even though our union would not have been previously sanctioned by Jewish law.

Our parents held our ketubah and passed it to us, symbolizing the blessing of the generations, and they wrapped us in my tallis. Honored members of our community blessed us, based on themes of the Sheva Brachot.

Our ceremony was transformative for us, for those in attendance, for Judaism itself. We claimed our right to have all the deep elements of a Jewish wedding, before God, and we made them our own. By doing so, under the *chuppah*, with the blessing of our rabbi, we insisted upon the inclusion of our love within the Jewish tradition.

TJ: Wow, Ali, it's beautiful to hear how you and Jessica have updated our customs in ways meaningful to you both, while preserving the sanctity of their origins.

I'm also trying to strike the balance between transformation and tradition. We both participate in the same lesbian, gay, bisexual, and transgender synagogue. But who doesn't notice the dominance among gay men first, then lesbian women? It seems as if bisexual and transgender Jews, as is the case with many community institutions, are erased. It is up to these individuals, not the congregation as a whole, to make efforts to fit in or not, educate others, or keep quiet.

I nonetheless find myself uncomfortable with all the tweaked passages, prayers, and melodies of the synagogue's siddur. Admittedly, there are times that I, and several of my friends, are annoyed that the neutralization of Hebrew has gone so overboard that the familiar Judaism we were raised with is no longer recognizable. Understandably though, the amended wording is highly significant to many congregants, mostly women, alienated by the original text.

So in addition to our progressive synagogue, I have alternatively sought out a more traditional place of worship that would welcome me as openly queer: namely, a neighborhood Chabad-Lubavitch house. While this young rabbi and rebbetzin have embraced me from the start, as Chassids, they observe *halachic* sex roles. Recently, while celebrating Simchas Torah there, I knew the rabbi sensed my disappointment at the need to have two separate circles of dancing. To avoid confrontation, it was, of course, vital that I locate myself among the women. But it was also strategically necessary for me to become one: the *mechitzah* has become a call for me to ally myself with those oppresssed by it. Interestingly, as the rabbi proceeded to offer rounds of *l'chaim* to the men, he poured shots of whiskey for his butch guest, too, opening the access of partaking in this particular *mitzvah* to all in attendance. Additionally, he has made it quite clear to me that I may bring whomever I please to his Shabbos table, and so I have.

To varying degrees, I apply pressure as well as applaud progress at both settings—be it the LGBT Reform congregation, where I was initially welcomed because of my queerness, or the ultra-Orthodox shul, where I was initially welcomed because of my Jewishness. Undoubtedly, as I flitter back and forth, I reinforce my location as an inhabitant of fluctuating margins. It is much easier to live in this body as a construction that I've carved out, rather than as a set of identities that were pushed out.

Judith Halberstam has suggested that "butches and FTMs alike think carefully about the kinds of men or masculine beings that we become and lay claim to: alternative masculinities, ultimately, will fail to change existing gender hierarchies to the extent that they fail to be feminist, antiracist, antielitist, and queer."

A Jewish FTM friend of mine likens Halberstam's *tikkun olam*-like call as embodying all that it means to be a mensch. Throughout our struggles, I think it would serve us well individually and as a community to keep this in mind as we continue to participate in our shuls, at our Shabbos tables and simchas, before God, as Jews. Just as we seek to interpret the positive values within our texts, so too, should we embody progressive definitions of our genders.

I would like to think that we each had a nascent version of Halberstam's vision, conscious or subconscious, when we each went to the Wall, motivating us to act accordingly, in ways truest to ourselves and our communities, given the constraints.

Ali: I think we each challenged the gender hierarchy that exists at the Wall by going there as transgender Jews while in a place of inventing ourselves. Our conversation has made connections in a way that no longer isolates our transgressive experiences in Israel. I'm hopeful about the manner in which we are bringing our trans selves to Jewish institutions, the way we are bringing Jewish identity into the transgender fold. Overall, the act of having this dialogue helps mediate the possibility of differently gendered understandings within the Jewish community, within Judaism itself.

NOTES

1. A quick note on pronouns: TJ has not, at this point, transitioned in medically—or, for the most part, socially—validated ways. The use of third-person feminine pronouns in no way is intended to suggest that surgical and/or hormonal transition is the requisite for linguistically conforming to the gender of one's choice. However, for various reasons beyond the scope of this essay, TJ is not discomforted by use of them. That notwithstanding, she is uncomfortable being attributed to feminine constructs of gendered nouns, such as, girl, lady, woman. For more on this, see TJ Michels, "Rants of a Label Whore," www.gay.com. As an FTM, Ali has transitioned socially and hormonally, and is referred to in masculine terminology. It would be inappropriate to do otherwise.

2. Gayle Rubin, "Of Catamites and Kings: Reflections on Butch, Gender, and Boundaries," in *The Persistent Desire: A Femme-Butch Reader*, Joan Nestle, ed. (Boston: Alyson, 1992) and Judith Halberstam and C. Jacob Hale, "Butch/FTM Border Wars: A Note on Collaboration" in *GLQ, A Journal of Lesbian and Gay Studies*, Vol. 4, No. 2, 1998.

3. See, for instance Rubin, Hale & Halberstam, and Halberstam, *Female Masculinity* (North Carolina: Duke UP, 1998). Additionally, Naomi Scheman's "Queering the Center by Centering the Queer: Reflections on Transsexuals and Secular Jews" in *Feminists Rethink the Self,* Diane Tietjens Myers, ed. (Boulder: Westview Press, 1997) pp. 24–162, does raise separate issues of Judaism and transsexuality as they conflict with social normalizing apparatus. However, her intent was not to explore transgender Jewish identity. See also Danya Ruttenberg's "Blood Simple: Transgender Theory Hits the Mikveh" in *Yentl's Revenge: The Next Wave of Jewish Feminism* (Seal Press, 2001). We are encouraged by and pleased to be in the company of other transgender Jewish contributors to this anthology.

4. Evelyn Torton Beck, ed. *Nice Jewish Girls* (Watertown, MA.: Persephone Press, 1982). The publication of Beck's anthology marked an emergence of theory and activism that sought to make lesbian Jews visible agents of change within lesbian feminist communities, and to some extent, broader mainstream Jewish communities.

5. From "My Visit to the Wall: The Lesbian Friends' View" by Ali Cannon, 1999.

6. The most infamous of these is Janice Raymond, whose *The Transsexual Empire: The Making of a She-Male* (Boston: Beacon, 1979) became a work that stood as "the" lesbian-feminist critique of transsexuality long after its publication and gave rise to another, more recent separatist tirade: Sheila Jeffreys, *The Lesbian Heresy: A Feminist Perspective on the Lesbian Sexual Revolution* (Melbourne: Spinifex, 1993). Other examples coming from the queer theory/gender studies camp that tend to trivialize or deny transgender agency: Marjorie Garber, *Vested Interests: Cross Dressing and Cultural Anxiety* (New York: Routledge, 1992); Elizabeth Grosz, *Volatile Bodies: Toward a Corporeal Feminism* (Bloomington: Indiana UP, 1994); and Bernice L. Hausman, *Changing Sex: Transsexualism, Technology, and the Idea of Gender* (Durham, NC: Duke UP, 1995).

7. Hale, "Tracing a Ghostly Memory in My Throat: Reflections on FTM Feminist

Voice and Agency," in *Men Doing Feminism*, Tom Digby, ed. (New York: Routledge, 1998), pp. 101–103.

8. While there are multiple formal and informal community sources for this, one of the earliest documented accounts of FTMs on their butch and lesbian affiliations is in Deva, "FTM/Female-to-Male: An Interview with Mike, Eric, Billy, Sky and Shadow," in *Dagger: On Butch Women*, Lily Burana, Roxxie, and Linnea Due, eds. (San Francisco: Cleis Press, 1994).

9. Halberstam, "An Introduction to Female Masculinity," p. 26.

10. The addition of the biblical matriarch Miriam was added to the traditional declaration at Ali and Jessica's wedding to denote female representations within the People of the Book.

IN THE *ARON KODESH*

WRESTLING WITH
THE RABBINIC CLOSET

Anonymous

ALTHOUGH I AM an advanced rabbinical student, nearing graduation and ordination, I am an invisible man—to my fellow students and to you, my reader. No one who looks at me sees the real me, they see only the outline of what they need/want/desire to see. They see a passionate, educated, dynamic man who is ready and willing to jump into the churning waters of twenty-first century American Judaism. What they do not see, what they cannot see, is my queerness, my gayness, my otherness. I am an invisible man who leads a double life. It is difficult and often trying; however, I do make the best of it. Never did I ever think that I would lead such a life. Unfortunately, in order for me to succeed in rabbinical school, it is a life that I have to lead. To be sure, there are movements of Judaism that would have allowed me to be openly gay and a rabbi; however, I am neither a Reform nor Reconstructionist Jew. I am a traditional Jew and wish to be a traditional rabbi in the Conservative movement.

I am a rabbinical student and a gay man, and every aspect of my life is interconnected. I cannot be one without the other. Now, while neither my being a rabbinical student nor my being gay is in any way remarkable, the movement with which I am affiliated has no room for me. Although the Reform and Reconstructionist movements now admit openly gay and lesbian rabbinic students, the Conservative movement would have no room for me if they found out about me. This movement does not allow openly gay or lesbian students to be ordained as rabbis. Hence, my double life.

To be honest, I did not always aspire to the rabbinate. I had chosen an entirely different career path: a career in which my sexuality would not be a liability. My original career plans, to firmly ensconce myself in academia, demanded only that I write well and produce meaningful scholarship. However, somewhere along the line, the siren call of the rabbinate reached my ears, and I was unable to ignore it. Part of this call was about me recognizing the need for rabbis who were not of the "old mold"—those who had no ability to relate to their congregants. I saw myself as being a rabbi who could reach and teach all types of people. While I thought that I would make a good rabbi, I never felt as if I had enough knowledge. I didn't grow up in an observant home, didn't attend day school or yeshiva and I thought these were required for admission. I was also of the thinking that one needed to have memorized *Mishnah, Gemara*, and all the codes in order to apply. However, I was living as an observant Jew, and I read and studied everything I could get my hands on, and thought I might have a chance. So, even though I felt inadequately prepared for rabbinical school, I took the plunge. I applied to one rabbinical school and was accepted. I packed my bags, left a career and friends, and prepared myself for one more trip to graduate school. This trip was both physically demanding, as I had to uproot myself and travel across the country, as well as psychologically demanding because I had to put myself back into the closet.

There was one thing that I promised myself when I came out as a gay man when I was around 24 years old. While I did not envision myself as a poster-child for gay pride, wearing my queerness on my sleeve, I would never deny my queerness if I were asked point-blank about it. I am one who passes easily for straight, and I am often met with disbelief when I tell someone that I am gay. Because of this, I have been able to move in circles that would be closed to me if my gayness was more apparent. My brother, who has been my strongest supporter and greatest ally has also been my *malach HaShem*, my guardian angel. He has always been there to talk and to listen. He was the first person to whom I came out and is my confidant. He warned me that since I was a single man with no visible "romantic ties," the issue of my sexual orientation might come up in my interviews and would almost definitely come up during my years of study. Thankfully that has not yet been a bridge I have had to cross. To be honest, I was, and still am, surprised that it has not come up. The case may be that the rabbinical school assumes that because of the movement's policy, no openly gay or lesbian student would apply. There is another reason why this issue may not have come up. It's likely the present administration of the rabbinical school does not want to institute "witch-hunts." Unless they are faced with overwhelming evidence, I do not think that the deans of the school will try to ferret out gay and lesbian students.

I was "out" in my pre-rabbinical school life, but I did not have a lover when I began rabbinical school. I did have several romantic "friends" and a couple of "fuck buddies," and I was active in the East Coast bar and club scenes during the early 1990s. I knew that once rabbinical school began, my life would have to change, and that I would have to do something that was going to be very difficult. When I realized that I was gay and that there was nothing wrong with loving men, I felt as if a great weight had been removed from my soul and that a heavy door had finally swung open. Now, I knew that I would have to reenter the closet and once again bear that weight.

Although it was a steep price, I stepped back into the closet, not too deeply, and gently closed the door. I knew that it would be very difficult, but I had no idea that it would be impossible. During the early weeks of my first year, I had very few problems. I was too busy with classes and with work to worry about much of anything else. That quickly changed. As the workload decreased and I became more comfortable with school, I began to have free time. And with free time came a wandering of my mind: I soon began thinking about my previous gay life and started to miss it and the men who populated it. I realized that I would not be able to remain fully closeted; I needed to find a way to express my queerness. So I found the gay neighborhoods and began to lead a double life. I do not think that anyone in the gay community here knows my real name or what I do. I miss being able to be open about who I am and what I do. Yes, I do many of the things I did when I was out of the closet; however, now I do them under the cover of a fake name. It is tiring and frustrating leading two lives.

Thus far, I suppose I have been successful at compartmentalizing my life. I have my rabbinic friends and I have my gay friends. I have my rabbinic life and I have my gay life. There is very little overlap between the two, although there is some. Early on in my rabbinical school career, I realized that I would need people whom I could trust. I came out to three people during my first two years at the school. One was a rabbinical student and another was working on a master's in Jewish education. The most difficult person to come out to was my *chevruta*, my study partner. I waited until my birthday and after a couple of drinks, I let the information slip. I had no idea how he would react, even though I had been studying with him for several months. In the larger Jewish community, there are few people who know that I am gay. I am worried that someone will let it slip that they know a gay rabbinical student and then it will get back to the deans. The people who do know are those who already have ties to the gay community and know that they need to be discreet. I do know a couple of gay rabbis. Although these rabbis are not affiliated with the movement, they have been tremendously supportive.

However, as I move closer to graduation and ordination, the lines between these lives are blurring. It is becoming increasingly difficult to separate the two. I guess the lines have always been blurred, a fact of which I am only now becoming aware. I am conscious of the fact that I have backed myself into a corner. With graduation comes my first full-time rabbinic position. I know full well that my life will cease to be my own: I wish to be a pulpit rabbi, working in a smallish congregation. My life, as some of my mentors have told me, will be lived in a fishbowl, with everyone looking at what I do. For pulpit rabbis, the private is public, as pulpit rabbis are not only community leaders, but also role models and exemplars. When people tell me that I will make a fine leader and role model, I want to scream at them, "But, I am a liar. I am hiding who I am so that you will accept me as a leader!" I don't feel like a role model. I feel like a coward. And the longer I remain in the closet, the more intense these feelings will become. I am relatively certain that my life would be a little easier if I were to take an academic or administrative position. However, I want to work with a congregation: I want to work with people and help them to find meaning in Judaism and in their lives. I want to help American Jews to become "fired up" about the traditions that have so much to offer us. Yet, for all my good intentions, my life will be difficult and lonely until the Conservative movement is populated by open-minded, liberal, feminist leaders with a passion and commitment toward Jewish tradition and values, and sees fit to change its archaic attitudes toward gays and lesbians in the rabbinate.

Battling loneliness is the most difficult part of my life. When I go to bed at night, I hope that someday a lover will join me. Right now, however, that is not an option. I do not think it would be fair to ask someone to lead the life I am leading. Moreover, I am busy with study and work; adding a lover to the mix would be more than I could handle. And if I do take a pulpit, it may never be an option. In the current political and social atmosphere of some synagogues, I may never be comfortable having a lover at my side. Sometimes I do feel that I am being a bit overly dramatic when I imagine myself never having a lover. Yet, when I see my friends pairing off in domestic bliss, I feel alone and empty inside. I do want to be with someone and to adopt children and have a home. However, I also want to have a career in the rabbinate. These two desires—to be a pulpit rabbi, leader, and mentor for my commu- nity and to be a lover, father, and friend—pull at me in opposite directions.

I know that there are options; nevertheless, I cannot accept the options currently available, because I see them as compromises. I could land a non- pulpit position or I could move outside the movement. And there is always the slight chance that I will find a congregation that will look beyond my sex- uality. However, these options all feel like I am selling out and compromising my true passion of leading a congregation into the twenty-first century. Yet, there is the chance, slight that it is, that soon the movement will see the light and change its attitude.

Besides the loneliness is the fear that I will be discovered, and subsequently outed. When I meet someone, I am always unsure what to tell them when they ask what I do. Sometimes I tell them I am a teacher, other times a grad- uate student. I never tell them that I am a rabbinical student. And it is not because I do not want to be known as "the rabbi" among gay men, but rather it is my paranoia that even in the most remote gay bar, somehow my sexual identity will be revealed to my rabbinic community. I have a perhaps paranoid fear of being called into my dean's office and told that he has heard that I am dating a cousin of one of his friends. My nightmare is that my name gets mentioned over dinner as "the gay rabbinical student." Maybe I am worried about nothing; however, I have come too far to lose it all, because I was care- less. If the administration found out, I would be expelled from the program and would not be ordained. Even if I were allowed to graduate, I would never land a rabbinic position within the movement.

I have done my best to beat back the beast of loneliness. I have made friends, both gay and straight, who have enriched my life beyond my wildest dreams. My straight friends have been very supportive, offering me comfort and love. They listen to me when I gush about an attractive man I met and they give me a shoulder to cry on when I am angry and frustrated. On the other side of the coin are my gay friends. They, too, are a wonderful support system. We laugh and cry together; we dish and are dished together. But most of all, we live and enjoy life together. These friends remind me of my pre-rabbinic school life—that it is possible to be gay and happy. They remind me that to be gay and Jewish is to be doubly blessed. For this, I am eternally grateful. However, there are times that my friends only increase my frustration. I know that they are always ready to listen and willing to put up with me, but I am not sure that they understand what I feel. They mean well, but they don't know what it is like to lead a double life. They are privileged not to lead a double life. They may see a gay Jew as doubly blessed, but as a future rabbi, I usually see my two identities conflicting rather than complementing each other.

I am often lonely and crave more than the companionship of a friend. Like many gay men, I am well acquainted with bars and clubs that offer more than drinks and dancing. And, like many gay men, I love sex. There was a time before I came out that I slept with women. During that time, I saw sex as dirty, something I had to do to prove my manhood. However, once I came out, sex became something wonderful. Sex was a way in which I could celebrate who I was. Sex was my way of connecting. In many ways, it is still my way of connecting: I want to touch and be touched. I want to connect with someone on many levels. It angers me that I am cheapening myself and those around me when I slink around dark, shadowy bars and clubs searching for companionship. I know that I will not find the love of my life there; however, I will find someone with whom I can connect on at least a physical level—someone who reminds me that I am not alone, that my touch means something.

The only emotion that can compete with loneliness is anger. Controlling my anger, especially what I say to people, is becoming increasingly difficult. It seems that I spend more time fighting back anger than doing anything else. I sit in classes, listening to seemingly intelligent people deride and belittle gays and lesbians. My classmates, who are liberal on almost every level, who support women's rights and fight against the death penalty, become right wing when it comes to gays and lesbians. Perhaps this is because my classmates, hard as it may be to believe, may have never knowingly met a gay or lesbian person and because of this, they know only the negative stereotypes. It never ceases to make me wonder: the same people who support women's ordination rail against gay and lesbian ordination. Moreover, some of my classmates have suggested that gays and lesbians be barred from positions of leadership in synagogues. How men and women in their twenties and thirties can hold such ideas in this day and age is beyond me. Some classmates have been very open in their disdain for gays and lesbians, as they fear no reprimand. I have suggested to some that they watch what they say because one never knows who may be listening. The usual response is, "There are none here, so what does it matter?" I wonder what we are unleashing upon the Jews of America. Yet, to be fair, there are some students and instructors who do speak out in support of gay and lesbian ordination and other gay issues. So far, their voices have been few. Even though my classmates have caused me to bite my tongue on more than one occasion, I remain hopeful for the future. New classes of rabbinical students at the rabbinical school show much promise. Several students are outspoken regarding gay and lesbian ordination and are less tolerant of people who make denigrating comments. They also are certain that the ban will soon be lifted. I hope they are right. I am especially hopeful because these liberal-minded rabbinical students chose to remain in this movement, rather than entering Reform or Reconstructionist rabbinical schools. As these gay- and lesbian-friendly students fill the rabbinic ranks, the homophobia of the movement will be eradicated.

In the end, I know that I am the one who is responsible for my anger and loneliness. I chose this particular rabbinic program. I chose this life. No one forced me to be a rabbi. To be sure, there have been times when I have wanted to throw it all away, to return to the security of my previous life. At one time, I applied to other rabbinical schools, places that would have welcomed me and my sexuality. However, when it came time to transfer, I was unable; I could not leave the movement that had given me so much pain, because it had also given my life direction. Without the movement, I am not sure that I would be a practicing Jew, much less a potential rabbi. Judaism came alive to me through the movement.

I have never in my life wanted to be a spokesperson for anything. However, sooner or later, I just may have to step out of the closet and take my place at the table where everyone else is seated. In the end, I believe that this is the reason why I remain at this particular school in this particular movement. It may be easier to change the movement from within. If I come out after ordination, after successfully completing the requirements, it may make it a bit easier for those who come after me. For the longest time I would cringe when people called me a role model because I felt not like a role model, but like a liar. I felt that I lied to get into school and that I continue to live that lie. But that all changed when I realized that someday all that I had been through would be worth it, that the doors that were closed would crash open and that those who denied us would welcome us. It is easier to change things from the inside: once enough of us graduate and come out, the movement will see that we, like our straight classmates, make fine rabbis. We will be the movement. We will define the movement, and its criteria for quality rabbinic leadership—a passion for Jewish life and learning, love for tradition and humanity, and a respect for love, relationships, and family, regardless of sexual orientation.

One of my favorite festivals is Passover. I have great memories of Seders spent with family and friends. However, once I came out, I began to think that we should have another son at the Pesach Seder. We should have a "Quiet son who was not allowed to speak." This fifth son, like his brothers, represents a part of all of us. When I yearned to see myself represented at the table as the silent son, I thought it would be better to sit at the table, albeit silently, than not to be represented at all. I no longer feel this way. I want to be at the table and I want to be able to ask, "Why? Why have we been shut out for so long?" I still want to ask these questions. I want to know why I, as well as others, have had to lead a double life. But there is something else I want to do: I want to change the movement from within. I want to make sure that future gay and lesbian rabbinical students do not need to lead double lives, but will be able to serve as role models for their communities as complete human beings.

May it happen speedily and in our days.

PART III

INSTITUTIONS

The sexual system is not a monolithic, omnipotent structure. There are continuous battles over the definitions, evaluations, arrangements, privileges, and costs of sexual behavior. —GAYLE RUBIN

Definitions have their uses in much the same way that road signs make it easy to travel: they point out the directions. But you don't get where you're going when you just stand underneath some sign, waiting for it to tell you what to do. —KATE BORNSTEIN

In order to feel fully safe I need to feel known. —EVELYN TORTON BECK

One must either accept some theory or else believe one's instinct or follow the world's opinion. —GERTRUDE STEIN

All truth passes through three stages. First, it is ridiculed. Second, it is violently opposed. Third, it is accepted as being self-evident. —ARTHUR SCHOPENHAUER

KOL SASON V'KOL SIMCHA, KOL KALAH V'KOL KALAH

SAME GENDER WEDDINGS AND

SPIRITUAL RENEWAL

Jane Rachel Litman

I OFFICIATED AT my first gay wedding in 1978. I was camping at the Michigan Womyn's Music Festival, and two giddy young women approached my tent one drizzly morning as I sat nursing my coffee. "We're Jewish lesbians in love," they announced loudly and joyfully. "Someone said you're a rabbi, and we want to get married. Will you marry us?"

They might as well have told me that they were space aliens and asked whether I could beam them up to the Pleides. Looking back, I wish I'd exclaimed, "*Mazel tov!*" Instead I asked, "Why in the world do you want to get married?"

In the radical feminist universe of 1978, no one was getting married. Lots of women were getting divorces, many were "becoming lesbians," others joining collective women's households. Some women just up and left their suburban homes and families. Marriage was considered an institution of the patriarchy, an oppressive relic of a time when women were chattel. Feminists frequently cited the statistic that although married men had a longer life span than single men, married women had a shorter life span than single women.

I remember a popular political pin that read, "The Surgeon General warns that marriage is harmful to women's health."

I "patiently" explained to the couple all the reasons why Jewish weddings were as patriarchal and politically incorrect as secular ones. I quoted the Bible about bride prices, and lectured them about the distinction in traditional *ketubot* (Jewish wedding contracts) between virgins and nonvirgins. "The central feature of a wedding is 'kinyan,' the acquisition of the woman by the man," I told them. "Don't you see? God has liberated lesbians from marriage so that we can practice free love unfettered by male needs for power and ownership." I was really warming to my topic.

But the happy optimistic women before me were not convinced. "Okay," they said, "we won't call it 'marriage,' but we want a *huppah* (Jewish wedding canopy) and we want to break the glass." That comment, and the attendant vision of two women under the *huppah* breaking the glass, clicked on a dim light in my imagination. I began to sense the radical political nature of the whole idea. I knew these two women wouldn't want a ceremony in which one of them was "the boy" breaking the glass. What would they want? My curiosity led me to ease up on my rhetoric a bit.

"Do you want to have two glasses or to break one together?" This was a question—a question that implied a level of both acceptance of Jewish tradition and willingness to transform it—and a metaphor, which had never previously entered my mind and would become a way of life for me in the many years ahead. "One together," they bubbled. "We want to do everything together." Oops! They had taken my curiosity for assent. They looked so happy, so hopeful, so certain. How would I get out of this now?

"I'm not actually a rabbi," I disclaimed, "only an exrabbinical student." I had dropped out of Hebrew Union College, the Reform movement's rabbinical seminary, two years earlier. Though the Reform movement is now quite supportive of gay rights, at that time openly queer students were not admitted or were asked to leave rabbinical school. In 1976, my first year of seminary, I was 20 years old, living in Israel—a foreign country—for the first time in my life, and trying to decide if I was a lesbian. It was all way too much for me, and I took a leave of absence.

By the summer of 1978, I had become a near-pagan radical feminist going to grad school in computer science at Berkeley, though still pondering the issue of sexuality. In the mid 1970s, "womyn's" community, bisexuality didn't exist. Lesbian or non-lesbian? (Revolutionary or victim/traitor?) That was the question. Even my summer camping trip amid several thousand mostly lesbian women in Michigan carried the subtext of my yearning and complete inability to "decide" my sexual orientation. But the two cute lovers in front of me were not privy to the depths of my personal inner struggle. They just wanted to tie the knot.

"We don't care if you're a real rabbi, just as long as you know what to do," they laughed and hugged. "It's not legal anyway." I sent them off with a list of items to gather: a Kiddush cup (Jewish ceremonial goblet), a wineglass to break, and material and branches for the *huppa*. We scribbled out handmade fliers inviting folks to the event. I busily rewrote the ring vows and *sheva brachot* (the seven blessings that form the climax of a Jewish wedding ceremony) from a Hebrew grammar that is gendered for a male subject to one with two female subjects. I even wrote out a ketubah that, despite my earlier lecture, contained many references to mutual respect and support, but nothing about virginity. In spite of myself, I enjoyed reengaging the knowledge gained through my years of study, and I liked the intellectual challenge. Without realizing it consciously, I was getting into the spirit of the rite.

The wedding was held in a grove of trees. Fortunately, the sun finally came out, but the world was still rather damp. There was a *huppa*, made of a huge tiedyed shawl held up on sticks by four women. I used a tree stump as a table for the kiddush cup, handwritten ketubah, and rings. We were the object of much curiosity, and a crowd of women who were attending the festival gathered around. The buzz was curious, some women expressed their displeasure with "the trappings of hetero-patriarchy," but mostly people were supportive of the ritual and Jewish visibility.

Unexpectedly, I found the ceremony very moving. I noticed that I was crying as each woman pledged to the other, *"Haray at mekudeshet li b'taba'at zo k'dat Miriam, Moshe, v'yisrael"* ("Behold, with this ring you are consecrated to me, as my beloved, according to the tradition of Miriam, Moses, and Israel"). The ceremony ended with the breaking of the glass, a resounding *"Mazel tov!"* from the crowd, and applause. To my knowledge, I've never met those women again. They would be in their late forties now. Given the fluid lives we led, the tumultuous personal and cultural tidal waves we rode, they are likely not together any more. However, I'm deeply grateful to them for giving me that precious opportunity to choose creative adaptation over alienation, Jewish faith over nihilism. I officiated at perhaps a half a dozen women's commitment rituals at women's festivals over the next several years.

In 1984 I returned to rabbinical school when the Reconstructionist Rabbinical College (RRC) began its internal process of moving toward publicly accepting opening gay students (Hebrew Union College officially changed its policy in 1989). I was "out" at my admissions interview, one of the first. Despite a rather bumpy time at RRC, and pretty much nonstop political confrontations with its faculty and administration, I remain very proud of that institution for its vision and courage in terms of GLBT rights. At RRC I felt exhilarated to be part of a community of educated Jews engaged in the exciting conversation about the same-gender weddings and their implications in relation to Jewish law and custom. Ironically, as a student rabbi, for the first time I also found myself asked to officiate at weddings of female/male couples.

The truth is that at that time I found those weddings difficult. Though most of the couples with whom I worked were decent loving people, many of them were far more focused on the party accompanying their ceremony than the ritual itself or the more profound spiritual values it symbolized. Almost all the couples with whom I worked were not affiliated with a congregation and as often as not told me they wanted a rabbi in order to please their parents. When I wanted to explore detailed aspects of the religious significance of various aspects of the service, couples often replied "just do whatever the Jewish way is." I was still very young and new to my rabbinate and did not yet understand the possibilities of that situation and how to develop the relationship.

Officiating at mixed gender weddings also brought up my own personal issues around sexual identity. By 1984, the word "bisexual" had entered the cultural vocabulary and that was how I identified. But much of my feminist political identity was deeply tied to lesbian women's culture. I dressed and talked "like a lesbian" (whatever that means!), and I don't think I really expected to spend my life in the context of a committed relationship to a man. Sometimes God has other plans. Several weeks before moving to Philadelphia to enter RRC, I fell in love with a man. Stewart and I have been together 17 years, have two fabulous children, and it's still a bit disconcerting. Neither mainstream society nor lesbian/gay culture was very supportive or understanding of the complexities of bisexuality. People have a hard time understanding that sexuality is about identity as much as relationship, and that for many reasons involving my own personal self-understanding and life experience, on a daily basis I think of myself as queer.

Meeting the world as a woman involved with a man particularly while officiating at "straight" weddings heightened my own personal sense of queer invisibility and isolation. The fact that same sex couples were (and still are) denied access to secular legalities is demeaning to me personally as a bisexual woman, the same way anti-miscegenation laws were degrading to all people of color without regard to the race of their partner of choice. Stew and I don't face the day-to-day discrimination same gender couples face (and I'm not discounting the deep level of injustice that this constitutes); however, I am acutely and painfully aware of the way society regards bisexual and all GLBT people. Every time I performed a "straight" wedding, this awareness would pervade my consciousness.

I tried to be a good rabbi for those female/male couples who came to me during my student years, but I had my doubts. By the 1980s "living together" was no longer in fashion, but the marriages that replaced it often held as little (or less of) a sense of responsibility and ego compromise, particularly on the part of the male partners. Television programs like *The Dating Game* and *The Newlywed Game* exploited and publicized the most shallow and materialistic aspects of human love relationships. The relatively recent top-rated beauty pageant style show, *I Want to Marry a Millionaire*, hit an all-time low for heterosexual relationships. The truth is that the 1970s radical feminist analysis of marriage as a social institution, though not entirely correct, wasn't entirely wrong either.

Even mixed gender couples who had every societal support experienced a divorce rate hovering at about 50 percent. Marriage as a profound and abiding commitment seemed to have lost much of its religious significance. It seemed to me that there was way too much pressure for these hetero couples to get married and equally too easy for them to dissolve the marriage. For good or for bad, the public exchange of vows and rings under the *huppa* didn't hold quite the power of communal expectation that it once did. At this point in my life, I had no ongoing relationships with the handful of lesbian couples at whose weddings I officiated. I often wondered if they stayed together; I hoped that their weddings gave them some support against an often hostile society, but I couldn't say whether their commitments survived any more or less than more mainstream brides.

After ordination, my first pulpit was with a large mainstream Reform congregation. My pastoral skills at weddings improved, but my general sense of dis-ease did not. In 1991 I had the very good fortune to become the rabbi of Congregation Kol Simcha, a GLBT outreach synagogue in Orange County, California. It was through serving the extraordinary members of that congregation that my view of marriage changed entirely.

Tom and Mark came to see me soon after I came to Kol Simcha. They were somewhat older and less effervescent than the lesbians in Michigan, but essentially told me the same thing, "We're a Jewish couple and we want to get married." Tom had full-blown AIDS. He was an elementary school teacher. Mark was a lawyer. They'd made out their durable powers of attorney, and written wills. They had done everything they could to provide the legal protections that society reluctantly grants to gay people who are willing to pay the money and jump through the hoops. But Tom and Mark wanted more. They wanted their Jewish faith to honor and recognize their love and commitment.

Tom was a Jew by choice. His family had disowned him when he came out. One sister still had a relationship with him. He didn't know if she would come to the wedding. Mark was from New York. His parents accepted his relationship, but had only recently been told that Tom had AIDS. They were having trouble understanding why the couple wanted to get married.

Though "straight" weddings might reflect a sense of unconscious social conformity, gay weddings are filled with intentionality. When same gender couples decide to get married, it's rarely due to social expectations. GLBT people want weddings despite ever-present unspoken cultural messages, not because of them. Gay children and teens rarely imagine themselves in a Barbie/Ken wedding spectacular. If little boys secretly long for Ken and young girls contemplate marrying Barbie, they know they are supposed to keep that fact utterly to themselves.

Tom and Mark wanted to get married as Jews under a *huppa* because they were in love and were committed to each other. That they were both men, and that Tom was very ill did not change that reality for the two of them. Mark wondered if I would talk to his parents, who were coming for a visit in a few weeks.

Mark's mother had barely sat down in my office when she started leaking tears. She clearly loved her son and his lover. She was having trouble imagining a Jewish wedding with two men, and she was deeply saddened by Tom's illness. She didn't want "a public spectacle." But as we talked, she eased up a bit. It clearly helped that a rabbi took the issues seriously and thought the wedding was within Jewish tradition. Mark's father was a cultural Jew, and wanted to give whatever support he could to his wife and son. They were very good people, all of them. Two days later I went over to Mark and Tom's home for brunch. It had been decided—the wedding was on for June. Even Tom's sister had agreed to come.

Summer arrived. It was a beautiful wedding: a lavishly floral bowered *huppa*, dozens of elegant tuxedoed men, the families, their whole community present. Tom and Mark wrote their own vows, and Tom quoted the Book of Ruth in his "aught but death will part you from me." Seven of their closest friends were honored to give the seven blessings. The glass was broken, and the lovers kissed.

Tom died before their second anniversary. Over the nights of *shiva*, we looked at pictures of the wedding. It's very difficult to be a 30-year-old widower. Even more difficult if you are gay. Even more difficult if mainstream society, your workplace, and your spouse's family refuse to acknowledge the relationship. But it helps to have the wedding ring and the memories, and the love and support of a Jewish community.

About a year later, I had an appointment with Ilene and Debra, each of whom were in their thirties. They were thinking of having a baby. But Debra couldn't even articulate the word "baby," and would have a mild anxiety attack every time they walked past a toy store. "Something doesn't feel right about it," was all she could say. "I didn't picture it quite this way. It doesn't feel real."

Ilene shrugged helplessly at me. "Maybe you need some kind of ritual," I suggested. "Perhaps something to make it seem more real." I searched my mind for an appropriate Jewish ceremony. Ilene turned to me, "I bought us rings. Can you think of any ritual for exchanging rings?" I laughed, "I think it's called . . . a wedding."

Debra's whole demeanor relaxed, "That's it. I knew something wasn't right. I'm sort of old fashioned. I want to get married before having a baby." Right there in my office, Ilene got down in front of Debra, took her hand, and asked, "Will you marry me?" Being a rabbi just doesn't get any better than that.

Over the years I've officiated at dozens of queer weddings, uniting over a hundred gay men, lesbian women, bisexual people, and transgender folk. It's the closest experience I know to sitting at lunch counters in the South during the 1960s. It is one of the holiest honors I have as a rabbi. The courage, integrity, steadfastness, and vision of people who are denied the basic human right of legal partnership has changed me. Quite simply, same gender and other queer couples have redeemed the institution of marriage in my spiritual life. Being part of these rites has given me a new insight and understanding into the radical religious nature of love and marriage. Many of my closest moments to God occur at weddings—both straight and gay—as I feel the mystical power of love to bless and heal the world. I believe that queer marriage is God's *tikkun*, spiritual rebuilding, of all marriage in our too often loveless narcissistic world.

On a practical level, I have spent a great deal of time reconstructing traditional Jewish forms and prayers so they work for queer couples. I've written or translated numerous texts to be used in gender-inclusive *ketubot*. A couple years ago I made the decision to standardize the Hebrew in the *sheva brachot*

I recite at all weddings. I now include the terms *"hatan v'hatan, kalah v'kalah, kalah v'hatan, and hatan v'kalah,"*—groom and groom, bride and bride, bride and groom, groom and bride—in all of the weddings I perform, without regard to the gender of the specific persons in front of me. I believe this choice increases inclusivity and the visibility of all beloveds.

I am blessed to be part of the Jewish weddings of so many couples filled with love and commitment. Secular society has something to learn from our religious observance. It is very difficult for all families, but particularly gay families, to stay healthy and functional when society constantly works to undermine the values of honesty, love, and support that weddings express. When I hear conservative politicians talk about "family values," I wonder whose families they mean. Queer people need custody equity, tax breaks, and decision-making powers in times of illness just as much as straight people do. In particular, the cruel practice by the U.S. Immigration and Naturalization Service of separating families (queer and straight) in which a member is undocumented is deplorable. Family values must include good childcare and equal rights for everyone. Gay rights are both symbolic and part of the big picture of justice and genuine compassion for all.

I feel deeply grateful to be part of this particular *tikkun olam*. I was present when the Central Conference of American Rabbis overwhelmingly passed a resolution in support of rabbinic officiation. A few weeks later, I stood in front of the Lincoln Memorial beside Reverend Troy Perry, founder of the Metropolitan Community Church, and Reverend Jimmy Creech who was expelled from The United Methodist Church for performing gay weddings. Before us was a sea of people who had come to stand for their legal human right to wed. This is a movement that cannot be stopped. Courage and stead-fast love are powerful forces. I believe with *emunah shleimah*—perfect faith—that it is only a matter of time before the laws against queer couples meet the same fate as those against interracial couples. In the meantime, people of faith will continue to practice our religious freedom and commitment by cel-ebrating queer marriage.

I am a far less cynical and doctrinaire person than I was that overcast morning in 1978. Though I am still very much a feminist, I'm more con-cerned about the societal aspects of materialism, social conformity, and dis-crimination than with about how individual people choose to lead their lives. So now when people—whatever their genders, class, or cultural back-grounds—come to me to and say, "We're in love and we want to get married," I always respond, "*Mazel tov!*" *Mazel tov* for them, and *mazel tov* for me.

WITHOUT STANDING DOWN

THE FIRST QUEER

JEWISH STREET PROTEST[1]

Jonathan Krasner

WHEN THE ORGANIZERS of the 1993 Salute to Israel Parade decided to ban New York's queer synagogue from participation, the controversy fostered debate within New York's queer Jewish community about an appropriate response to the perceived affront. In one response, Congregation Beth Simchat Torah (CBST), the queer synagogue of New York, and many of its supporters, including the Reform movement's leadership and its Zionist association, held an alternative celebration at a midtown synagogue. But some queer Jews, feeling disenfranchised by the so-called gay Jewish establishment, decided to attend the parade and protest the organizers' decision from the sidelines. The protest was small—no more than between 20 and 30 individuals at its height—but it managed to attract media attention and constituted a visible gay Jewish presence at the parade. The demonstration also had a transformative impact on both the identity construction of the protesters and the direction of their fledgling organization.

Conventional wisdom in the mainstream Jewish community, especially among the more observant, was that the protesters were disaffected, alienated

Jews with little Jewish background and weak Jewish identities. To put it bluntly, it was assumed that the activists were more gay identified than Jewish identified.

In fact, most of the protesters were affiliated with a nascent gay and lesbian Jewish organization called Jewish Young Gays and Lesbians (JYGL). It was made up primarily of strongly affiliated individuals in their twenties and early thirties. Most came from traditional Jewish homes, and many maintained a high level of Jewish practice since their coming out. Almost without exception, they were products of Jewish day schools, summer camps, and/or youth organizations. Advocates of an integrationist agenda, they criticized CBST for what they perceived to be its isolationist response to the synagogue's exclusion. It was precisely their status as Jewish insiders that caused them to experience indignation at CBST's exclusion.

JYGL members resented what they saw as an attempt by the organized Jewish community to push queer Jews back into the closet. They were particularly critical of CBST Rabbi Sharon Kleinbaum and the synagogue, viewing them as unwitting collaborators. Interestingly, while some of the protesters criticized CBST for being too "closeted," many of these same individuals identified their participation in the parade protest as a decisive event in their own coming-out processes.

For most JYGL members, the parade was their first experience being "out" in the larger Jewish community. Universally described as empowering, the protest served to justify and reinforce JYGL members in their convictions and integrationist agenda. The drama surrounding the parade also helped facilitate a process of organizational self-definition, through which it was decided to prioritize community education and activism over socializing and to privilege the homophile politics of persuasion over the confrontational politics of transgression.

THE FORMATION OF JYGL/JAGL²

The group that would eventually become known as Jewish Activist Gays and Lesbians (JAGL) was conceived at a January 1993 student conference sponsored by *Tikkun*, a progressive Jewish bimonthly magazine. The conference opened with a panel comprised of disparate Jewish voices, including that of Tamara Cohen, a lesbian Jewish activist enrolled in a joint program at Barnard College and the Conservative Jewish movement's Jewish Theological Seminary (JTS).

Tamara also facilitated a subsequent, smaller group discussion of Jewish queers and their allies. It was there that the idea for a gay Jewish group was first floated. The discussion was small, no more than ten people, not all of whom were gay identified. But among the group were individuals who would soon become key players in the queer Jewish organization. Jonathan Springer, who at the time was a 25-year-old former programmer for the New Israel Fund, and a newcomer to New York, was there with a recent acquaintance, Ron Dayan, a 29-year-old Israeli, who was pursuing graduate studies at Columbia. Also among the participants were Natan (Tani) Meir and Andrew Ingall, students at Columbia College, and Julie Blumenfeld, another Barnard-JTS student. The group decided to meet the following day at a local Chinese restaurant to continue their discussion.

"There was a real feeling of excitement," remembered one participant. The group "came to a consensus that more activism was needed in the Jewish community on gay and lesbian issues." Increasing Jewish visibility within the queer community was also discussed, but group members seemed far more interested in activities and projects aimed at promoting queer visibility and integration within the Jewish community. Julie remembered that the JTS's recently articulated policy against ordaining openly identified lesbians and gay men as rabbis, and the general attitude of the Conservative movement toward gays, dominated the conversation.

Given the make up of the group, it is not surprising that their discussion was focused on effecting change within traditional Jewish circles. Tamara and Julie were JTS students, while Tani's family had strong ties to JTS and the Conservative movement. Both Tani and Tamara had attended a Conservative-affiliated Jewish day school, and Jonathan's sister was a JTS rabbinical school graduate who had applied to intern at CBST and was told by JTS that she could not take the job. It is also useful to remember that traditional Jews comprise a larger and more influential segment of the New York Jewish community than they do elsewhere in the United States.

After the conference, the group held a couple of meetings and a Purim party in individuals' homes. As word of the embryonic group spread at Barnard, Columbia, and JTS and in queer Jewish and politically progressive circles, the group began to attract individuals who had not attended the conference. It was becoming clear that there was an enduring interest in forming an organization. Less clear were the goals and orientation of this new group.

From the beginning there was tension between those who envisioned the group as primarily activist and those who were looking for a social outlet and saw the group as an opportunity to engage in community building. The minutes from an early meeting indicate that the group considered organizing a public demonstration marking its formation, complete with the sounding of *shofarot* (rams' horns), traditionally the Jewish call to action and a symbol of beginnings. There was also talk about "kiss-in" kiddush disruptions in area synagogues. As conceived by Tamara, the kiss-ins would be "fun, in-your-face" political theater—the type of activism perfected by media-savvy groups like ACT UP—aimed at heightening the Jewish community's awareness of the existence of queers within their midst, even in their houses of worship. Neither of these activities ever made it past the planning stages. Opponents questioned the effectiveness of such tactics in affecting change, particularly in the traditional community.

In addition, many group members had themselves only recently come out of the closet and some were still enmeshed in their own coming-out processes. Drawn to the group for social reasons, they would later embrace a more activist posture. But at this point, they may have felt threatened by the idea of publicly outing themselves.

One of the questions that occupied group members in the early meetings was what to call the new organization. The choice of the name JYGL—Jewish Young Gays and Lesbians—reflected the direction (or lack thereof) in which the group seemed to be headed before the parade controversy. Conspicuously absent was any mention of activism. JYGL was first and foremost a safe and supportive environment for Jewishly committed gays, lesbians, and bisexuals to socialize and commiserate. Many of the individuals whom I interviewed explained that prior to the formation of the group they had felt that their lives were compartmentalized. Many were searching for a venue in which their Jewish selves could be integrated with their queer identities.

Aside from the tension that existed between the activists and the socializers, personality conflicts also developed. In addition, despite members' protests that theirs was a group more progressive than the "gay establishment," JYGL replicated the identity politics of the queer community at large (including CBST), in other words, the tensions between men and women and the invisibility of bisexuals and transgendered people.

THE DECISION TO PROTEST

By late April of 1993, the group had chosen a name, successfully orchestrated a couple of social events, and begun expanding its membership. What was lacking was direction, an issue or a cause. But on May 6, 1993, just before 11:00 P.M., JYGL's drifting came abruptly to a halt when officials at the American Zionist Youth Federation (AZYF), the parade's sponsor, sent a fax to CBST's office officially banning the synagogue from marching in the parade. With what appeared to be a blatant case of anti-gay discrimination by the organized Jewish community staring them in the face, JYGL's mission suddenly seemed clear.

Traditionally, members of the various secular Zionist youth organizations comprised the core of parade marchers. But in the 1970s and 1980s, these groups experienced a decline in membership and support. Since then, Orthodox groups, particularly the constellation of New York area yeshiva day schools, comprised the single largest group of marchers. When many Orthodox groups threatened to boycott the parade if CBST were allowed to march, organizers ultimately felt forced to give in. Without the Orthodox marchers, and their families and friends on the sidelines, organizers feared that the parade would be a pitiful affair.

Founded in 1973, CBST was only the second gay and lesbian synagogue in the United States. The synagogue maintained an independent and religiously inclusive posture, declining even to affiliate with any particular branch of Judaism, even after the more liberal denominations began taking steps toward the full acceptance of homosexuals in the late 1970s and early 1980s. By 1993 the Greenwich Village synagogue boasted over a thousand members. Anthropologist Moshe Shokeid, who spent 13 months studying CBST in the early 1990s, pointed out that its congregants "display an impulse familiar among American Jews, to build a synagogue comfortable for its particular constituency, in a style borrowed from mainstream society."[3] Nevertheless, most CBST members considered it to be a maverick institution. When it was first founded, openly identified lesbians, bisexuals, and gay men were largely shunned in America's synagogues. Following the example of successful gay churches, CBST and a handful of other gay synagogues sought to provide their members with "safe spaces" to integrate their dual identities while raising the visibility of homosexual Jews on the American Jewish landscape.

CBST's recently installed rabbi was meeting with her synagogue board when the fax from AZYF came through. Rabbi Kleinbaum had been negotiating with the parade organizers for months. For a time, it seemed that a compromise had been worked out. CBST would march as part of the Reform Zionists of America (ARZA) contingent. The combined group would sport a banner that read "ARZA Proudly Marches with Congregation Beth Simchat

Torah in Salute to Israel." At first, the AZYF supported the compromise. But, ultimately, under pressure from Orthodox rabbis, institutions, and funders, AZYF felt compelled to issue a last-minute "dis-invitation." Naturally, Kleinbaum and the synagogue's president, Catherine Sull, were dismayed with AZYF's determination, but they were furious that the organization had waited until three days before the parade to make a final decision (or to apprise the synagogue of their decision).

Kleinbaum informed her congregants of the synagogue's quandary in an impromptu meeting after Friday night services on May 7. It was on the basis of that discussion, and a later meeting with the synagogue board, that Kleinbaum made her decision: CBST would hold an alternate celebration at Central Synagogue, not far from the parade route. It would not seek to disrupt the parade or demonstrate from the parade's sidelines. Kleinbaum reluctantly accepted the Reform Zionists of America's invitation to hold an alternate celebration because she did not want CBST to be perceived as a polarizing force. Some opponents of CBST's participation in the parade contended that the synagogue's desire to march stemmed more from a desire to promote a "gay agenda" than a genuine concern for Israel's welfare. According to a number of congregants, Kleinbaum was concerned that any protest of the parade by CBST might, inadvertently, play into the hands of anti-Zionists or anti-semites.

Kleinbaum also had to contend with a diverse membership. While some would have preferred a more conspicuous response, others were uncomfortable with the inevitable media attention. Synagogue President Sull acknowledged that Kleinbaum was compelled to take into account fears of "outing" expressed by congregants. Sull asserted that CBST's original application to march had been daring in and of itself for a community that had traditionally opted for a low profile, partially in order to protect its closeted congregants.

The Reform movement's Union of American Hebrew Congregations and ARZA joined CBST at the celebration. Reform congregations and religious schools were encouraged to attend both the parade and the alternate celebration. About 700 people attended the alternate celebration, including leaders of the Reform movement. According to the *New York Times*, police estimated that 73,000 spectators attended the parade.

Sitting among the congregants at Beth Simchat Torah on the Friday evening prior to the parade was Ron Dayan, who was livid with the AZYF's last-minute expulsion of CBST. Ron had a special interest in the parade controversy because he had served in the Israeli army. He thought it was scandalous that as a gay man he could serve in the Israeli Defense Forces but could not march in the Salute to Israel Parade. As he listened to Kleinbaum's discussion of CBST's contingency plan he was becoming equally disillusioned with CBST's response. Ron was convinced that AZYF's action should be met head-on with a protest at the parade. For Ron, it was important that gay Jews be a visible force at the parade in defiance of the wishes of the AZYF and the Orthodox community.

Ron found out that the AZYF had broken its deal with CBST late Thursday night, shortly after the decision had been faxed. He immediately called Jonathan Springer and Tani Meir to discuss a response. JYGL members had discussed the parade at previous meetings. The group agreed that it would be a visible presence at the parade, but adopted a wait-and-see attitude about strategy due to uncertainty about the final outcome of the controversy. Given the latest developments, a couple of possible scenarios were floated, including disrupting the parade by staging a sit-in. But the civil disobedience option was quickly rejected because JYGL members did not wish to antagonize the parade goers. It was decided that JYGL would protest the parade nonviolently on the sidelines, by holding placards and chanting songs and slogans. The articulated objectives of the protest were visibility and education—the former was to be the primary route of achieving the latter. With decisions being made virtually on the eve of the parade, there was little time to reflect on personal insecurities.

JYGL's modest membership was quickly informed about the protest. Members shared the group's plans with friends, and papered the Columbia and JTS campuses with leaflets announcing the location and time of the demonstration. They also handed out leaflets at a queer student dance on the Columbia campus that weekend.

Ron announced JYGL's planned protest at the Friday evening CBST meeting, inviting members of the congregation to join in. According to one witness, his announcement upset some congregants. Many felt that CBST was taking the high road by staging a counter-celebration, as opposed to a demonstration; CBST was keeping the focus on celebrating Israel's independence day rather then on the controversy with the AZYF and members of the Orthodox community. Some of these congregants believed that a demonstration at the parade would dilute this message. Other members feared that a protest might play into the hands of anti-semites and the media, which was perceived to be hostile toward Israel. Still others were afraid to be visible for fear of being "outed." As for Kleinbaum, according to CBST board member

Glenn Mones, "She didn't want the synagogue to be seen as upsetting the peace of the community."

On the Saturday night prior to the parade, six core JYGL members met in the living room of Tamara's apartment and made about 30 signs and placards. The signs had slogans like "*Yisrael l'kol ha-Yehudim*" ("Israel for all Jews") and "*V'ahavta l're'akha kamokha*" ("Love your neighbor as yourself"). One sign had an Israeli flag drawn in pink. Ron notified various newspapers and television stations of the planned protest and its location. Tani put together a song sheet, which would be handed out to protesters. The songs were carefully chosen to reflect the message of the protesters: that all Jews should be allowed to march in the parade, and hopes for the future acceptance by the mainstream Jewish community of gay, lesbian, and bisexual Jews. Songs included "*Hineh ma tov u'manayim/ Shevet ahim gam yahad*" ("How good it is for brothers [and sisters] to sit together"), "*Im tirtzu ain zo agada*" ("If you will it, it is no dream"), and "*Lo alekha ha'melakha ligmor/ V'lo ata ben horin l'hibatel mimena*" ("It is not your duty to complete the work/Nor are you free to desist from it"). The songs are popular standbys in Jewish summer camps and religious schools. Significantly, most of the signs and all of the songs were in Hebrew. Intentionally or not, the protesters were telegraphing their status as knowledgeable insiders.

Also helpful in reconstructing the mindset and goals of the protesters is the copy that appeared on the various leaflets that JYGL members distributed prior to and during the parade. One leaflet screamed in big block letters, "Jewish Queers: We Have Been Betrayed," and instructed the reader to "protest the expulsion of gay Jews from the Salute to Israel Parade and show your support to Israel." This leaflet is fascinating because, on the one hand, its message appears to be militant—the use of the word "queer" as opposed to gay connotes an activist, radical posture, while the word "betrayed" is unmistakably angry. But its injunction to both protest the expulsion of gay Jews and support Israel indicates that the protesters wished to make clear JYGL members' more general allegiance to the Jewish community. There was no desire on the part of the protesters to make common cause with anti-Zionists or anyone else that might have wished to protest the parade's purpose.

Between 20 and 30 individuals ultimately participated in the demonstration. Some were completely new to JYGL. Standing behind the police barricades that lined the parade route, demonstrators held signs, sang songs, waved at the marchers, and socialized. Some protesters handed out leaflets to passers-by and tried to explain to them the reasons for the demonstration.

There were few overt incidents of gay bashing or scuffles between protesters and parade goers.

Some protesters brought their families to the site. Miryam Kabakow remembered dragging her father to the protest. "I brought my father—what was I thinking?!—I said to him, 'You know Dad, we're going to the Israeli Day Parade [sic], and there's going to be this demonstration.' And I said, 'You know Dad, you think you're a liberal, why don't you come check it out.' And he came, you know, in his baseball hat, and walked by and said, 'Okay, I've seen enough.' And he left."

THE PROTEST AND IDENTITY CONSTRUCTION

For many protesters, the excitement of being involved in their first queer Jewish street protest was mixed with other strong emotions, like fear, trepidation, exhilaration, an emphatic sense of virtue, even vehemence. For most JYGL members, the parade constituted the first time in which they were "coming out" in a public setting, certainly to the larger Jewish community. While some protesters may have reveled in the attention, many others were nervous and felt vulnerable knowing that they would likely become the object of gossip, possibly derision. "That morning, as I started to hand out leaflets, I started out with great trepidation," Tani recalled.

> I was afraid to go over to people—I was afraid of being judged. I didn't want to be reduced to a symbol. I was myself. I didn't want to lose that. Ron noticed my hesitation and told me, "Tani, we have to do this without trepidation, without standing down. You have to think of the message we are trying to send." I realized this was one of the first times that I was out there in the larger Jewish community—not just at Columbia. . . . There were people marching in the parade that I knew—so I was nervous. But as it went on, I felt empowerment, strength from it. And little by little, my fear went away. It was a very important experience for me.

Protesters' experiences were not uniformly positive. Daniel Chesir was a 23-year-old graduate of the Orthodox-affiliated Yeshiva University. At the time, he was working at the Gay Men's Health Crisis and received a lesson in the lengths to which his Orthodox sister would go to avoid having their father, a teacher at an Orthodox girl's high school, associated with his gay son and the protest. "I saw my father walking by [the protest] with his girls [students] and I was there. And he saw me and was going to come over and talk to me, and suddenly, out of nowhere, my sister, on the other side of the street, pops up, runs over to my father, and pulls him over so his students wouldn't see him talking to me with this whole gay group. And I was like, 'Hey, Oh shit!'"

But if Daniel felt wounded by the rejection of his sister, he soon experienced affirmation from other marchers:

> I remember being really sort of excited because I went to yeshiva high school in New York when each of those groups passed by and seeing people that I knew. And I sort of remember that the only group [of marchers] that was really bad toward us was MTA—Yeshiva University High School for Boys—and the boys were going like "boo," "hiss," sort of stuff. They were making some comments. But Central High School, which is YU's high school for girls were all cheering and stuff. Kids at Ramaz [a modern Orthodox high school] were definitely cheering us, like a lot of the schools. . . . It made me feel good. I was like, hey, that's really cool that the students are like, into us, and stuff. I remember when Yeshiva of Flatbush walked by, which was where I went to high school, a few of the teachers who knew me came over and said hello, or were being friendly, and that was a cool thing.

Tani recalled that when his old elementary school, Solomon Schechter of Bergen County, New Jersey, marched past, most students were wearing pink ribbons as a demonstration of support for CBST.

Eric Cohen, a graduate of Ramaz, spoke of similar feelings: "[The parade] was exciting and nerve-racking. . . . I was standing there while Ramaz passed and I felt somewhat empowered. Ramaz brought back mixed feelings. Here I was, as out as one can be in a situation as close as one can get to a childhood experience."

Daniel, Tani, Eric, and the others were cognizant that they had caught the attention of friends, acquaintances, and strangers, even the media. They felt a sense of pride in their protest, but were reassured when marchers signaled their support and approval. Daniel, who had kept his distance from the Orthodox world after his decision to come out, was nevertheless still consumed with a sense of belonging. Eric, who also left Orthodoxy since coming, out was likewise engulfed by visceral feelings. For a fair number of protesters, the parade was nothing less than a confrontation with childhood and a coming to terms with the rejection of their childhood communities.

For Tamara, protesting at the parade was an act of defiance brought on by a sense of entitlement: "A lot of us had marched in this parade as kids for years. It just seemed like a clear instance of discrimination. We knew it was homophobia, we knew it was *halachic* homophobia. . . . " Tamara's comments reinforce my contention that the parade protesters were, as a matter of fact and their own perception, insiders. Having participated in the parade as youngsters, Tamara and others weren't suddenly seeking a right they had never known. It was only as a result of asserting their sexual orientation that they were suddenly barred.

Those associated with the organized demonstration signaled their defiance with relative reserve. At least one queer protester, however, broke ranks with JYGL and adopted the tactic of street theater. Sandi DuBowski, a film student at New York University (and a contributor in this anthology), dashed up and down the parade route in a pair of tight purple pants and a *talit* (traditional prayer shawl) draped over his bare skin. As opposed to the organized protesters, Sandi openly courted engagement and confrontation with his fellow parade goers. Sandi reveled in the shock value of his display. He and a friend captured his escapade on video. Of course, shock was precisely the emotion that Sandi hoped to elicit.

Sandi's aesthetic sense coupled with his embrace of a celebratory subversion surely caught the attention of those who encountered him. If he succeeded, the apparent incongruence of the picture that he painted with his body caused parade goers to reexamine their assumptions about gays and Judaism. For others, it may have served to reinforce existing prejudices. In retrospect, however, what is most significant about Sandi's protest is that it was a solo affair.

According to Tamara, Jonathan, and others, JYGL members felt that the Jewish community would respond more positively to education, restrained protest, and even shaming. JYGL members' gravitation toward homophile tactics over street theater and confrontational protest was also a reflection of their identification as Jewish community insiders. Tamara asserted that visibility was crucial in any strategy to effect greater acceptance and normalization, particularly within the traditional Jewish world. She believed that the most effective way to break down barriers was through challenging stereotypes. She realized that when her parents' friends became acquainted with her personal story, and came to realize that "the 'great lavender threat' was actually good ol' Tamara Cohen," their attitudes changed.

It is not surprising that after the parade, the group's political/educational agenda gradually eclipsed its social programs. Perhaps the most symbolic reflection of the shift in orientation—or solidification of mission—was the changing of the group's name from JYGL to JAGL (Jewish Activist Gays and Lesbians), which occurred that summer. The parade also served to attract a cadre of new faces. JYGL/JAGL was expanding from a group of primarily Columbia University and JTS students to encompass a more demographically, geographically, and religiously diverse population. In Tani's words, JAGL "had become more than just a bunch of people who basically all knew each other, who were interested in the same thing."

Demonstrator Bob Goldfarb told one reporter that JYGL members' integrationist agenda stemmed from a desire to create in the "real world," the multicultural climate of tolerance typified by their college experiences. In my view, Goldfarb, at the time a 45-year-old marketer of classical music, correctly isolated college as a formative experience for many JAGL members. For group members like Tani and Tamara, the integration of their Jewishness and their gayness was a central project of their college years. Even those who did not "come out" until after college were able to access paradigms of social integration and cultural nationalism or pride that they had learned from their college experience. Implicit in these models was the recognition that identity in America is necessarily hyphenated.

For many group members, college was an introduction to activism as a political tool. Jonathan and Glenn, both of whom came out after college, were heavily involved in Zionist politics on their college campuses, Jonathan on the left and Glenn on the right. Political activism was also celebrated in the feminist theory classes that had a tremendous impact in constructing the mind-sets of Tamara and Miryam. Both spoke of their involvement in gay Jewish activism as a natural progression from their earlier activism. These initial experiences provided the archetypes for future behavior in the service of (often) different political ends.

JYGL VERSUS CBST

JYGL members' protest was directed as much toward the gay Jewish establishment, as represented by CBST, as it was to the parade organizers and the mainstream Jewish community. Many JAGL members, as well as journalists, have neatly characterized the relationship between CBST and JAGL as a conflict between an older separatist institution and a younger group of integrationist upstarts. Tani contrasted JAGL's integrationist mission and the educational work that JAGL had done since the parade, in predominantly straight settings like summer camps and rabbinical seminaries, with his perceptions of CBST. "For myself, CBST was just a little too non-activist, passive. CBST allows itself to be marginalized. It is located as far west as it can be [in Greenwich Village], hidden in a courtyard. It is basically 'closety space.'"

"It was typical of CBST to be accomodationist," he continued. "Their attitude was, 'fine, we'll do whatever you want.' It was outrageous that CBST didn't protest with us. Nothing would ever change if *we* didn't do something." Interestingly, while Tani considered CBST to be "closeted," the parade proved to be a decisive step in his own coming-out experience.

Jonathan, echoing Tani's disappointment with CBST's "passivity," used generational imagery and the integrationist-separatist paradigm to distinguish the activist group from the synagogue. "I guess some people have conjured up the image of the older generation with its struggle for a separate gay and lesbian Jewish community because that was what was appropriate at the time, as opposed to the younger generation, which has benefited from those separate communities and has role models in them and has decided to take the next step, which is to work toward integration." But he tried to place CBST's predicament in a more sympathetic light, calling attention to CBST's diverse membership, and its desire to win respectability, which, he believed, explained its decision not to protest.

As Shokeid asserted in his ethnography of CBST, *A Gay Synagogue in New York*, one can easily conclude that CBST provides a classic example of the type of in-group behavior documented by Erving Goffman in his study, *Stigma*: "Members of a group stigmatized by society tend to ghettoize themselves and adopt that dimension of their existence as the major component of their identity."[4] (Shokeid, 1995: 29) Goffman argued that "loyalty" and "authenticity" become synonymous with in-group identification. Further, leaders within the in-group may go so far as "favoring a secessionist ideology."[5]

Goffman's model provides a partial interpretive lens through which to view CBST. But Shokeid discovered from his extensive interviews and year-long study of the synagogue as a participant-observer that there are a myriad of motivations that drive worshippers to CBST's *terra sancta*. Many congregants interviewed by Shokeid spoke of their affiliation with CBST as "a return to roots," an act of reclamation of a Jewish identity that had been purged as part of the coming-out process. Conversely, a smaller group spoke of the synagogue as a place to reconcile suppressed expressions of gay identity with a primary and abiding sense of Jewishness. Others spoke of the synagogue fulfilling "spiritual needs," while still others identified the synagogue as primarily a social venue. While the search for "social comfort and inclusion" may serve as a common denominator for CBST's members, many congregants clearly experience CBST as integrative—both on a personal and on a communal level.

Thus, a wholesale acceptance of an integrationist-separatist dichotomy between JYGL/JAGL and CBST is reductionist. Moreover, recent attempts by the synagogue to attract media attention and participate in "mainstream" Jewish communal life—as epitomized by their petition to march in the parade—indicate that the synagogue has become more integrationist. In fact, CBST board member and JAGL activist Glenn, convinced the board, in 1995, to reject a compromise that would have allowed the synagogue to march in the parade as part of ARZA's contingent and called on synagogue members to join JAGL's protest of the parade that year. In 1998, with the parade under new sponsorship, congregants were finally allowed to march behind their own banner. In the years following the parade controversy, CBST has become even more aggressively involved in pressing for inclusion within the mainstream Jewish community. At the same time, UJA-Federation and other Jewish communal organizations adopted a more welcoming posture. A measure of the extent of change is that JAGL became defunct in 1999.

JAGL members' attitudes toward the "gay synagogue" as a paradigm likewise defy reductionist categorization. For many, integrated congregations like B'nai Jeshurun, a gay-friendly, progressive Conservative synagogue on Manhattan's Upper West Side, provided an ideal model for Jewish communal life; while for others, CBST, with its primary identity as a gay shul, was their synagogue of choice. Daniel explained that "through the work [JAGL] was doing and what we were able to create, I felt more empowered to go to CBST and find my niche there." Significantly, observance level was by no means a reliable barometer of feelings toward the synagogue. Consider also the example of Glenn, who was active in both organizations and ultimately decided to affect change at CBST from the inside.

In the early stages of the group's coalescence, members did not link their interest in JYGL to dissatisfaction with CBST. Although some were regular congregants at the synagogue, it was an unspoken given that affiliation with CBST could not fulfill their needs. When asked, in retrospect, why they wished to create a venue outside of CBST, their reasons naturally varied. But a common theme among group members was a desire to engage in the creative process of organization building. Joining a much larger group where they would have little control could not satisfy this impulse. The alienation that group members felt from the "gay Jewish establishment," as epitomized by CBST, encouraged them to create a voluntary association that would better respond to their needs and more closely resemble the intimate, consensus-based groups they had been involved with at university.

Regardless of how an outsider chooses to understand the relationship between CBST and JYGL/JAGL, it is evident that engaging in comparison served as a useful exercise for JYGL members, furthering the group's own enterprise of self definition. If JYGL members remained unsure of their group's raison d'être, they could effectively use CBST as a foil to the end of negative self-definition: JYGL was *not* closeted, it was *not* passive, and it was *not* separatist. The fact that their perceptions about CBST may have been inaccurate or simplistic was beside the point.

Taken in tandem with the parade's function as a vehicle for identity affirmation, the parade experience helped JYGL members perceive the dual potential for personal growth, and increased public awareness and political change in gay Jewish activism. Miryam's comments provide a perfect illustration of the nexus of these two dispositions in fostering group identification and definition:

> I have to say, remembering my feelings of being at the parade in 1993, that I was really proud. I just felt, first of all, I'm not a member of CBST, and although I'm going to their counter demonstration, I feel closer to this group [JYGL] that's doing this protest here because I marched in the Israel Day Parade [sic] in Ramaz, and so I felt like this is really amazing. . . . So I felt like we're not CBST, but I'm feeling close to this group. And look what we're saying. We're saying something important.

NOTES

1. My thanks to Sylvia Barack Fishman for her valuable criticisms of an earlier draft of this essay.
2. My research was carried out in the fall of 1995. It included extensive interviews with JAGL members and CBST leaders as well as a systematic review of press accounts in the English language *Jewish Forward*, the New York *Jewish Week*, and the *New York Times*. Crucial to my study was the assistance provided by JAGL archivist Eric Cohen and member Natan Meir, who supplied me with a wealth of JAGL materials, including parade flyers, song sheets, steering committee minutes, and press clippings. Miryam Kabakow graciously lent me a home video, which included footage of JAGL activities.

3. Moshe Shokeid, *A Gay Synagogue in New York* (New York: Columbia, 1995), p. 234.
4. Shokeid, *A Gay Synagogue*, p. 29.
5. Erving Goffman, *Stigma: Notes on the Management of Spoiled Identity* (Englewood Cliffs, NJ, Prentice-Hall, 1963), p. 113.

OUT AT SCHOOL

A QUEER JEWISH EDUCATION

David Shneer

STANDING AT THE front of her fifth grade classroom, Jennifer Levinson, a long-time teacher at Congregation Sha'ar Zahav's Kadimah religious school, introduced a lesson on family history. "Today we are going to be making family trees," said Jennifer to her class of energetic, bright Jewish children. She had examined the materials that were part of a curriculum used for Jewish family history projects. The trees she was to hand out to her children had prepackaged spaces for them to fill in: two slots labeled "mother" and "father," and above that, grandparents, and so on. Before class began, Jennifer went through her class list and realized that only one of her eight children would be able to fill in the slots as presented on the curricular materials. In the end, this creative teacher did not hand out the trees. Instead, she asked her students to create their own models of their families, and what resulted was revolutionary. They produced bushes, multibranched trees with vines growing in various places. One student produced a spider web–like image with intersecting lines and round forms encircling the student whose name was at the middle of her "family web." What we were witnessing was the queering of Jewish education, and the queering of Jewish families.

In just 15 years, policies of the Reform Jewish movement have undergone a radical transformation toward the inclusion of queer Jews in their structures. In 1990, the Union of American Hebrew Congregations began ordaining openly gay and lesbian rabbis; in 2000, the Central Conference of American Rabbis agreed to support Reform rabbis who officiated at same-sex weddings. In 2001, the head of Reform Judaism called on Reform synagogues to halt all interactions with the Boy Scouts of America due to the latter's anti-homosexual policies. But progressive Jewish education has not undergone such a transformation. The family structures presented to Jewish children in their school settings are still heteronormative, stressing the traditional Jewish ideal of one mother and one father.

The first steps toward change began in the late 1980s and early 1990s. In the groundbreaking book, *Twice Blessed*, Rabbi Denise Eger and Lesley Silverstone's essay on education lamented that discussion of homosexuality very rarely makes it into any classroom, let alone a Jewish one. They suggested using a text-centered approach and personal speakers to create a more tolerant environment in which to discuss difficult issues of sexuality. Their goal was to "show how the Jewish educator can be more sensitive to the issue of homosexuality," and was visionary for its time in prescribing change within Jewish education. In the early 1990s, some Jewish schools began including units on "tolerance" and "diversity." These units used traditional Jewish values such as being kind to and welcoming of strangers and accepting all people who are made in "God's image," some of the concepts that Eger and Silverstone had proposed in their article. In 1994, Rabbi Camille Shira Angel and Shifra Teitelbaum published "Intimate Connections: Integrating Human Love with God's Love," a curriculum that uses "Jewish values to sensitize students of all ages to the lesbian/gay experience." The curriculum "takes the perspective that challenging anti-lesbian and gay biases, and embracing lesbian and gay members of our community are ways to offer our students a fuller understanding and appreciation of the breadth of human love." (p. ii) The material and structure Angel and Teitelbaum present picked up where Silverstone and Eger left off. They provided Jewish educators of high school students a methodology and resources for educating about sexual diversity and about making a more inclusive community. Other progressive high school programs have incorporated single units about sexual diversity into their curricula. The nondenominational high school program Midrasha located in the San Francisco Bay Area has a unit in its 1996 ninth grade identity curriculum on homosexuality, homophobia, and tolerance called "Do Not Disdain Any Person."

What do both of these pathbreaking curricula have in common? First, that issues of sexual diversity and Jewish values have been reserved for high school–aged children; and second, that both have structured discussions around the question of tolerance, inclusiveness, and combating homophobia. These were the first steps in Jewish education to introduce students to issues of homosexuality in the classroom.

Even with these efforts at educating diversity and tolerance in Judaism's most progressive institutions, there is much more work to be done. The Gay, Lesbian, and Straight Education Network (GLSEN) recently completed a national survey of queer students and found that:

- More than 90 percent reported that they sometimes or frequently hear homophobic remarks in their school.
- More than one-third reported hearing homophobic remarks from faculty or school staff.
- Nearly 40 percent reported that no one ever intervened in these circumstances.

Within Jewish contexts, homophobia and queer invisibility are still the norm. Despite the great strides the Reform and Reconstructionist movements have made in ordaining queer clergy and officiating at same-sex ceremonies, there is still a glass ceiling for queer rabbis. And keep in mind that none of this essay's discussion about change has mentioned the more traditional forms of Conservative Judaism and Orthodoxy. There are limits to tolerance, even in the increasingly open rabbinical schools. Jewish schools have even further to go. But given GLSEN's statistics and the persisting homophobia in the Jewish establishment, tolerance education needs to be a significant aspect of any educational system, and training teachers to be more aware of or proactive on issues of homosexuality must be the first step of such an education.

Although appropriate for many school settings, the tolerance model does not address the changes that have altered American and Jewish society. In 1990, you could count the number of out rabbis on your fingers, and nearly all of them worked in gay Jewish synagogues, where being openly queer was part of the job description. In the past ten years, two social movements have changed the face of the Jewish community. On the one hand, the movement to establish queer Jewish institutions has expanded into new geographic areas and new social arenas. There are queer synagogues all over the country including Seattle, Fort Lauderdale, Louisville, Philadelphia, Chicago, and other cities. There is a gay and lesbian Jewish family camp in Northern California, and gay and lesbian Jewish youth groups on college campuses across the country. And as queer Jews have made Jewish spaces for themselves, progressive non-queer Jewish institutions are responding with a new, unprecedented inclusiveness. There are openly queer rabbis on the *bimah* in mainstream Reform synagogues, gay and lesbian *chavurot*, gay-straight alliances, and other forms of institutional change that point to a new openness in defining and creating the liberal Jewish community.

Despite all of these changes in institutions aimed at adult Jews, no such reform has happened in Jewish education. Education is the place where the Jewish community has, in theory, the most invested in the questions of Jewish continuity, community, and the future of Judaism in America, questions that still, unfortunately, shape Jewish policy-making in the United States.

Jewish education does not reflect the changing diversity of the adult Jewish communities. For example, not a single Jewish children's book explores sexual diversity. Congregation Sha'ar Zahav's children's library includes the ever-popular, but not explicitly Jewish, *Heather Has Two Mommies* and *Daddy's Roommate*, which virtually monopolize the market of children's books that address queer family issues. This suggests either that publishers feel there is no market for Jewish children's books that address sexual diversity, or that the subject is still too politically taboo for a publishing house to address. As individual consumers, queer Jewish families are demanding representation of themselves in children's books, but unfortunately, individual families do not generate the Jewish children's book market—Jewish educational institutions do. Among Jewish schools, there is still only a tiny market for queer Jewish children's books. Hebrew language education still works in the bi-polar world of *aba* (father) and *ima* (mother), even when such concepts do not ring with meaning for children of same-sex families. As queer Jews have more children, the demand for a queer-identified Jewish education will only become stronger, and Jewish educational institutions and publishers need to respond to this emerging demand.

WORKING AT THE OTHER END OF THE SPECTRUM

As the former director of the first (and for a long time only) Jewish school at a GLBT synagogue, I have seen how difficult it has been to effect institutional change in Jewish education. The appearance of Congregation Sha'ar Zahav's religious school, Kadimah, in 1988, was a result of the new demographics of the GLBT community—Jewish lesbians, and later gay men, began to have children, and they wanted their children to learn in their synagogue. At the time, the parents saw a queer Jewish school at their queer synagogue as a safe haven from the homophobic world. It mirrored the purpose of the synagogue as a whole—a place where their children would not feel isolated for their different family structures. Parents got together and formed a cooperative school as part of the synagogue—the birth of the first queer Jewish school.

The school was officially founded by several families, the then rabbi of Congregation Sha'ar Zahav, Yoel Kahn, and long-time Jewish educator Phyllis Mintzer. With just a handful of students, Kadimah felt like a one-room schoolhouse. The curriculum reflected the content of other progressive Jewish educational establishments with special attention paid to finding ways of representing diverse family structures. According to Mintzer, the guiding objectives of the curriculum were "to develop literate, functional Jews, who identified as Jews in their own terms and were members of a diverse community with diverse families." The school was to be a safe space for all of the children to talk about their diverse families and the consequences they faced for being children of diverse families. It is important to note that the founding school had three straight families, showing that from its inception, a "queer" curriculum included all forms of diversity. The content of the curriculum was similar to that of other synagogues: holidays, lifecycles, Torah, ethics/values, and later, included more history and text. Kahn and Mintzer aimed for a rigorous Jewish education with the diversity of the community as the guiding philosophy.

As time has evolved, so has the school. Kadimah now has more than 40 children enrolled, and more than 150 children involved in various children's and family activities, from GLBT families and mixed-gender families as well. And just as Kadimah's student and parent population becomes more diverse, the notion of a queer Jewish school has arrived at other institutions. Queer synagogues from New York, Los Angeles, and in other large metropolitan areas are finally experiencing what Sha'ar Zahav experienced 15 years ago: the emergence of the queer Jewish family constituency as shaping the queer Jewish synagogue. In many ways, Kadimah is the face of the future of queer Jewish institutions' educational systems, and perhaps, for Jewish institutions in general.

The demographics of Kadimah have expanded, as more mixed-gender couples join the synagogue and enroll their children in the school. Simultaneously, other progressive synagogues in Northern California have more GLBT families. Demographically speaking, then, in the most progressive areas of the country, the queer Jewish synagogue movement and the most progressive non-queer synagogues are moving *toward* each other. As part of this milieu on the forefront of change in American Judaism, the school has been forced to define what it means to offer a "queer Jewish education."

QUEERING THE CURRICULUM

To conceive of a Jewish education at a queer synagogue, the school needed to examine the ways that the synagogue as a whole differentiated itself from other communities, aside from the demographic makeup of the congregation. Were there particular practices or liturgy that defined a queer synagogue? Sha'ar Zahav's Friday Night Siddur includes a special reading as part of the Kaddish that reads, "We remember our gay brothers and sisters who were martyred in years past . . . " and everyone, queer or not, stands and reads this moving and powerful statement together, a collective Kaddish that defines the congregation as queer, regardless of the sexual identity of the person reading it. The Sha'ar Zahav Yahrzeit list includes friends and companions as well as spouses, parents, and children, since for many gays and lesbians, friends were their chosen family. The synagogue board was, until last year, made up entirely of queer-identified people. Adult education classes often have a queer focus to them, such as "Queer Talmud" or "Gay and Lesbian Parenting and Judaism." Was there a way to mirror these signifiers of queer community in children's education?

Given that what identifies queer people as such is, at root, complex sexual identities, dealing with queer issues is especially challenging for children for several reasons. First, talking about issues around sex and sexuality with children makes adults uncomfortable. In public schools, official discussion of sex and sexual identity (if they even cover the second) does not begin until middle or high school, when students themselves are developing and are reflecting on their own sexuality. Second, for those children who might not be consciously thinking about their sexuality, adults are often afraid of raising the subject of sexual identity, fearing that talking about the ideas will plant them in their moldable minds. Eger and Silverstone felt obliged to mention in their 1989 article that "no one can teach another person to be gay or lesbian." With such fears and stereotypes to deal with, approaching queer issues with prepubescent children can be even more challenging. How do these questions play out in a queer context?

To affirm their queer family structures and the identity of their parents while not sexualizing the educational experience is a tricky path to walk down. For the 1998 San Francisco Israel Fair, Kadimah's sixth grade class did a series of poetry readings of contemporary queer Israeli poets, most of which dealt with the theme of love, and some of which bordered on the erotic. While most parents were very excited to see our creative fusion of queer issues and Israeli culture and politics, some were concerned that the poetry reading sexualized our youth. This event was one of the most contentious in the school's history. It highlighted the challenges implicit in creating an affirming educational experience and one that openly discussed issues of love and sexuality, what I call a "queer-identified" educational experience, while providing the children a context in which to deal with the sexual nature of that which identifies the community as queer. For these sixth graders, same-sex love poetry struck a great balance between textuality, history, Jewish culture, and the identity issues that are part of our curriculum and part of their lives.

Kadimah only educates children up to age 13 (through their Bar/Bat Mitzvah), so the very discussion of sex and sexuality was framed by questions of age appropriateness. At an education board retreat, the board and I out-lined the key values that were to guide our curriculum development process. Among such Jewish values or content skills as "provides quality Hebrew edu-cation" and "gives children synagogue skills" was included the statement, "cre-ates a sex-positive environment"—not something Mintzer mentioned as one of the original guiding goals of Kadimah. As the education director, I strug-gled with the idea of a sex-positive children's education. Did that mean talk-ing about sex with eight year olds? Did it mean not shielding children from Biblical innuendos of sex? Did it mean broaching the subject of sexual iden-tity with the older children in the school? To some extent, the school found a balance between creating an environment where talking about sex and sexu-ality are not taboo, while not bringing up sex in ways that children cannot developmentally understand.

I had a discussion with the seventh grade class about the Biblical injunc-tion against homosexuality from Leviticus. The kids were ready and willing to tackle the text in a direct manner. We talked about the difference between sex acts and sexuality, the injunction against male acts but not female acts, and the historical context in which these injunctions occurred. All the gloves were off, and the children were completely engaged. As parents started arriv-ing, one poked her head into the room, and the kids in chorus screamed out, "No adults. We're having a serious conversation." They understood that we were talking about topics that are traditionally taboo, but also recognized that they were ready and interested in talking about sex and sexuality seriously. In essence, the children determined the boundaries of their "sex-positive" education and, as Jennifer Levinson discovered in her family tree project, the children help us shape a queer Jewish education.

The story also raises the subject of the teacher's role in this process, and her/his own sexuality. There seem to be two variables in exploring the intersections of a teacher's role and discussions of sexuality: the teaching environment and the sexual identity of the teacher. In my discussion with the seventh graders, I, a gay man, was teaching at the queer synagogue. Did it matter that these students knew that I identify as queer? Did they ask me questions they might not ask a teacher whom they knew identified as straight? What if they did not know the sexual identity of the teacher? Would I have been allowed to or felt comfortable enough to have this discussion in a non-queer environment? Could a teacher who identified as straight have had the same experience in that classroom that I had? I'm not sure.

The sexual identities of Kadimah's teaching staff reflect the diversity of the community. There are straight-identified, queer-identified, lesbian, gay, and transgendered teachers. As director, I did not ask prospective teachers their sexual orientation. It is in fact illegal to do so, although there are ways to ascertain that kind of information without asking point blank. All of them were able to bring the values of diversity and community to their teaching and all agreed that quality teaching and experience with diversity were the most important parts about teaching at Kadimah. That said, board members, parents, and teachers always asked me if a new teacher was "gay or straight." Always. And there was a right answer. There are two reasons I see for this persistent question. First, parents wanted their children to see queer people represented in positions of authority. Second, and this is what I see as a teacher and director, when a teacher identifies as queer, it changes the interactions s/he has with the students. The students can ask questions that use the second person, "Do you feel oppressed by the Leviticus text, David?" and perhaps are more able to articulate for themselves their own "I" statements. In a queer context, most agree that it changes the dynamics for the better.

In a non-queer context, some think that it changes them for the worse. Straight teachers who discuss sexuality in non-queer environments have more latitude for sensitive discussions about sexuality and queer issues, because the conversations tend to be *less* "I" centered and more abstract. In other words, they can be more distanced from questions of identity. Queer

teachers are often afraid to broach the subject of sexuality in non-queer contexts for the very fears that others have—the fear of "teaching queer" or
planting ideas in impressionable children about diverse sexualities.

In 1995, I taught in the Bay Area Midrasha program that I mentioned
above. The students and teachers were all on a weekend retreat, and the topic
of the weekend's curriculum was "identity." Each of the approximately 15
teachers was asked to teach a lesson about identity. I brought in the Leviticus
ban on homosexuality and the David and Jonathon story to talk about
polyvocality and sexuality in the Torah with the 16 and 17 year olds. Of the
150 students on the retreat, 50 of them attended my session, and the discussion, scheduled for one hour, lasted more than two hours. Students were
interested, angry, excited, and impressed that a teacher would talk this
"openly" with them. To drive home the point about identity, I wore a queer-
identified shirt about safe sex to the study session. Two students asked if they
could borrow my shirt. The session was a huge success.

That is, until the director of the program began getting calls from parents
about a teacher who wore some "gay shirt" and talked about homosexuality.
The director adamantly defended the program and the class to the parents,
but felt obliged to respond to the parents' concerns. The director called me to
have a "frank" discussion about "how far" we can go in this program. He was
straight-identified, but very supportive of the study session, and asked that I
not wear such "sexually explicit" clothing to the camp. I had hit the boundaries. Sexuality in text was one thing; in real life, it was another. Letting students, rather than their parents, determine the boundaries of their education
was clearly the direction I favored, and was the direction the parents seemed
to fear. They feared that their students might start using "I" statements. In
contrast, at Kadimah, after telling the parents about the Leviticus discussion
I had with the seventh graders, I received a hearty congratulations from
straight and queer parents alike, and was encouraged to keep up the good
work. (No, I did not wear the safe sex T-shirt to the seventh grade class.
Should I have? Were they too young to see a teacher wearing such a T-shirt?
Would the parents have reacted differently to my lesson? This is where the
debates of a queer education lie.)

For older kids, queering the curriculum can actually involve discussions
about that which makes their parents, and possibly themselves, queer—their
particular form of love and their sexuality. As we move down the curriculum,
"queering" is about breaking normative models of Jewish values, heroes, and
history and emphasizing different aspects of Jewish culture and tradition. In

this, queering has much in common with feminist efforts to change curricula in order to remake what it is to be Jewish. Kadimah's fourth grade class studies Jewish history through heroes and heroines. They study some of the old favorites like Solomon, Abraham, and Sarah, but we include the David and Jonathon story and explore the varieties of love that the Torah exposes. They learn about the medieval Hebrew poets, Yehuda Ha-Levi and Solomon Ibn Ezra, who wrote same-sex love poetry, and use that as a jumping off point for discussing Sephardic culture. They also study contemporary Jewish history by learning about Magnus Hirschfeld, the Jewish founder of the Institute of Sexology in Berlin, an institution destroyed when the Nazis came to power, and Bella Abzug, one of the earliest female U.S. senators. In other words, the curriculum "queers" Jewish history by exposing the children to exemplars rarely, if ever, included in canonical Jewish histories.

The Bnei Mitzvah class studies life cycles and learns the Sha'ar Zahav kaddish. In addition, the children watch a video of a same-sex Jewish wedding officiated by a cantor and explore the meaning of a Jewish wedding. For the youngest children, the concept of queering the curriculum is much more abstract, and involves affirming family diversity and exposing the children to queer relationships through example, which were the guiding principles behind the original Kadimah curriculum. Kadimah's children participate in *aufrufs* of queer couples. They watch two men sneak a kiss in the corner of the oneg room; they watch the synagogue's rabbi interact with her same sex partner, as rabbi and rebbetzin.

IS "QUEER" ONLY A SEXUAL IDENTITY?

A second problem about "queering the curriculum" is the tendency many queer Jews have of projecting the congregation's "identity" onto all of its members, including its children. As members of a queer synagogue, Kadimah's students are all exposed to images of queer couples showing affection for each other in Jewish spaces, seeing non-traditional families as normative, not exceptional, and embracing the philosophy of openness and *tikkun olam* that form the foundation of the congregation's Jewish values. However, most of our children have not explored their own sexual identity, and are part of our congregation by association with queer Jews—notably their parents, adult friends, and relatives. So are these children of gays and lesbians "queer" in any way?

Most definitely. The very fact of having queer parents defines these chil-

dren as "other" because of issues around sexual identity and family relationships. These children face multiple differences in their schools—as Jews and
as children of queer people. As their haven, the school's job is to empower
them to embrace their difference, both in their religion and in the sexual
identity of their family and congregation. The school also gives them the
pride and knowledge they need to brave a world that sees them as different,
because of their families. Social homophobia oppresses these children by
association, and therefore, society "queers" them. Some of our children are
teased on playgrounds for having two mothers; they do not see themselves
represented in classroom textbooks or in the media. Many of our children
have invented their own defense mechanisms to mask their identity to their
peers, in the same way that queer people do in various places in their lives.
Most of our Bnei Mitzvah kids have "stories" to explain who that second
woman is who picks them up from school on occasion: "It's my aunt." "It's my
mom's friend." Queerness, for children of gays and lesbians, is an ascribed
identity; no one knows the sexual identity these children will have when they
are old enough to articulate such ideas for themselves. But homophobia
brings oppression into their lives in a similar way that anti-semitism makes
many people "Jewish" who do not think of themselves that way. I'm thinking
in particular about how Nazi definitions of Jewishness defined people raised
Christian as Jews if they had Jewish grandparents. Or the way Orthodox
Judaism defines anyone born of a Jewish mother as Jewish despite personal
practice or identity. Ascribed identities may not be self-defined, but they are
real. In this way, Kadimah's children of gays and lesbians are queer.

Now, what if I told you that, as a result of the demographic changes of the
1990s, nearly half of Kadimah's children were not children of gays and lesbians. Are they being queered by their association with queer families and a
queer congregation, like the children of queer parents are queered by their
associations with their parents? The congregation does not know the sexual
identity of all of its members, but it does know the family arrangements of
the children in the religious school. To date, about forty to fifty percent of
Kadimah families are "mixed gender," or in heteronormative parlance,
"straight." When asked why a "straight" family joins the "gay shul," most
respond that it has to do with two things: the values and the strong sense of
community. These families seek a place with progressive values that embrace
diversity—diversity of religious background, race, learning styles, and sexual
orientation. We have a high number of interracial and interfaith families. We
have a high percentage of students with learning disabilities. These families

sought out the "gay shul" for its loving openness and strong sense of grass-roots community organizing, and often because they were close friends with other queer people who were members of the synagogue. Are these "straight" families queered by being part of this community? How about their children?

Here, we reach both the limit of and the endless opportunities presented by a queered curriculum. These straight folk are still straight, and when asked "are you queer," by and large, only those who have had experience with queer sexuality, not just queer community, answer in the affirmative. Their kids, in ten years, will probably have the same answers. For some queer members of the synagogue, this is a source of sadness. Ten years ago, the synagogue had a queer-centric model that made "queer" normative as a counterbalance to the heteronormativity of the rest of the world and especially the rest of the Jewish establishment. The curriculum of the school, however, always rested on the principles of non-normativity, or a least making diversity normative. It shows diversity of family structures including same-gender, interracial, and other diversities, and does so in order to make sure that all of the childrens' families (including the straight ones) are represented. The mission statement of the synagogue now includes heterosexuals as a key constituent of the congregation, and the school's constituents were largely responsible for the shift. The kaddish for gay martyrs is still part of the Siddur, but ten years from now, I predict that the wording will be changed to reflect all martyrs of oppression, not just those oppressed because of their sexual orientation.

The school and its curriculum are at the heart of this shift in demographics. It is true that the growing presence of straight-identified families who come to this synagogue precisely for its queer curriculum and community values threatens the queerness of the institution, if we define "queer" as queer normativity. But this aspect only looks at the limits of a queer curriculum and a queer synagogue. The opportunities presented by a queer curriculum are, in fact, endless.

The basic values that inform a queer curriculum—multiple family arrangements, progressive politics, sex-positive environment, all underpinning a rigorous Jewish education—must form the basis of *all* Jewish education's curricula as we move into the twenty-first century. All children should be exposed to queer couples kissing in the oneg room, to discussions about the Leviticus's ban on homosexuality. All children should be exposed to the many interpretations of David and Jonathon's love (at Sha'ar Zahav, we used to push the homosexual reading, and now we argue for multiple readings of their relationship). All children should be part of a community that embraces interfaith and interracial couples looking for a spiritual place that supports them. Once they are written and published, all school libraries should have books that reflect queer families in a Jewish context. At the roots of a queer curriculum are the Jewish values of *tikkun olam*, love, the idea that each person is created *be-tselem elohim* (in the image of God), and a space where the lives of children of gays and lesbians are as normative as every other child's life. Some may argue that these are simply quality, progressive educational values. I agree. But only a queer curriculum at the gay synagogue could push Jewish institutions from the "tolerance" model of progressive Jewish education's approach to sexual orientation (which is still a heteronormative approach) and dismantle the very idea of normativity within Jewish education and Jewish institutions.

BREAKING GROUND

A TRADITIONAL JEWISH
LESBIAN WEDDING

Inbal Kashtan

KATHY AND I had a sense before, during, and after our wedding that we were making history—breaking ground in positioning lesbian weddings within traditional Judaism. We wanted to record this history, and so along with our thank-you cards, we sent out a request for guests to write us a note about their experience of our wedding. We received numerous responses, most from people who were deeply moved by the ceremony and who felt in some way transformed by it. One of our guests, a heterosexual modern Orthodox woman, wrote:

> I was quite impacted by my sense of the courage it required of you both to stand so boldly in your love and commitment to one another. It seemed to me, given the innovative and "untraditional" nature of your "traditional" wedding, that there were few places for the two of you to hide.

Another friend expressed his difficulty in grappling with the image of two women in a traditional Jewish ceremony. He wrote: "The lesbian piece shook me up a little. It was just totally new to see a traditional Jewish wedding [in which] my eyes kept seeing . . . two dresses, two pairs of breasts . . . A challenging new image." Another heterosexual friend, who had been a vocal supporter of gay and lesbian rights for years, understood the event differently from how she expected to. "I get it now," she wrote. "It wasn't just a wedding; it was a political rally." And a relative wrote: "Your wedding was truthfully one of the deepest and most beautiful I've seen. Every little bit of exposure I get to gays and lesbians expands my vision of what is 'normal.'"

In different ways, each of these responses captured something of the essence of our traditional Jewish wedding. The first two responses reflected the dichotomy of tradition and innovation, the shock of "two pairs of breasts" at the most traditional locus of heterosexual union. The third response grasped the radical political statement still inherent in the act of lesbian and gay marriage. The fourth response and a number of others like it attested to the way our wedding resonated for Jews—many of an older generation— connecting it with their own heterosexual experience. All of these responses confirmed that our attempt to create a recognizably "normal" Eastern-European Jewish wedding had succeeded; these people were able to resonate with the sacredness and power of the day in a way that profoundly affected their understanding of the meaning of a "lesbian" and a "Jewish" wedding.

In creating a traditional Jewish lesbian wedding, Kathy and I joined a generation of Jews who are seeking a more meaningful relationship with Judaism. Many contemporary Jews are seeking to connect to Judaism by turning to older traditions, ancient texts, and spiritual practices. However, our unique relationship to Judaism as queer Jews presents a poignant paradox: the deeper we delve into tradition, the more it seems to reject our sexualities, our loves, our unions, our families.

How, then, do we struggle with this seeming rejection and still fulfill our yearning for tradition and connection to Judaism? Kathy's and my response to this question was to stake our relationship at the center of Jewish ritual by creating a wedding utterly grounded in Jewish tradition, yet boldly asserting our queerness. For us, this meant taking a traditional Orthodox wedding and wrestling with every ritual and text that we could uncover, taking our wedding beyond the realm of a "political rally" and squarely into the sphere of cultural transformation. Choosing any framework other than traditional Judaism for our wedding was unthinkable for us, because the particular rituals of our tradition are the ones we find most meaningful for marking our important life-cycle events.

One of the reasons that our lesbian wedding resonated so powerfully for our mostly heterosexual guests is that it took them not only into their own experience but, more profoundly, *beyond* their experience, touching on their own yearning for a spiritual connection with Jewish tradition. Our wedding looked like an Orthodox wedding—aside from the two pairs of breasts. Yet because it was a wedding of two women, it was an inclusive Orthodoxy, one that held a promise to queer *and* straight Jews of the possibility of finding themselves in the tradition.

Figuring out how to create a traditional Jewish lesbian wedding was a bittersweet challenge. We struggled with how to capture in the texts of the ceremony two of the deep truths about the day. First, that this was a wedding like the countless weddings that had gone before it in the history of our people, in the sense that it publicly expressed, in Jewish idiom, a commitment to a life together. Second, that this wedding was something new and different and radical and traditionally inconceivable.

Originally, the *halachic* requirements that made a wedding Jewish were simple: "the bride accepts an object worth more than a dime from the groom, the groom recites a ritual formula of acquisition and consecration, and these two actions must be witnessed."[1] The other rituals familiar to most Jews, such as the wedding canopy (*huppa*), having a rabbi officiate, and even breaking the glass, are customs that developed over centuries, and that varied between locations and times, suggesting that the tradition has been flexible and open to interpretation and modification. We relied on this understanding of the imperative to interpret texts and make them relevant to contemporary Jews in the design of our wedding.

Our interpretive work varied with each element of the traditional Jewish wedding. Some texts we were able to keep with very few changes, some required a great deal of work to make them both relevant to our particular situation and still clearly resonant with the original text. The text of *Birkat Erusin* (engagement blessing), for example, praises God for creating marriage as a vehicle for intimacy, but also records the teachings regarding forbidden marriages (such as those between siblings). We chose to abbreviate the text slightly to emphasize the delight over the very existence of rituals to sanctify a relationship, and cut completely the section on forbidden marriages. This was one of the easiest choices for us.

One very brief yet key text we changed was the spoken formula during the exchange of rings, the key text marking the union: "You are hereby sanctified unto me, with this ring, *according to the religious law of Moses and Israel.*" Kathy and I wrestled with the question of whether we can, with full integrity, claim this wedding as falling within our people's explicit legal framework. We ended up deciding that we could not make such a claim, and so we changed the wording to reflect what we felt we could claim. We said to each other, and wrote in our ketubah, the wedding contract: "You are hereby sanctified unto me, with this ring, *in the tradition of the Jewish people.*" This was the one choice we made that we later regretted. In retrospect, we wished we had made the claim of legality, because our wedding was so profoundly an expression of Jewish life and tradition that it made more clear to us the imperative to chart a path toward making it legal. As our rabbi and friend Rona Shapiro said at the wedding, it marked the direction that Jewish law *should* follow:

> If *halachic* principles, followed strictly, yield unjust conclusions, then it is our duty according to *halacha* to exercise civil disobedience. At such times brave individuals and communities must be willing to stand in front of the *halacha*, to walk as Abraham did in front of God, and to say, "this is where we're going," trusting that *halacha* will catch up with us. We stand on the edge of a *halachic* limb and assert stubbornly that this limb is part of the tree. We say, *this* is *halacha*, *this* is Torah, and we wait for the rest of the community to join us.

Other texts presented different challenges. We almost entirely rewrote the text of the ketubah. Written in Aramaic (Jews' lingua franca when the text was being formulated in the early centuries C.E.), the ketubah was essentially a legal contract in which the woman's dowry and her monetary settlement in case of divorce or the death of the husband were specified. The different branches of Judaism have devised alternate, more egalitarian ketubot; some couples create their own. Since we could not find great meaning in the original text, we did not want to use it as a base for creating a same-sex ketubah. Instead, we chose to retain the text's framing structure while constructing a new document composed of quotations from Jewish texts. The first paragraph follows the traditional text stating the facts of the marriage—with an embellishment at the end. The second paragraph begins as a quotation from the last of the wedding ceremony's seven blessings, while our commitments to one another are primarily amended quotations of verses from the books of Hosea and Ruth. And in keeping with the Jewish tradition of not making explicit vows—as well as with our own understanding of human nature—we stated our commitments as intentions rather than promises. The text of the ketubah follows:

> On Monday, the fourth of Elul in the year 5756, August 19, 1996, in Berkeley, California, Katherine Grace Simon, daughter of Anna, of

blessed memory, and Jerome, and Inbal Kashtan, daughter of Rivka and Mordechai, of blessed memory, entered into a covenant of kiddushin, according to the traditions of the Jewish people, and as is the practice of lovers in all the nations of the world.

In joy and happiness, gladness and delight, love and companionship, mindfulness and seriousness, Inbal and Kathy committed to one another to do their utmost to continue cultivating their shared and unique paths, deepening their love, and renewing their relationship.

Inbal and Kathy said to one another: You are hereby sanctified unto me, with this ring, in the tradition of the Jewish people. I sanctify you unto me for life; I sanctify you unto me in justice and righteousness, in loving kindness and compassion; I sanctify you unto me in faithfulness. Where thou goest I will go, where thou dwellest I will dwell.

All this was done and said under God's wings and with the support and presence of family and friends.

All this is valid and binding.

A pastiche of biblical and rabbinic verses and framed by the traditional structure of the ketubah the text is more *midrash*, or textual interpretation, than contemporary marriage agreement.

Unlike the ketubah, which we crafted ourselves, the text of the Seven Blessings we were able to retain almost entirely, struggling principally with producing a clear translation and gleaning the different blessings' themes. We asked seven different people to "bless" us by reading the texts. Most simply, where the blessings traditionally speak of "the bridegroom and the bride," we used alternate constructions. Other changes reflected more theological and political concerns. In order to highlight God's many manifestations, we used alternate names for God in addition to the traditional, "Lord, our God, King of the Universe." After much discussion, we replaced "the cities of Judah" with "the cities of Israel and the hearts of the world" to acknowledge our sadness about continued Israeli occupation of Palestinian land in the Judean Hills and our wishes for peace and joy for all peoples.

In addition to the original blessings, we also suggested a theme that the people giving each blessing might use as the basis of a brief personal blessing for us. We derived these themes from traditional commentaries, which explain why these particular blessings are used at wedding ceremonies, as well as our own interpretations:

First blessing
Blessed are you, Adonai our God, ruler of the universe, creator of the fruit of the vine.

Theme: Abundance, sweetness, joy[2]

Second blessing
Blessed are you, Shchina, creator of the universe, who created all for your glory.

Theme: Creating relationships adds to the glory of creation

Third blessing
Blessed are you, source of life, creator of the first human beings.

Theme: A new relationship is like a fresh creation of humanity.

Fourth blessing
Blessed are you, spring of life, who created human beings in her image, humanity in the image of divinity, and patterned for humanity the perpetuation of life. Blessed are you, spring of life, creator of humanity.

Theme: The divinity in human beings, and the ability to give life through procreation and nurturing.

Fifth blessing
May the barren one rejoice in the ingathering of her children in gladness and peace. Blessed are you, righter of the world, who brings Tzion joy in her children.

Theme: Hope that those who are separated will come together and unite in peace and joy, and that we may return to a whole relationship with the earth.

Sixth blessing
Delight these beloved companions as you delighted your creations in the Garden of Eden of yore. Blessed are you, heart of the world, delighter of beloved companions.

Theme: This union is a little glimpse of the delight of the Garden of Eden

Seventh blessing
Blessed are you, embracer of the world, who created joy and happiness, bride and bride, mirth, merriment, gladness, delight, love and compan-

ionship, peace and partnership. Quickly, embracer of the world, may there be heard in the cities of Israel and in the hearts of nations the voice of joy and the voice of happiness, the voice of the bride and the voice of the bride, the mirthful shouts of beloveds under their *huppas,* of young women and men feasting and singing. Blessed are you, Adonai our God, delighter of the beloved companions.

Theme: Through the union of loving people, the possibility of joy and healing in the world is increased

We framed the ceremony with rituals that also reflected the melding of tradition and radical innovation. We appropriated the custom of a *tish,* in which (traditionally) the groom takes a few minutes before the ceremony to speak some words of Torah, known as *dvar Torah* (with his male guests seated with him around a table—*tish* in Yiddish). Traditionally, too, the groom is nervous, and not much in the mood to teach, so his friends interrupt his talk with teasing and song. At our wedding, we declared ourselves teachers and transmitters of Jewish tradition by having two separate *tishes* (we were separate so as not to see each other until the ceremony began), where we each gave a *dvar Torah* and were each joyously interrupted. After the ceremony, our wedding turned into a raucous celebration, with guests partaking in the traditional Eastern European *freilakh*—lifting us up in chairs, dancing in whirling circles, and sitting us down to watch mirthful acrobatics, a rap song, a rhyme on our relationship, and impromptu merry-making.

▼

As Jews who grew up disconnected from traditional Judaism because of our sexual orientation, we have the challenge of making our connection to Judaism meaningful and personally authentic. In order to build a significant and meaningful relationship with traditional Judaism we had to wrestle with the tradition. What we saw at our wedding was that, although as queer Jews, we are *forced* to struggle with tradition, every Jew who wishes to engage with Judaism, to make meaning out of Judaism *should* struggle, because the tradition does not lend itself readily to our modern sensibilities. Many Jews feel alienated by their tradition, and queer Jews have the tools to make it meaningful for *everyone.* The gift some queer Jews have is that we come into this engagement with Judaism from a feminist and queer critical awareness. We have experience with teasing meaning out of history that has traditionally felt exclusive and alienating to us. If we can harness this awareness with an impulse for finding connection, love, and meaning in these traditions and texts rather than abdicating what is uncomfortable to us, we can actually find the threads of dissent and internal critique. Our tradition has been built on interpretation and multivocality. And therein lies the true paradox: the more we delve into a tradition that seems to exclude us, the more we find embedded within it the principles and voices we can use to transform it. Daniel Boyarin, an Orthodox professor of talmudic culture, writes:

> My endeavor is to justify my love [of rabbinic texts and culture], that is, both to explain it and to make it just. . . . I cannot . . . paper over, ignore, explain away, or apologize for the oppressions of women and lesbigay people that this culture has practiced, and therefore I endeavor . . . to render it just by presenting a way of reading the tradition that may help it surmount or expunge—in time—that which I and many others can no longer live with.[3]

As queer Jews who wish to participate in Judaism's ritual traditions, we must engage in cultural transformation. Through our endeavor we forge a path for other Jews seeking to make their relationships to Judaism fully engaged and meaningful. Mining our tradition for meaning—contemporary, relevant, and deeply rooted—we open it up to all Jews who do not see themselves reflected in an unexamined Judaism.

NOTES

1. Anita Diamant, *The New Jewish Wedding* (New York: Simon & Schuster, 1985), pp. 18–19. While the book's title suggests a break from tradition, Diamant convincingly argues that customizing the tradition is in fact part of the traditional Jewish wedding.
2. Kathy's father gave us this blessing, which many of our guests found particularly moving. He said:
   > In trying to think of what I could say to bless the two of you on the theme of abundance, sweetness, and joy, it finally occurred to me that the most sincere and deepest thing I could say to you is to remind you that I, in my lifetime, was blessed with marriage with two wonderful people. And I enjoyed with each of my wives the sweetness and the abundance and the joy in such measure that if I could wish it for you, it would be the most wonderful thing of all. And that's what I wish for you.
3. Daniel Boyarin, *Unheroic Conduct: The Rise of Heterosexuality and the Invention of the Jewish Man* (Berkeley: University of California Press, 1997), p. xvii. For more on the multivocality of talmudic Judaism, see his *Intertextuality and the Reading of Midrash* (Bloomington: Indiana University Press, 1990), and *Carnal Israel: Reading Sex in Talmudic Culture* (Berkeley: University of California Press, 1993).

REMAKING FAMILY

CANADIAN JEWS, SEXUALITY,

AND RELATIONSHIPS[1]

oscar wolfman

> I go home for the holidays—except Yom Kippur; why be with family if
> you're not going to eat?

IN ONE PITHY phrase, this statement about identity, relationships, and sexuality encapsulates my study on queer Jews, Jewish holiday celebrations, and family.[2] I interviewed 40 lesbian and gay Jews across Canada's urban centers (where both Jews and queers tend to congregate) to examine how Jewish and queer identities are maintained, practiced, and resisted through families and religious holidays, and how queer Jews respond to Jewish institutional homophobia.[3] As this paper is part of a larger study on how people create their identities, even when aspects of their identities conflict with each other, the focus here is on how the participants maintain religious belief despite religious laws that frown upon some same-sex sexual practices.[4]

Visiting families for the holidays is not unique to Jews or to queers. But what are the consequences of sexual orientation on family traditions? What explanations can be given when a religious identity is connected to family, so that sitting at the family table means "being Jewish"? And what constitutes the family for these queer Jews?

Judaism, like all religions, is a social construction. It is a system of thoughts, beliefs, and discourses created by people, by which they may establish collective identities and cultural practices. Within Judaism, the two cultural practices that were most central for explaining how my participants related to their Jewish identity were social responsibility (*"tikkun olam"*) and struggle ("Israel"). These Jewish practices are not unique to my participants, but I will illustrate how the emphasis on these two foundational practices signals an important shift in integrating one's same-sex sexuality with a homophobic religion, while at the same time contributing to a general shift within contemporary Judaism.

QUEER JEWISH *MISHPUKHA*

Before I describe the Jewish family (*mishpukha*), it is important to know how the participants in my interviews understand concepts of family and Judaism, and how the Canadian context of this study shapes my participants' understandings of these concepts. The first element of a same-sex sexual identity is to be able to recognize one's difference from what constitutes "the norm."[5] The ease with which such acknowledgment occurs is related to one's social context. National laws contribute to the identity of Canadian queer Jews, because to speak publicly about one's sexual identity, a person requires the words and social concepts that allow for self-definition and that provide the safety to speak publicly about one's identity. To identify oneself according to a marginalized sexual orientation requires living in a society and a state in which queer relationships are something to be known and discussed. But such a social and political context is only the first step. Individual understanding and personal practices of identity are vital, as they explain how one moves from a political "subject" to an individual who can accept, alter, or resist legal and social identities.[6]

"I'm Lucky to be Alive at This Time in Canada"

In terms of popular culture, Canadians share many similarities with people from the United States, but we differ when it comes to issues of multiculturalism and diversity, and the legal rights for same-sex sexually identified people. Canada, in its census, asks people of their marital status, wherein they include the category "same-sex relationship." Therefore, the Canadian government acknowledges the identity and the legitimacy of gays and lesbians in ways the United States does not. These differences are important because we cannot homogenize all Jewish culture, nor can we homogenize queer culture. As so much of what has been written about lesbians/gays/queers comes from the United States, researchers tend to present the American gay/lesbian/queer as the universal (within a particular historical and economic system) identity.[7] As such, ignoring differences between modern capitalist countries carries the potential of homogenizing all lesbian and gay Jews, as well as transforming queer theory into yet another strategy of American imperialism. To reduce that potential, I discuss Canadian lesbian and gay Jews within the Canadian legal and social context.

THE LITERATURE ON QUEERS, JEWS, AND FAMILY

Much has been written on queers and on their families, but it tends to focus on youths, their families, and "coming out." Much of this work has overtones of pathology, as it is largely written by social workers and psychologists, and deals with the problems of encountering homophobic families. One sociological book on the subject is John Preston's *A Member of the Family: Gay Men Write about Their Families* (New York, 1992). As the title suggests, it only discusses men. The book is a series of personal accounts, with no analysis of patterns or issues revealed in the narratives, and no account of religion.

Likewise, books on queers and spirituality tend to focus on Christian denominations. Some books that deal with a wider range of religious groups, such as David Shallenberger's *Reclaiming the Spirit: Gay Men and Lesbians Come to Terms with Their Religion* (Rutgers, 1998) and Catherine Lake's *ReCreations: Religion and Spirituality in the Lives of Queer People* (Queer Press, 1999) are also narratives that do not deal with the relationship of the family and celebrations as a component of their religious practices. Rebecca Alpert's *Like Bread on the Seder Plate: Jewish Lesbians and the Transformation of Tradition* (Columbia, 1998) is the book most related to my research, although it focuses specifically on women. In general, what is written on Jews and same-sex sexuality has focused, largely, on biblical interpretations of sexuality. This is somewhat odd, considering the disproportionate number of queer Jews within the field of lesbian and gay studies and queer studies. And I found nothing dealing specifically with queer Jews in Canada, let alone their religious family practices.

Aaron Cooper's "No Longer Invisible: Gay and Lesbian Jews Build a Movement" (*Journal of Homosexuality*, 1989–90 [3/4], pp. 83–94) provides a history of the lesbian and gay Jewish movement, focusing, largely, on the

United States. Cooper describes movements that developed in response to institutional and legalized homophobia. Certainly there is homophobia within Canada and within Canadian Judaism, but Canadian queers have protected rights that people in the United States have not yet gained. Both Annie Goldflam ("Queerer than Queer: Reflections of a Kike Dyke," *Journal of Homosexuality*, 1999, 36; pp. 135–142) and Hinde Ena Burstin ("Looking Out, Looking In: Anti-Semitism and Racism in Lesbian Communities," *Journal of Homosexuality*, 36, pp. 143–157) provide personal narratives on being Jewish and lesbian in Australia. Goldflam notes the importance of geographic location within the country as significant to forming a Jewish identity. Burstein discusses the anti-Semitism within the queer community as creating an outsider status of queer Jews within an already marginalized group.

THE CANADIAN CONTEXT

Canada, in fact the English colony of Lower Canada, became the first area of British Dominion to grant legal rights to the Jews on June 5, 1832, in *An Act to Declare Persons Professing the Jewish Religion Entitled to All the Rights and Privileges of the Other Subjects of His Majesty in This Province* [of Canada]. Certainly, discrimination continued to occur, with the refusal of the Canadian government to accept Jewish refugees from Nazi Europe as one of the most overt acts of Jewish discrimination. However, Jews, as a cultural and religious group, were protected and well integrated into the Canadian "multicultural" (if largely, Christian-centered) society. Ironically, the original Act invoking Jewish citizenship gave Jews the equal rights of "other subjects," whereas it has only recently given those rights to "other" subjects, like gays and lesbians.

In Canada, homosexuality was legalized on December 21, 1967 (one and one-half years before the Stonewall Riots ignited the "gay lib" movement in the United States), by then minister of justice, Pierre Elliott Trudeau. His famous comment (the following day), "There is no place for the state in the bedrooms of the nation," propelled a liberation of sexual freedom—at least in theory. While Canadians could not be arrested for same-sex activities, new focus was put on the definitions of public and private. The *Charter of Human Rights and Freedoms*, enacted in 1982, made any discrimination based on sex illegal, and the courts usually interpreted this to include sexual orientation. Finally, in 1996, the *Canadian Human Rights Act* included sexual orientation as a category protected from discrimination—20 years after the Canadian

Human Rights Commission first proposed it. The government passed Bill C-23, on June 29, 2000,which provides equal benefits (and obligations) to same-sex couples as to mixed-sex couples; and, on January 14, 2001, the first two (one gay, one lesbian) couples were married in Canada.

DEFINING TERMS

With this political and cultural context, I turn now toward understandings of family. For the respondents to my interviews, the most important factor in altering their conception of family was the general discrimination against same-sex relationships. Legally, they could not consider their partners as part of their family (during the time that the interviews took place) but, personally, they acknowledged their partners as such. In some cases, the partner was defined as the basic component of the family, and membership in the extended family was defined through its acceptance of the partner. This notion was prevalent in how the interviewees celebrated Jewish holidays, as will be discussed below.

   In addition to their partners, the interviewees' families included chosen members. The participants criticized the oppressive nature of the nuclear "traditional" family as "heteronormative" and patriarchal, but they did not critique the concept of the family or their ascribed place as a family member. What they did was to modify and expand the parameters of the definition. Friends were often included as family members. This did not mean that family was not important, but that it was so important that it could not be restricted to only those affiliated by blood or marriage.

HOMOPHOBIA AND FAMILY

The importance of family was compounded by the homophobia of some in the biological family. Some respondents were disowned. Some were tortured through psychiatric "treatments," including aversion therapy, at the parents' request. Verbal and emotional homophobia caused some participants to separate geographically (and with Canada's size, this has great meaning) and emotionally from their blood families, and to transfer their familial needs onto friends: "My brother came out as gay in unfortunate circumstances. Because I witnessed the horrible reactions from the [Jewish] community to him and my family, I knew I couldn't come out in the Jewish community . . . I knew to live as gay, I had to move away from my family and that city."

For some, the connection of religion and family were so intertwined that they questioned whether they could still live as a Jew: "I was told, by some members of my family, that I can't be [both] Jewish and lesbian."

Sibling relations, or extended family members of similar ages, were the sources of anger for some interviewees. Even when overt homophobia was not apparent in the family, or the extended family, the differences between the treatments of heterosexual members and gay members revealed discrimination in practices: "My sister's getting married. She's getting all the attention of the family. All sorts of showers; people flying in from all over. I don't get any of it, because I'm not allowed to get married. I won't get ten blenders. My family doesn't wish my partner and I 'happy anniversary' because our relationship isn't 'real.'"

Honesty about one's sexual identity and the risk of being rejected in the process highlighted the importance of the family in constructing identity and forming social relationships. More than half my respondents were out to their family, while a few more mentioned that they were out to some family members. Those who were not out to their families tended to have negative feelings about their lives and their situation as gays/lesbians.

Not only did many of the participants connect their Jewish identity to their families, but they also believed that a profound connection to family was a main difference between Judaism and other religions. Family was the essential element in defining their religious heritage: either one was born from Jewish or non-Jewish parents. Thirty-four participants had Jewish parents, which gave them Judaism that "remains with you," even for those who experimented with other religions. Unlike their sexual identity, which most thought stemmed from biology, religion was perceived as inherited through family.[8]

In my exploration to see if some Jews were more homophobic than others, I was surprised to find no correlation between a family's chosen Jewish denomination and familial homophobia.[9] Some Orthodox Jewish families were more supportive of their queer children than were some Reconstructionist Jewish families: "I grew up in an ultra-Orthodox home. . . . When I came out, I wasn't shunned. The people I cared about cared about me. They made it clear that they didn't agree with [my sexual choices], but they still cared for me as a person." And one respondent said, "A rabbi said homosexuality gave him a bad feeling inside; it made him sick—and that's a Reconstructionist rabbi!"

Age was also not a factor in determining one's personal homophobia. Some elderly relatives were queer-positive, such as a grandmother who helped her granddaughter to find "a nice Jewish girl," while some children of lesbian/gay parents directed homophobic comments at their queer parents, illustrated by the comment, "Why can't you be normal?"

CANADIAN QUEERS CONNECT TO THEIR JUDAISM

Most of the participants viewed their Judaism as spiritual, particularly through the lens of *tikkun olam*. The phrase translates as "to repair the world" and, while its meaning has changed, for the respondents of my study, it implied an interdependence with, and a responsibility for, others: "I really do not know what a Jew is, since I was born this way . . . I guess a good person, someone who works hard, a moral person, a giving, selfless, spiritual, logical person."

As Jews and often as queers, these participants believed they had a role to perform in creating a better world, as "cocreators" with God. For these respondents, "fixing" did not mean proselytizing the world to a Jewish ideology, but to live ethically, as an example to others, and to be proactive in correcting injustice. All the respondents who mentioned this spirituality connected it with homophobia, among other forms of injustice. To repair the world, they wanted to start with themselves, their family's attitude, and then their community's attitude.

"You can be a Buddhist by yourself, but a Jew? No." As this quote notes, Judaism was perceived as something more than a system of introspection. It was also a community identity, not one that is independent of a unit larger than oneself. All the participants noted introspection as essential to their understanding of their identity as queers and Jews. Yet even when turning inward through spirituality, the participants felt the need to share their experiences with others to encourage their growth.

For the majority of the respondents, being Jewish meant connecting with a family (and for converted Jews, choosing to modify their family) and bridging the traditions of the family to their community. Few of the interviewees related Jewish identity to Jewish law, and explained this as due to the institutional homophobia noted within the Jewish communities, particularly in synagogues:

> The looks, whispers, nonacceptance in the synagogue
> from everyone.

> Religion can be used to promote homophobia. There
> is a very prominent rabbi in our city who writes

homophobic books and newspaper articles. He is taken
as the voice of the [Jewish] community.

> During my divorce, the Jewish community started
> discussing my right to have custody of my child, and
> there were accusations of paedophilia. The rabbi said
> that homosexuality was a sickness. . . . My family and I
> left that shul.

Almost half the interviewees stated that the heteronormativity and homophobia of the synagogues deterred them from attending, while those who
went to pray felt like "exiles" who did not belong: "If rabbis won't accept me
as gay, then I won't go. They don't want gays in their congregation [even
though there's only one aspect of my life that's different from (heterosexual)
Jews]."

Interviewees, for the most part, were damaged by the homophobia
expressed in the synagogues in which they grew up or tried to join, or by con-
ceding to their families' requests to be closeted in the Jewish community, in
order to protect the family from embarrassment. This estrangement from the
organized Jewish community affected how religious holidays could be celebrated, and how the Jewish identity of these queers could be maintained.

The homophobia in many synagogues discouraged queer Jews from taking
part in the communal element of prayer, resulting in several strategies: affiliating with queer-positive congregations, hiding their sexuality within the
conventional Jewish community, containing their religion within family settings, or focusing on noninstitutional forms of Judaism, such as spirituality.

That said, despite some respondents' willingness to closet themselves to be
part of organized Judaism, the family remained the central site of Jewish
tradition and culture.[10] For many, Judaism has shifted from a public religion
of the synagogue to a private one of the home and of individual spirituality,
and as part of this shift, Jewish families have cooperated with their queer
family members.

YONTIF

> "Judaism is based on the family—it's as important as the
> the laws—so I feel less need to go to synagogue."

Celebrating Jewish holidays or family events in a Jewish manner was the primary means of maintaining a Jewish identity, particularly for those, the

majority, who were not observant of Jewish laws. Not surprisingly, the majority of the participants mentioned the observance of major holidays (Rosh Hashanah, Yom Kippur, Chanukah, and Passover) when talking about maintaining their Jewish identity. They occasionally mentioned large family gatherings (weddings and Bat/Bar Mitzvahs[11]), which occur infrequently among families with small numbers of children, as is typical of non-Orthodox Jews in Canada. However, the frequency in which these events were listed denotes that they are key events in Jewish family culture.

For holiday observance, attending synagogue with family was rarely mentioned, but virtually all the respondents who had Jewish parents talked about religious events in the home, and the most important among those, festivals involving food: Shabbos, Rosh Hashanah dinners, Passover Seders, breaking the Yom Kippur fast, Chanukah parties, weddings, and Bat/Bar Mitzvah receptions. This can be explained by the communal aspect of sharing food. Food is sensual, which connects the body to pleasure, as well as, for many of the respondents, the occasions in which to eat traditional Jewish foods. In its symbolism, ingesting food that is in a particular environment and of a particular form is connected to a religion, a form of communion.

The Sabbath meal, whether held with a larger family, or with one's partner, had a spiritual component that transcended the act of eating, and was often noted as connecting the people to a larger Jewish community and history, as well as to the commitment to one's partner: "[My partner] takes part in our Sabbath dinners, including saying the prayers." Another respondent explicitly included a non-Jewish partner in Shabbat celebrations. And a third said, "I believe it is a mitzvah to make love with my partner on Shabbos. Afterward, we pray together, thanking God for making us sexual beings and capable of love."

Yom Kippur was most often brought up in the context of breaking the fast. The familial aspect of the holiday was stressed, as the contents of the Yom Kippur service made the holiday difficult for some interviewees to attend. "At Yom Kippur, they recite Leviticus [on forbidden relationships]. I cannot attend [synagogue] without thinking about the prohibitions declared on my life."

NEGOTIATING FAMILY

During all Jewish-oriented events, the relationship between the queer Jew's biological family and her/his partner was often central in determining the quality of the experience. For these respondents, Jewish identity was usually maintained through family events, but given the choice between being with the partner and the biological family, the partner was almost consistently chosen. Queer Jews, when asked not to bring their partner, did not attend events, and the family relationships were strained until the families accepted and invited the partner to all future events: "My parents don't want me to bring my partner, so I don't go either." Occasionally, partners were asked, under restrictions: "I'm asked to bring a date, when invited, but we're not expected to dance together." Interestingly, those who defied the request not to express intimacy or dance together at religious or family events usually received positive responses from others attending.

In discussing the inclusion of one's partner at family events, the overwhelming majority responded that their partners were treated as a member of the family. This seemingly surprising result does not represent an immediate acceptance of same-sex partners. Everyone described acceptance and incorporation as a gradual process. The longer the relationship between partners, the more likely that the partner would be treated as a member of the family.

Because fostering acceptance was a long process, participants often would not ask their new partners to attend family functions, and would only raise the issue of one's partner to families once the relationship became "serious."

Expressing intimacy in front of family members was often a key litmus test for a partner's integration into the family. Most queer Jews in this study felt comfortable holding hands, hugging, kissing, and dancing. "We do what heterosexuals can do in public." Verbal intimacy was mentioned, such as how they talked to each other, discussing incidents that implied a shared intimate history, and using "we." "You know when you've been with somebody so long you know how they'll answer, and you start finishing their sentences."

When respondents and their partners were visiting from out of town, families offered them rooms with one bed, acknowledging the sexual component of the relationship (although the respondents were quick to note that they did not have sex during those visits).

"My family buys presents for my partner, as they do for me." Gift giving was another way in which partners were included in family events. Some participants mentioned that their partners were included in family photos and portraits. As with attendance at wedding or Bat/Bar Mitzvah celebrations, photographs acknowledge the same-sex element as part of the family component to a larger audience than a quiet immediate family dinner can. Overall, given the importance of family to maintaining Jewish identity, the integration of a partner into family celebrations was a source of great pride: "My partner is expected to attend all events with me."

ISRAEL

"Israel" translates as "he who struggles with God." Abraham, the first Jew, negotiated with God, at Sodom, over how many people should be saved; Jacob wrestled with an angel: these are but two of the many stories in the Torah of the questioning and debate between Jews and God. The Holocaust is a pivotal event of how modern Jews have had to question their understanding of Judaism, and what being the "chosen people" entails.[12] In this sense, Israel can be interpreted as not just a passive belief, but also a methodological engagement with God.

Queer Jews in Canada see their role as questioning the concept of "normal." Queers and Jews are marginalized in multiple ways in our society, and struggle is an everyday practice. As all the respondents noted, their outsider position in mainstream (Christian heterosexual) society forced them to reflect on identity more than for those whose social centrality allows them to simply accept their privileges. For queer Jews, finding their place includes a space not only within the straight Christian world, but also within a straight Jewish community.

Several respondents noted that there are queer-positive rabbis, congregations, and affiliations. But changes in attitude toward queer members did not occur spontaneously from within any Jewish community. As a respondent noted:

> Gay Jews are not welcome in congregations. Where we have been
> included, we've had to struggle with the Jewish community to create
> that space for ourselves.

Some respondents challenged homophobic comments by rabbis and congregation members and, when change was not tolerated, respondents left synagogues, often with their family members.

Canada is one of the few countries where the number of Jews is growing—although that growth may be related to immigration from areas of the world where the number of Jews is disappearing. This influx of Jews from different cultures, as well as the increase of young Jews from the mini baby-boomer generation, suggests that queer inclusion in Judaism may be part of a more general shift in Judaism due to changing demographics. There is a new generation of Jews who, due to already existing laws, are prepared to speak up for their rights, rather than remain grateful for what little they are given. As several of the participants in my study have had to fight for their rights as lesbians and gays, and for women's equality, in society at large, it is not surprising that most were prepared to speak out for their rights within Jewish communities. As a response to queer Jews, and changing trends in legal and social policies, many Jewish congregations have had to reexamine their biblical interpretations of same-sex sexuality.

Part of that reassessment has been through the development of queer Jewish groups, which supply Jewish cultural and/or religious practices for their members, and which serve as a bridge between the queer and Jewish communities. All five of the cities in Canada, where my interviews took place, had at least one queer Jewish group: "I went to a Seder arranged by [a queer Jewish group]. It was moving to celebrate with people who were like me."

Queer Jewish women have had a particularly important role in this movement, and some respondents suggested that this might be the case, because Judaism has ostracized women through its traditional rituals and practices and even by its architecture: "As a woman and as a lesbian, I feel separated—literally—with the *mechitza*."

The role of women in the private sphere, including the role of mother, and exclusion from much Jewish education, has limited the opportunities for women who do not reproduce or who are in same-sex relationships. At the same time, one respondent suggested that traditional Jewish men's ignorance about women has provided the opportunity for some women to modify or subvert the patriarchal dominion of Judaism: "Jewish men are in the public but, because women are left alone, they can create their own rituals."

Thanks to feminism, this reworking of Judaism has grown in the Jewish queer community, both in terms of family and religious events, making a struggle for place part of the struggle with God and one's *tikkun olam*:

> We had a Jewish wedding. Family, friends, relatives, food, presents: the whole thing! . . . It wasn't legal, but it showed our friends and family how committed we are to each other, and that we expected the same treatment as our straight relatives get.

> I invite my chosen and blood family to my Seders. I write a Haggada that contains the communal rituals, and use poems that convey the spirit of the holiday, not an exclusionary story of the Jews as a chosen

people. Passover is about being marginalized in society and looking for a safe home. That's something we all share.

CONCLUSIONS

There were many variations in how the respondents of my study saw their identities as Jewish and queer, but they all saw both identities as important, if not the most important, elements in how they understood themselves and lived their lives. There was a range of Jewish practices, but Judaism was always somehow connected with family events, often around food. Like pride events, the Jewish family celebrations were about a heritage of struggle and celebration of perseverance. Like sex, events involving food acknowledge pleasure and sensuality, and link sharing with mitzvah.

For these queer Jews, the importance of families was less to be resisted than to be modified for more inclusion. While queer Jews examine how oppression is structured in the family and in religion, the interpretive and flexible nature of the religion provides a framework to reform from within. Judaism is also on the margins of Western society, although the myth of a "Judeo-Christian" tradition has been discursively used to justify oppression. In fact, this myth provides an historic example of how a group (Jews) can integrate with, yet remain different from, the mainstream, and use that position to question the mainstream. (According to the respondents, non-Jewish queers do not appear to question the Christian normativity of society. This calls into question "who qualifies as queer.") Future research on understanding queer Jewish identity should include not only how to queer the Jewish family, but how the Jewish family was *always* queer.[13] Queer Jews can introduce elements of traditional Judaism, such as the proactive ethical practices of *tikkun olam*, as a "traditional" way to queer non-Jewish society, or as an example of how a lesser-observed element of one's religion can be highlighted to shift religious practices.

Attachment to the Jewish family was, in part, due to the homophobia within the greater Jewish community. Where else could one share Jewish celebrations if not with the family, biological or chosen? However, it should be noted that respondents were not always being silenced by the heteronormativity of the Jewish communities. Some respondents were vocal in their criticism toward homophobic rabbis, were challenging homophobic statements in synagogues, were representing themselves as queer in Jewish parades, and, most importantly, were forming Jewish queer organizations and holding queer Jewish services. They were making spaces for themselves within the Jewish community. It is the heteronormative Jewish community that has had to respond to queer inclusion. The mainstream Jewish community has to remember that the Canadian legislation that protects Jews is the same one that now protects queers.

I found that the idea of religion as a process of debate validates Jews' examination of the problematic of identity. Such questions are not heretical. At the same time, the idea that a religious person is one who creates a socially just world gives Judaism a flexibility to change and include new social identities. Most importantly, these participants revealed that being Jewish was inherently tied to the family unit and to family celebrations. While family rituals could be spaces for family tensions, these very tensions emphasized the connections for the participants. If the connections could strain, they could also stretch, rather than break. In a world where being queer often means leaving or substituting one's religion and/or one's family, the Canadian queer Jews in this study provide alternatives. They reveal how Canada's queer Jews may be at the forefront of remaking family, not only for themselves, but also for everyone.

NOTES

1. I would like to thank Dick Butcher, Robert Monro, Gottfried Paasche, Randy Schnoor, Stuart Schoenfeld, and the editors of this book for their excellent suggestions.
2. As with all quotes used, this one is representative of the general attitude of the entire sample, unless otherwise stated. I have not identified the subjects in this paper, as the small sample size within each city I studied (eight) would threaten the anonymity of some participants.
3. My participants responded to advertisements about this study inserted in gay and Jewish newspapers and magazines, and through email announcements to lesbian, gay, and Jewish internet clubs. Each was given a standardized set of questions, from which their responses were noted. Due to last-minute cancellations, four people were found through a snowball sample (friends of participants). As intended in the quota, participants were to be divided into an equal number by sex and location. Diversity by age and religious background was attempted, but I did not succeed in getting an equal number of Sephardic and Ashkenazi Jews. I have rationalized this discrepancy as representative of the unequal proportion of these two groups in the Canadian Jewish population. I also found some Jews of mixed Sephardic and Ashkenazi families. In addition, my sample includes Jews, raised in Christian families, who converted to Judaism. As Canada does not have any laws dealing with bisexuals, only those who identified as "lesbian" or "gay" were included in this study, even if they did have mixed-

sex sexual relations presently or in the past. I was not willing to impose my definitions onto people. Likewise, the study included those who identified as Jewish, even if some religious Jews would not consider them Jewish (for instance, those practicing Judaism, but who had a non-Jewish mother, and those who were still in the process of converting).

4. Among the 40 participants, none were legally married, although several had commitment ceremonies. Five participants had previously been married to members of the opposite sex. Seven had children; two had grandchildren. Seventeen were currently in same-sex couples, seven of whom were partnered with other Jews; six with non-Jews, and four who did not specify. There was a 40-year age range (from twenties to sixties) with an equal distribution of ages among females and males. The majority of participants were in their mid thirties to mid forties. The majority of converted Jews came from the western areas of the study, areas noted for smaller Jewish communities and, in Vancouver, more separation between the lesbian and gay communities.

5. See Kenneth Plummer, *Telling Sexual Stories: Power, Change, and Social Worlds* (New York: Routledge, 1995).

6. Michel Foucault, *The History of Sexuality: An Introduction* (New York: Vintage, 1978).

7. I use gay and lesbian as problematically related to queer. Many of the books on queers use the word interchangeably with lesbian/gay, even when they say that queer is distinct from gay and lesbian, as a social group from a particular era, as ideologically unrelated, and as a group that is more inclusive of other identities. Based on the responses from my participants, the majority used the words interchangeably. Some hated the word "queer," yet others hated the words "gay" or "lesbian."

8. Five respondents chose Judaism and converted. Some claimed that they did not "feel right" in their previous religion, which implied an inherent drive to connect with their "true" religion, and none discussed the possibility of reconverting. Since these conversions took place through Orthodox Jewish affiliations—although some Orthodox rabbis will not convert someone openly lesbian or gay—these five respondents were very knowledgeable about the laws and rituals of Judaism. These new Jews were among the respondents who defined Judaism as based on religious law rather than family inheritance.

9. Michael C. LaScala studied 20 gay couples in New York. He discusses the stress in-laws put on gay relationships and the inclusion/exclusion of partners in family events and holidays. LaScala also reviews earlier studies, which show that the age of the parent, the age of the child, the number of siblings, and the socioeconomic status all affect parents' responses to their children's same-sex partners. These are important issues not discussed in my work, and will be included in future research. See Michael LaScala, "Gay Male Couples: The Importance of Coming Out and Being Out to Parents," *Journal of Homosexuality*: 39, pp. 47–69.

10. For more on "domestic religion," see Barbara Myerhoff, *Number Our Days* (New York: Simon and Schuster, 1980).

11. It was surprising that funerals were not mentioned, considering how many people thought that coming out to their parents or grandparents would kill them. My expla-

nation is that people focused on the grief they felt, rather than the others gathered. This may be naïve.

12. Some respondents, particularly those whose parents come from post-Holocaust Europe, as well as those who converted to Judaism, discussed how the Holocaust related to their religious beliefs and practices, and their understanding of who God is and what God does.

13. Daniel Boyarin's book on gender and Judaism, *Unheroic Conduct* (Berkeley: University of California, 1997), strongly alludes to a queer (non-normative for mainstream Europe) illustration of Jewish families.

REMEMBERING THE STRANGER

IDENTITY, COMMUNITY,

AND SAME-SEX MARRIAGE

Joanne Cohen

WHO ARE WE and where are we headed as twenty-first century queer Jews? I am anything but certain. In this fragmentary political memoir, I wish to explore this uncertainty and demonstrate the importance of working with our memories of alienation and remembering our experiences of estrangement. I hope this work might somehow reflect and inform diverse efforts to integrate queer and Jewish identities, to work creatively with personal and political history, and to build enduring, warm, vibrant, and viable communities and relationships. In particular, I'd like to raise some disquieting questions and practical/political concerns posed by endorsing same-sex unions (as affirmed by the CCAR, the Central Conference of American Rabbis) as a contemporary model for queer Jewish community development and identity integration. I argue against exclusively assimilationist or isolationist strategies in advocating diverse queer participation and ongoing struggle in mainstream Jewish life.

I hope this essay will stimulate intelligent discussion, shatter complacency in some quarters, and pointedly question the informal positive consensus that has developed around same-sex union ceremonies and the marriage model. First, I'll outline some of my premises, with a view to reducing some anticipated reactionary invective at the outset.

For queer Jews, as for any historically marginalized minority, I regard thoughtfully taking up and investigating multiply stigmatized identities, affiliating with communities, and choosing to interpose oneself in history to be courageous acts entailing ongoing struggles with fear, oppression, resistance, self-hatred, doubt, and conflict. I imagine the community of queer Jews to be international; largely secularized and unaffiliated; sexually, religiously, and politically diverse; and pursuing wide-ranging strategies to create viable queer Jewish identities and communities. I don't assume that any solution will work for all of us at all times, that any solution is necessarily valid by being chosen, nor that our own struggles will necessarily make it any easier for future generations.

I also assume that thinking that is alive and contemporary can allow for provisionality, uncertainty, and change. Thinking with a sense of historic responsibility requires an unflinching willingness to consider the negative underside and discomfiting implications of apparently positive developments to avoid naïve surprises. And, incorporating an appreciation of irony, indeterminacy, and paradox is helpful to a postmodern view of history. So, to write a memoir is to write a kind of fiction. Writing rhetorically and in diverse voices is regrettably to risk being (mis)read literally. Raising unpopular ideas, colorfully characterizing diverse extremes of political style, and asking disquieting questions of our community is to risk being accused of advocating these extremes or working against rather than worrying with one's community.

Please know that I am as taken aback and disappointed as anyone by the loss of certain idealized hopes implied by my argument, but that there lurks beneath a negative space of hope. I believe our ongoing struggles to understand and create our identities and communities, even in opposition, may be more valuable than realizing our most fervent utopian, static dreams of unconflicted families and communities and permanently positively integrated identities. Mine is not a vision for everyone, but it is a kind of loving hope, if you can see it.

Like many queer Jews, I have struggled, not altogether unsuccessfully, with issues of queer and Jewish identity and community, ethics, power, equality, and resistance in virtually every aspect of my life for as long as I can remember. From the time I was a precocious Hebrew dayschool tomboy wearing blue jeans under my school uniform skirt and successfully arguing with my rabbi teachers, I have yearned for equal and equitable participation in Jewish and secular life.

In our perpetual seats in our small town Orthodox synagogue, I would regularly amaze my mother at my ability to find our place, to the word, in the Hebrew prayers the moment we walked in, without a page number being announced. I wish I could find my place as easily now in my own queer Jewish identity, relationships, and community, but I can't, and not for lack of trying.

I am viewed publicly as an accomplished adult, who helped build an internet community of diverse queer Jewish women, has appeared on television, spoken publicly, and published articles on queer Jewish identity. I am active, respected, and openly queer in a large mainstream Conservative synagogue, close to my family, and have demonstrated cultural literacy and competence in diverse social, academic, and professional settings. Despite this, I am personally, practically, philosophically, and politically about as far as one could get from being a role model or poster-child for completely proud, positive, enduringly integrated queer Jewish identity. (I don't set this standard for myself, but recognize the implicit hopes raised by my inclusion in this anthology and by frequent requests to assume leadership roles.)

I have begun to accept that whatever our compensatory accomplishments as individuals, no single person's skills and experience could possibly achieve a permanent and positive integration of queer Jewish identity, however fervently many of us may have tried. Even the couple or family unit is an insufficient base for identity formation, without a framework of culture, history, and community. None of us can possibly do this alone, nor should we try to do so in isolation, either as individuals, or as queer Jews in insular communities.

To affirm proud queer and Jewish marginal identities in an historical and cultural context of genocide, anti-semitism, homophobia, and anti-religious secularism requires that we repeatedly deal with internal and external moments of conflict, oppression, doubt, resistance, and self-loathing. My personal and academic experiences would suggest that our struggles with alienation, identity integration, and community formation are likely to be inherently ongoing. Every historic triumph and personal success should be viewed provisionally, requiring extensive rethinking as new developments and understandings emerge. The imperfect personal and communal means available may sometimes be insufficient for us to form enduringly integrated queer Jewish identities, relationships, and communities. Perhaps provisional, imperfect, and somewhat compartmentalized moments of integrated identity may be more reasonable goals.

As well, we need to consider unintended consequences and blind spots in our efforts to develop our identities and communities to prevent worsening the problems of alienation we hope to resolve by forming relationships and joining communities in the first place. A longer and wider view is needed to bring perspective to every personal and community success we achieve, to prevent developing dangerously complacent, impractical, or unintentionally damaging approaches to community development that could lead some queer Jews to retreat completely from community life.

We must pay attention to the fragmentation and alienation many queer Jews experience to counter the apparently limited consideration many community leaders often seem to give to the painful estrangements and conflicts many of us face in our everyday lives. We are often simplistically exhorted to participate in communal life without adequate appreciation of the justifiable pain and ambivalence we may sometimes feel, which could prevent our taking on communal roles for a time.

Once we join queer or Jewish communities to develop our identities, we may experience unanticipated and powerful conflicts inside and outside ourselves. We may experience moments of integration and later disappointment when we realize that, despite our fervent hopes, no solution is likely to be permanent or perfect. Our work to overcome alienation and integrate our queer Jewish identities will likely never be complete. We may need to compromise on some of our most ideal hopes, to prevent naïve setbacks we can ill afford, and recognize that no solution and no community is likely to serve all our needs all the time.

I have sometimes feared that my inability to find a cozy, unrelentingly positive niche as a queer Jew in relationships and community represents a developmental failing on my part, despite all my arguments. Am I being too critical? I have a disquieting awareness that some of us have already successfully struggled to reach adult milestones of integrated queer Jewish identities, positive community affiliations, and successful permanent partnerships (albeit many in ways I would not choose, and in ways that may appear more solid from outside than from within). Nevertheless, my own unfulfilled yearnings for these largely unmet goals are still sometimes troubling to me.

Like many single people, I have often felt alienated in queer and Jewish communal settings that overwhelmingly and simplistically celebrate monogamy and the family, both queer and conventional. I have experienced the pleasures of home, family, shared culture, and holiday celebrations with Jewish lovers, only to experience the losses of those relationships so profoundly that it became too painful to participate in queer or Jewish communal life for a time. I have looked around at my surrounding queer and Jewish communities and wondered whether I could really identify with these people who seem both reassuringly familiar and disconcertingly different, and who sometimes demonstrate the negatively stereotyped behaviors I have sometimes feared and disliked in myself. I have found the complacent sanctimony of some Jewish religious communities and the apparently dissolute nihilism of some queer settings less than fulfilling. At times I have been perplexed by my own sexuality and gender expression—as both sacrament and sacrilege it is sometimes haunting and disturbing at its most raw and vulnerable. As a postmodern intellectual and queer feminist, I have sometimes felt completely absurd as I tried to fit my experience into various Jewish, feminist, or queer cultural models and rituals. And, as a 30-something single person facing a widely acknowledged postmodern decline of public life, I am still seeking admirable models of successful queer Jewish aging.

I believe we need to explore, document, and share our moments of disillusionment, doubt, conflict, confusion, loneliness, and alienation as much as our celebratory moments if we're going to be honest about our needs, experiences, and our real challenges as queer Jews. And yes, the reality of our break ups needs to be considered whenever we think about forming healthy queer Jewish communities and identities.

In writing this piece, I learned that my own reluctance, anguish, and struggles to confront, understand, and share my imperfect experiences are symptomatic of the problems many of us face. We try to reconcile histories of persecution, stigmatized and stereotyped identities as queers and Jews, self-hatred and pride, pain, conflict, ambivalence, and personal experiences of pain, loss, and trauma.

These *personal* struggles as a single queer Jew helped me remember old lessons from political theory and my early Jewish education, paradoxically demonstrating how much our *community* development may depend on each of us remembering and sharing our painful experiences of estrangement and alienation. The Jewish tradition teaches us to befriend and remember the stranger, because we were strangers in the land of Egypt (Exodus 23:9, Deuteronomy 10:19). This fundamental awareness of the pain of alienation, estrangement, and exile underlies many valuable Jewish and secular ethical teachings on identity and community obligation, inspiring diverse charitable works, acts of decency, and struggles against oppression. Our ability to befriend and empathize with others, especially those who are socially distant from us, may be the very foundation for ethical community development.

In short, Blanche Dubois was right. From the time we were Israelite strangers in Egypt, and throughout our frequently precarious historical experiences as queers and as Jews, our very survival has often depended on the "kindness of strangers." Because we know what it means to be different, displaced, vilified, struggling, violated, and oppressed, we are expected to learn empathy, and not to impose needless suffering on others. Even when we rejoice at our personal and communal successes, we are taught to remember those who are different, alone, and struggling, and to demonstrate friendship, hospitality, decency, and solidarity. The Exodus from Egypt marks not only the historical beginning of ethical Jewish identity and nationhood, but is also a liberatory lesson recalled daily in Jewish religious practice.

Many of us have been estranged and vilified as queers within our own families and Jewish communities, and have faced anti-semitism in secular contexts. By remembering estrangement in our personal and community experiences, both Jewish and secular, we might learn to be kinder, to ourselves and each other, and to build more livable communities, within and beyond our immediate personal relationship networks.

If we remind the mainstream Jewish community of this key teaching, we might assert a powerful religious and ethical claim for better treatment of queers and all of us who are oppressed in our communities. Far too many contemporary Jewish communities often overemphasize material prosperity and private family relationships, at the expense of recalling our origins as an ethical community. As well, as Jews in secular queer communities, we might proudly reclaim our Jewish origins and inform our secular activism by remembering alienation.

When the Central Conference of American Rabbis (CCAR) of the U.S. Reform movement announced its willingness to perform and recognize Jewish same-sex union ceremonies, many of my friends rejoiced. They believed this to be a clear signal that at long last, queer Jews were beginning to be more fully accepted in Jewish life. Although this is an important symbolic historical milestone, I tend to regard this development far more cautiously.

The challenges of integrating our queer and Jewish identities are so great, and our historic pain of exclusion is so deep, it would not be surprising for us to leap at each new theory or cultural development, hoping for it to resolve our long-standing fragmentation. While it would be a welcome respite from our usual anxieties, failing to consider the implications of the CCAR decision could lead us to dangerously alienating disappointments that we can ill afford. We need to be realistic and inclusive of our diversity as queer Jews.

There are a number of theological and practical limitations posed by CCAR's decision to allow same-sex unions, however much it presents a valuable statement of acceptance and affirmation of Jewish same-sex relationships. First, from a traditional Jewish perspective, which includes many queer Jews and their families and communities, the CCAR decision is not based in religious law (*halacha*), and would not be regarded as theologically valid religious practice, however well intentioned.

Second, the CCAR decision has been affirmed even in the absence of correlative civil recognition of these ceremonies. Currently, most civil authorities legally recognize traditional religious marriage ceremonies across denominations. Such would not be the case with a same-sex ceremony, where civil recognition of same-sex marriage does not yet exist in most jurisdictions. Thus, the CCAR ceremony would lack secular legal validity.

Third, even if one were to assume that these unions were valid in religious and civil law, given the realities of serial monogamy and relationship break ups in both heterosexual and same-sex Jewish relationships, would it not have been prudent to develop a Jewish same-sex divorce ceremony at the same time? Note that the traditional Jewish wedding includes the reading of the *ketubah*, or marriage contract, which includes a statement of the parties' respective responsibilities, should the relationship dissolve. Could the absence of a same-sex Jewish divorce ceremony create a queer religious status similar to that of *agunot*, Jewish women who have obtained civil, but not religious, divorces from their husbands? Most contracts include conditions for their dissolution. The CCAR ceremony may require further development to avoid imposing unintentional religious legal disabilities on queer Jewish couples.

Fourth, however creative and well intentioned CCAR's development of a same-sex union ceremony, it would be helpful to learn how CCAR explains this innovation in relation to the historic prohibitions of Jewish same-sex marriages and lesbianism implied by Leviticus 18:3. Traditional Jewish authorities interpreted this biblical passage, which forbids following the practices of the land of Egypt, to prohibit not only lesbian sexuality, but also same-sex marriages.[1] How has CCAR acknowledged its departure from these traditional religious and cultural prohibitions?

Fifth, considering the theological innovation involved in celebrating same-sex relationships, it would be helpful for CCAR to respond more fully to traditional biblical prohibitions of male homosexual behavior (Leviticus 18:22, 20:13), as well as prohibitions of taking on appurtenances of the opposite sex (Deuteronomy 22:5). To have greater influence across Jewish denominations, and to avoid worsening doctrinal schisms (including within the Reform movement), it would be helpful for CCAR to provide some coherent theological definition of its same-sex union ceremony in relation to traditional Jewish practice.

What are the religious and legal assumptions of dependence and economic support underlying the CCAR decision? My suspicion is that CCAR's development of the same-sex union ceremony was well intentioned as a courageous symbolic statement and affirmative service to Jewish same-sex couples seeking religious and cultural recognition of their relationships, but that many of the practical and religious implications require further consideration.

As well, there are pressing practical issues to consider when we imagine diverse queer Jews seeking to affirm their relationships through a CCAR ceremony. Whether we are secular, of other liberal denominations, or traditional Jews, laypeople and rabbis alike cannot easily change their enduring theological commitments to accommodate contemporary political developments. Many queer Jews would be unable to affiliate with the Reform movement, even temporarily, to gain access to a same-sex union ceremony. Those of us who are single or in nonmonogamous or interfaith partnerships would not be included in a CCAR ceremony. Given the anticipated controversy, it would not be surprising for some Reform rabbis to be reluctant to officiate at the unions of couples who are not temple members or who are unable to affirm a commitment to Reform theology and practice. Thus, many queer Jews would not be easily served by this innovation.

As has already occurred in the mainstream Reform community's backlash against the CCAR decision, some Reform and feminist rabbis have already refused to officiate at same-sex union ceremonies for anyone, anticipating congregational and community resistance. Note that the CCAR decision is not a binding directive on Reform rabbis, but is a theological statement affirming the legitimacy of these ceremonies. Regardless of its theological status, the real practical decisions on allowing same-sex unions would likely be made locally by senior rabbis, synagogue boards, and ritual committees who are often socially and religiously conservative. Thus, due to career and political considerations, many well-intentioned Reform rabbis may be unable to officiate at these ceremonies, even for queer Reform couples who are members of their congregations.

Considering general Jewish and queer political interests, it might be help-ful to ensure that the pioneering couples for whom these ceremonies would be performed have likely prospects of enduring relationships. Imagine the negative repercussions if a happy couple were to break up a year or two later, after the strain brought by their unanticipated prominence and celebrity in the congregation and wider community. Thus, willing Reform rabbis might be especially selective about choosing "suitable" couples for whom they would be willing to perform same-sex unions, perhaps requiring years of personal acquaintance and "pre-marital" classes and counseling. It will likely be quite some time before any queer Jewish couple breaks a glass under a *huppa*, with a rabbi officiating, at least in Canada.

Contemporary Canadian legal developments might also make couples reconsider organizing their relationships on the marriage model. Currently, cohabiting same-sex partners are deemed legally equivalent to common-law spouses, with the requisite requirement to divide jointly held property and negotiate income-equalization payments through legal processes on the dis-solution of the relationship. Cohabiting same-sex partners are required to report their status on tax returns, census forms, and applications for social benefits. These developments could have an ironic chilling effect on our abil-ity to form and dissolve diverse same-sex relationships freely, particularly if there are economic disparities between the partners. As well, law has perverse effects, often punishing the very marginal communities it seeks to protect. Given a history of disproportionate policing and monitoring of queers and social activists, many of us are concerned about registering our partnerships with government agencies who have historically persecuted us or that have troubling histories of misusing personal information. Informal blacklisting and inappropriate disclosure are not unreasonable concerns.

Far from being an easy answer to our problems of exclusion as queer Jews, the CCAR decision presents many practical issues needing further consider-ation. Our initial jubilation rapidly leads to the realization that this innova-tion far from resolves our fragmentation as queer Jews. The CCAR decision would not include traditional Jews, those in interfaith partnerships, those in nonmonogamous relationships, and those who are uncoupled. Even same-sex Reform couples could encounter alienating difficulties in seeking to affirm their relationships. Rather than "widening the parameters of queer Jewish belonging," as some have argued, the practical implications could tragically raise and then deny expectations, ironically narrowing opportunities for inclusion.

The prospect of religious same-sex unions makes me uneasy, much as I would want to support diverse relationship options. I am troubled by attempts to legitimize our relationships in a religious framework that has historically vilified queer sexuality and gender-bending behavior, limiting sexuality to monogamous and mainly procreative heterosexual marriage and property relationships. While pioneering theologians have affirmed ethical same-sex sexuality, many queer Jews cannot help but remain conflicted by the vehement disapproval of our sexuality and gender expression in the Jewish tradition that makes up a key part of our identities. I suspect many of us engage in a kind of double-minded denial when we want to function sexually, or make uneasy compromises in our own minds, communities, and bedrooms. We need to talk more about this in safe ways that do not assume that those struggling with these issues are foolish dupes of traditional religious thinking, or that the sexual adventurers among us are inherently morally unfit.

As much as I value diversity and choice, I question what values are potentially affirmed by endorsing CCAR's religiously sanctioned model of marital monogamy as a template for queer Jewish relationships. Sanctification implies exclusion—to hallow something is to render other things profane. Might our support for religious same-sex marriage inadvertently imply that those who are ethically nonmonogamous, who date outside our faith, who pursue monogamy outside of "marriage," or who remain uncoupled are inherently less morally worthy? Would we be reasserting a kind of monogamous "missionary position" for politically and religiously legitimate queer Jewish sexuality? Considering the privatizing and alienating effects of family-centered celebrations (queer and straight) in many congregations, how might celebrating an individual couple's relationship necessarily contribute to affirming community values, and reconnecting with those who are estranged within the community? Recalling our historic exclusion as queers by virtue of our distinctly nonmissionary, nonprocreative sexuality and nontraditional gender behaviors, and reiterating the value of remembering our own and others' estrangement, I'd suggest that we think carefully before endorsing religiously sanctioned monogamy as a moral ideal for ethical queer Jewish relationships.

While some political compromise, discretion, and respect for our surrounding communities is required for our integration and ethical participation in Jewish life, I would advocate a moderate course between outright assimilationism and outright isolationism. Overemphasizing traditional marriage models and private family ceremonies may lead both queer Jews and mainstream Jewish communities to neglect the needs of those outside these models. Because every new legal recognition of queer rights and coupled status is often accompanied by regressive policing and persecution of less well-protected sexual minorities and queer sites, queer Jews cannot afford to forget our powerful queer antecedents or the strangers among us. Given the lessons of the Holocaust on the irrelevance of assimilation, many of us would find any approach to community building and identity formation that would seem to separate "good queer Jewish sexuality" from "bad queer Jewish sexuality" to be highly questionable.

In the same way that assimilated and parochial Jews alike have contributed to a vibrant Jewish culture, pride in our diverse queer community requires that all of us contribute to advancing wider awareness and acceptance, from closeted middle class professionals to "in-your-face" sexual libertines and social activists. As queer Jews, we need to celebrate our diverse sexualities and religious beliefs, even when these sexualities and beliefs are troubling, and when we may be disturbed by elements of Jewish religious culture, by the apparent nihilism of some queer settings, or by the overwhelming tendency in both settings to privilege personal relationships above the principle of community.

As diverse queer Jews, our challenges are too complex to be resolved by a single denomination, religious ceremony, or relationship model. One of the greatest hurdles preventing us from taking our places in diverse mainstream Jewish communities is a rightful fear of homophobia. Traditional Jewish social prohibitions of homosexuality and nontraditional gender expression continue to be invoked even by nonobservant Jewish families and communities, because these challenge enduring Jewish cultural values emphasizing marriage, family, children, cultural transmission, and continuity. The social sanctions we face may range from raised eyebrows to casual social ostracism to being utterly disowned by one's family and community. Aside from other factors encouraging secular assimilation, this "*naches* machine" of the mainstream Jewish community (which seeks gratification through its children's marriages, offspring, and professional attainments) has presented negative pressures leading many Jews to leave Judaism, a cultural loss the community can no longer afford.

Gradually, the mainstream Jewish community has begun to learn about the needless trauma and fragmentation caused by obstinately enforcing traditional Jewish values of heterosexuality, marital monogamy, and procreation at all costs. The attendant informal social controls are powerful, enduring, and potentially devastating. In the last five years, I have informally counselled two young queer university students who were coming out in nonobservant Jewish middle-class families. As I once was, they were being threatened with forced psychotherapy and economic dislocation by their well-meaning Jewish parents who were working with the best of anguished intentions. Thankfully, there were community resources, including a queer Jewish coming-out group, to which I could direct my young friends for support. However much institutional recognition may improve, serious risks still remain for queer youth in many mainstream communities.

Every secular and religious struggle queer people have undertaken, with the attendant media coverage, has improved awareness, as has coming out in diverse contexts. It is no longer unusual to hear of Jewish coming-out groups, Jewish Parents and Friends of Lesbians and Gays, or Jewish AIDS committees meeting at mainstream synagogues and Jewish community centers. One increasingly sees same-sex couples attending mainstream Jewish weddings, funerals, and other family functions. Even in Orthodox settings, one Jewish ex-lover and I were informally acknowledged as a couple by family, friends, and community members, even though no words to that effect were explicitly spoken.

The rise of queer Jewish congregations across North America, and their gradual acceptance, despite vehement resistance, in local and international Jewish federations has been extremely important in fostering greater awareness of our needs as queer Jews. One also cannot underestimate the importance of arts, literature, liturgy, cultural events, and local and virtual communities reflecting our life interests and providing information, social support, and networking opportunities for many gay and lesbian Jews, secular to religious.

Despite the importance of gay and lesbian congregations, I believe it's now time for those of us who can to stop working in isolation and to come out in our mainstream Jewish communities, preferably with support networks in place. For too long, the mainstream Jewish community has been able to ignore our needs through outright homophobia or by capitalizing on our retreat to insular queer Jewish communities. Despite the personal challenges, we need to return and claim our rightful places in our mainstream communities, as committed Jews and visible queers who are respectful but no longer self-annihilating through absence or assimilation. This is especially important in a time when mainstream Jewish identities and communities have never been more fragile and fragmented. Rather than justifiably criticizing homophobia from outside the mainstream, we might best achieve recognition by showing the courage to become involved and share some communal responsibilities. In joining, but not assimilating, we might powerfully demonstrate that those of us who are single, queer, or in alternative families may have as great a need for and commitment to Jewish community and cultural continuity as those in traditional families.

I took my own advice to heart, after years of involvement in a traditional alternative synagogue, and affiliated with one of North America's largest and most affluent Conservative congregations. My choice included careful consideration of my theological commitments, political and learning opportunities, my family's needs, proximity to my home, and genuine affection for the congregation. I have been moved by the warmth, respect, and encouragement I have received from most congregants, simply for being myself—a discreet, respectful, but openly queer, articulate, educated, and active contributor to ritual and study. I have support from the rabbinate and lay leadership, and have been asked to help develop anti-homophobia teaching materials. My involvement has provided an unanticipated and deep source of identity and community in an otherwise anonymous city. While being visible brings moments of self-consciousness, I believe more of us should try this, providing we do so sincerely, responsibly, and honestly, in ways consistent with our convictions. As mainstream Jewish communities learn to deal with queer Jews as diverse real people, with lives, families, and moments of mourning and celebration similar to their own, the less likely they may be to oppress us unthinkingly. Our presence makes a difference.

In advocating respectful involvement with our surrounding mainstream communities, I have deliberately recommended a provisional, grounded, moderate, and flexible strategy for queer Jewish identity integration and community development. I hope this approach might serve our community's needs responsibly and work for diverse queer Jews, respecting both a range of political and doctrinal commitments and *halacha*. This approach uses key Jewish values to provide an immanent critique of homophobia in mainstream Jewish contexts, and does not require ritual innovation or one-size-fits-all solutions. By reclaiming our places, we might effectively become the stranger they know and dare not oppress.

In a time when programmatic progressive, queer, and feminist politics are largely in decline, and in which many of us have already retreated from public life, it might be helpful to revisit the alienation and fear many of us have experienced. We might consider relearning the simple friendship, empathy, and support for diversity many of us first found in the gay and lesbian community. Remember the stranger. Let me know how it goes.

NOTES

1. See Rebecca Alpert, *Like Bread on the Seder Plate: Jewish Lesbians and the Transformation of Tradition* (New York: Columbia, 1997), who cites *Sifra Ahare Mot*, Genesis Rabbah 26:6 and Leviticus Rabbah 23:9.

PART IV

CULTURE

It is impossible to write about sex and not reveal too much of yourself. Whereas I think it is possible to have sex and reveal nothing of yourself whatsoever.

—TONY KUSHNER

Jews and homosexuals are the outstanding creative minorities in contemporary urban culture. Creative, that is, in the truest sense; they are creators of sensibilities. The two pioneering forces of modern sensibility are Jewish moral seriousness and homosexual aestheticism and irony. —SUSAN SONTAG

I assume everyone is gay unless I'm told otherwise.

—HARVEY FIERSTEIN

Sexuality is something that we ourselves create. It is our own creation, and much more than the discovery of a secret side of our desire. We have to understand that with our desires go new forms of relationships, new forms of love, new forms of creation. Sex is not a fatality; it's a possibility of creative life. It's not enough to affirm that we are gay but we must also create a gay life.

—MICHEL FOUCAULT

I don't want life to imitate art. I want life to be art.

—CARRIE FISHER

LOST JEWISH (MALE) SOULS

A MIDRASH ON *ANGELS IN AMERICA*

AND *THE PRODUCERS*

Jyl Lynn Felman

TONY KUSHNER'S 1993 Pulitzer Prize–winning play, *Angels in America*, is very gay. And Jewish. It's about assimilation, self-loathing, men with lost souls, the betrayal of the faith, and the abandonment of a moral vision. Depending on who the viewer is, there are two versions of the play, playing simultaneously. There's the deeply moving, virus-infected, goyishe-gay-who-divinely-hallucinates and the Mr. Married Mormon, coming-out-of-the-closet-to-pill-popping, straight soon-to-be-happy-ex, Mrs. Mormon, AIDS version. Then there's the culturally lost, wandering-in-secular-exile, ambiva-lent *treif*, quasi-civil-libertarian-melting-pot-mess, full-of-self-deception, painfully revealing JEWISH version, located in the extremely bizarre tri-umvirate of Roy Cohn, Ethel Rosenberg, and the imaginatively invented totally believable (character of) Louis Ironson. Ultimately one plot informs the other as the characters move in out of their tightly woven, interrelated narratives. But *Angels in America* will always be my *Jewish Fantasia on National Themes*. It resounds in my ears like the long, hard, final sound of the shofar calling the People Israel to worship in a postmodern, Hillary Clinton–

reconstructed, school-prayer-reinstated, third-wave, neo–Newt Gingrich era, in which, lying at the foot of the Statue of Liberty, Jewish identity is in fragments, while lost Jewish (read male) souls seek solace in the exact same, singular, super-clean anus of a closeted, self-righteous, god-fearing married Mormon faggot. Yes, *Angels* is about Jewish male self-loathing in the twentieth century held tightly within the ever-expanding embrace of Miss Liberty's very tired, porous hands.

Angels opens with a quintessential North American Jewish moment. A very old rabbi with a heavy Eastern European accent, long beard, and stooped shoulders presides over the funeral of a woman who has spent the last ten years of her life at the Bronx Home of Aged Hebrews without a visit from her grandson who lives minutes away. At the funeral, the rabbi reads out loud the names of the family mourners whose roster by the third generation is generously sprinkled with one gentile appellation after another. For the Jew who dies alone without family or community, Kushner has written the new "diaspora *Kaddish*." Rabbi Chemolwitz publicly admits that he doesn't know the deceased Sarah Ironson or her family. But he knows Sarah's journey and the meaning of that journey which in the end, is more important than knowing the person herself. For it is in the irreversible departure from Eastern Europe to the climactic but culturally dislocating arrival at Ellis Island where Jewish continuity is affirmed. Listen to the rabbi:

> Rabbi: (He speaks sonorously, with a heavy Eastern European accent, unapologetically consulting a sheet of notes for the family names): . . . This woman. I did not know this woman. . . . She was . . . (He touches the coffin)
>
> . . . not a person but a whole kind of person, the ones who crossed the ocean, who brought with us to America the villages of Russia and Lithuania—and how we struggled, and how we fought, for the family, for the Jewish home, so that you would not grow up here, in this strange place, in the melting pot where nothing melted . . . (page 10)

By using the plural "we" rather than the singular "she" the rabbi purposefully includes himself in the historic crossing of Ashkenazi Jews from the old country to the "new" country. And with the public insertion of himself into his "eulogy for the unknown," he affirms Jewish continuity in spite of the fact that he is presiding over the funeral of a Jew he did not know for a family he does not know. Then, through the brilliant use of the second person "you,"

Kushner personalizes the impersonal space of the estranged diaspora Jew from his/her cultural roots. Alone in the middle of a pitch black stage with the coffin of our ancestors the stooped rabbi stands facing the void. At the exact same moment, the audience is dramatically transformed into the future generations—not only of Sarah Ironson's family, but of the Jewish people in general. Then to us, as Jews, the rabbi speaks:

> Descendants of this immigrant woman, you do not grow up in
> America, you and your children and their children with the goyische
> names. You do not live in America. No such place exists. Your clay is
> the clay of some Litvak shtetl, your air the air of the steppes—because
> she carried the old world on her back across the ocean, in a boat, and
> she put it down on Grand Concourse Avenue, or in Flatbush, and she
> worked that earth into your bones, and you pass it to your children, this
> ancient, ancient culture and home. (little pause)

When the audience is secured as the next generation, the rabbi ends his eulogy with a bitter, painful admonition:

> You can never make that crossing that she made, for such Great
> Voyages in this world do not any more exist. But every day of your lives
> the miles that voyage between that place and this one you cross. Every
> day. You understand me? In you that journey is. (pages 10, 11)

In *us* that journey *is*. Even if we want to forget where we came from, we can't. It's impossible. The journey lives in us, in spite of us—not only as cultural, but also as spiritual inheritance.

By opening *Angels* with this scene, Kushner claims his rightful place in the Jewish lexicon of post-Holocaust writers confronting secular Jewish identity in the diaspora. Yet the questions *Angels* ask around sexuality, autonomy, and cultural preservation belong within the ethnic, narrative tradition that began in the old country with Sholem Aleichem's Tevye, asking *The Almighty* for guidance in raising his Jewish daughters in a secular world. And that particular ethnic tradition continues on today (in the New World) with the "all-American, Jewish everyman" plays of Arthur Miller, Paddy Cheyefsky, Nathanial West, and Neil Simon's *Broadway Bound*. But Kushner, writing in a poststructuralist age, explodes the boundary of tribal sensitivities. He uses a sexuality clearly constructed outside of procreative, nuclear, heterosexual marriage as the postmodern metaphor for the new, self-loathing Willy Loman. Willy has become "Nelly" and so very *fey* at that.

Louis Ironson is the post-'Nam, civil rights–redux, contemporary Jewish Nelly, not a likeable, hardly sympathetic liberal, Jew-boy fella. The son of good Jewish lefties and a failure by his own admission, he's a word processor working in the courthouse basement of the second Court of Appeals in Brooklyn. (He never made it to law school.) After his grandmother's funeral, he confides to his shiksa boyfriend Prior Walter that he hadn't visited Bubbe Sarah for ten years. She reminded him too much of his mother. With this confession, Kushner appears to play into the Philip Roth/Norman Mailer, Metro-Goldwyn-Mayer, hate-your-mother, *yidishe* mamma's boy stereotype.

But Louis's absence from his family must also be read in the context of the historical abandonment of an entire people and the shame that abandonment produced. Louis doesn't visit Sarah because he is afraid of his mother's shame— the shame of the little *feygeleh* who leaves home not to marry and make a for- tune, but to fuck other little *feygelehs*, Jew and Gentile alike. Louis has internal- ized the family shame and projects this shame onto his grandmother, so he cannot visit her out of fear of revisiting his own (Jewish male) self-loathing. This singular act of abandonment of an immigrant grandmother, by a self- loathing Jew, forms the controlling metaphor upon which Kushner seeks to negotiate the question of morality in human relations in the age of AIDS.

Louis Ironson abandons his virus-infected lover just as he abandoned his grandmother. Ignorant of Jewish tradition and afraid of what he's about to do, Louis checks with the rabbi after Sarah's funeral:

> Louis: Rabbi, what does the Holy Writ say about someone who aban- dons someone he loves at a time of great need?
>
> Rabbi: Why would a person do such a thing?
>
> Louis: Maybe because this person's sense of the world, that it will change for the better with struggle, maybe a person who has this new- Hegelian positivist sense of constant historical progress towards happi- ness or perfection or something, who feels very powerful because he feels connected to these forces, moving uphill all the time . . . maybe that person can't, um, incorporate sickness into his sense of how things are supposed to go. Maybe vomit . . . and sores and disease . . . really frighten him, maybe . . . he isn't so good with death.
>
> Rabbi: The Holy Scriptures have nothing to say about such a person. (page 25)

For Kushner, speaking rabbinically, abandonment is an act of moral as well as spiritual impotence. For Jews—Israeli and diaspora— abandonment is not only a twentieth century (Jewish) leitmotif but also a historical obsession. And, in the age of AIDS, both public—medical, governmental, religious— and private—family, friends, colleagues—abandonment has become a controlling metaphor for gay suffering. Appropriately then, Kushner uses a gay Jew as cultural icon, representative of the "desertion dilemma," so central to both the Jewish and gay communities.

Out of his internalized self-loathing, Louis abandons his grandmother— his roots. Because of his shame, he is unable to comprehend that he is about to abandon his lover Prior in the exact same way. With the creation of Louis Ironson—secular Jewish faggot that he is—Kushner locates the question of abandonment outside a religious context. Throughout *Angels*, Louis seeks to locate moral justification for the immoral abandonment of those he loves.

Enter the character of Roy Cohn who has built a career on the totally fallacious moral justification of the stupendously grotesque, immoral act. Kushner uses Roy Cohn's assimilated self-loathing Jew-boy persona to mirror the self-loathing Louis Ironson. Are they identical characters? In the play, Louis abandons his literal family, the mother of his mother. And he deserts his life partner sick with AIDS. Roy abandons his metaphoric mother, Ethel Rosenberg. And he forsakes his homosexual brothers by always fucking in a locked closet. Both men are isolationists, living in *galut* (contemporary Jewish exile). Louis lives outside Jewish communal life, whereas Roy is completely acommunal. Thus, the narrative function of Roy Cohn (in *Angels*) is to create an alter ego for Louis, a point counter point from which Kushner positions assimilated and estranged, very middle-class Jewish male identity. In this context, the audience sits as the *bet din*, a Jewish court, judging the morality of Louis Ironson—the newly wandering, perpetually meandering, diaspora Jew. Next to Roy Cohn, Louis looks good, or so it would appear.

But why make the central characters of your play self-loathing gay Jews? Because Kushner, himself a gay Jew, employs one identity to dramatically inform upon the other. Ultimately he uses the condition or state of diaspora, and male "Jewishness" as cultural signifier for "gayness." He draws thematic parallels between assimilation and self-loathing within the Jewish male psyche and location and dislocation within the gay male psyche. (The only women in the play are dead, angels, or crazy.) And—for the first time in contemporary mainstream Broadway theater—Kushner dares to use the homosexual persona to reveal Jewish male neurosis. Thus, there is a certain poststructuralist symmetry being constructed around the social identities of Jewish and queer. Kushner exposes the vices of one identity with the other, and vice versa.

The challenge, then, lies with the heterosexual audience—both Gentile and Jew. As innocent bystander, the Gentile must resist the desire to distance the self from these characters precisely because of their Jewishness and/or their homosexuality. But for the male, heterosexual Jew to identify himself with either Louis Ironson or Roy Cohn is a far more difficult predicament. To identify with them as Jew is to locate the exiled self in a pattern of familiar, albeit uncomfortable, neurosis about "Hebrew" circumcised maleness and to face the internalized shame of the classic pariah.

The queerness of Roy Cohn and Louis Ironson does not invalidate their Jewishness; on the contrary, it illuminates it. For the author, the social (not to mention historical) link between Jew and homosexual is clearly potent. He knows personally that it is in the intersection between assimilation and selfloathing that both Jews and homosexuals are caught.

Kushner then collapses the borders between sexuality and ethnicity. A fragmented ID becomes a fluid ego, although often a despised one at that. Finally, as if he is writing *responsa* to Harvey Fierstein's "mother" in the groundbreaking *Torch Song Trilogy*, when she forbids her son to mention Jewish and gay in the same *Kaddish*, Kushner refuses to split off the self. The problem is that what he offers in the characters of Louis and Roy, point counter point, is too easy to reject precisely because they are so full of self-loathing. So Kushner strategically introduces (into the play) the "sacred" secular Jewish mother Ethel Rosenberg, who was betrayed by all the prodigal Jewish sons: Irving R. Kaufman, Irving Saypol, Roy Cohn, and her own brother David Greenglass. She is the final link between the men, Jewish identity, assimilation, and self-loathing. It is the presence of Ethel Rosenberg in *Angels in America* that calls into question Jewish male morality in the postmodern era. The first scene when Ethel appears, Roy is very sick—so sick he can barely function and is about to collapse. In a chilling moment, which leaves the audience psychically suspended, Ethel Rosenberg calls 911 for an ambulance to take Roy Cohn to the emergency room. Throughout *Angels*, Cohn reflects on his proudest moment; his greatest singular accomplishment, according to him—the epitome of his power (and the height of his assimilation and self-loathing)—was when he persuaded Judge Kaufman to sentence Ethel to death in the electric chair. Kushner successfully exposes Roy's misogyny and internalized anti-Semitism. So when Ethel calls for the ambulance, it becomes apparent that she has come back to haunt her executioner and to witness his demise. In the last weeks of his life, Kushner has made Roy Cohn dependent on Ethel Rosenberg. Face to face, the Jewish son meets the (Jewish) mother he ruthlessly betrayed.

The next time Ethel appears it is at Cohn's hospital bedside. She announces that the end is near. Cohn is about to be disbarred, and Ethel has come back for the hearings. Slowly, almost imperceptibly the balance of power shifts between the abandoned mother and the son who abandoned her. Until now Roy was in charge. But with his impending disbarment, his total collapse—political and physical—is imminent.

At the same time, Louis has taken a lover, left the lover, and (near the end of part two) begged Prior to take him back. Tightening the symmetry in the play, Kushner parallels Roy's disbarment with Prior's refusal to take Louis back. Because of their immoral and unethical behavior, both Louis and Roy are thrown out and rejected by their own people. But unlike Louis, Roy has no shame. Thus, by the play's end, the characters of Louis Ironson and Roy Cohn are distinguishable. The audience slowly develops a limited sympathy (but never compassion) for Louis, whose lover will not take him back. But for Cohn, there is nothing. Ethel is there to witness it all. Her appearance at Roy Cohn's hospital bed, in the middle of the AIDS epidemic, is a *coup d'theatre*. Kushner has brought Ethel back to say *Kaddish* for Roy, the "infected" Jew for whom there is no prayer.

Framing the "Jewish play" within the play, Kushner begins and ends *Angels* with a *Kaddish*. The first *Kaddish* was not just for Sarah Ironson, Louis's grandmother, but rather for an entire era including a lost sense of Jewish peoplehood. The last *Prayer for the Dead*, coming almost at the end of part two in *Perestroika*, is truly a restructuring of the post-immigrant Jewish experience. The *Kaddish* has been transformed into a postmodern mourning prayer for lost Jewish souls. And it is in the final act of *davening* that Louis, Ethel, and Roy become the unholy triumvirate.

At the request of Prior's nurse, Belize (who stole Cohn's personal supply of AZT), Louis has come unwillingly to say *Kaddish* for Cohn. When he begins, Louis mixes up several Hebrew prayers until, out of nowhere, Ethel appears at the foot of the bed to lead Louis in the *Kaddish*. In this moment, Kushner exposes the true condition of the exiled Jew. Louis is the post-Holocaust Jew who quotes Hegel, but does not even know the *Kaddish*. He is truly lost; the product of his own shame and self-loathing, he cannot mourn properly. And Ethel, dead already 42 years and for whom we still say *Kaddish*, is the only one who knows the words.

The scene is both emotionally satisfying—Roy Cohn is disbarred and finally dead—and equally disquieting. The new diaspora Jew wanders around and around in *galut*, intellectually informed but culturally ignorant, sexually despised and profoundly isolated. This, then is the consequence of Louis's abandonment of those he loves. Having been only for himself, who is he? A combination of Willy Loman redux and Tevye's nightmare of a son-in-law. And who are we, Jews, Gentiles, and heterosexuals who disassociate ourselves from Louis Ironson, as though his dilemma is not our dilemma? In the diaspora, as Tony Kushner deftly shows with his "Gay Fantasia on National Themes," the question of abandonment simmers in the melting pot, boiling over whenever the temperature gets too hot, scalding everybody in sight.

POSTSCRIPT: *THE PRODUCERS* 2001

The year was 1968 when Mel Brooks's *The Producers,* or *Camp Feygeleh* as I like to call it, hit the Hollywood screen. One year before Stonewall. The day when drag queens and butch kings ran furiously out of a New York Greenwich Village bar spewing their live *cock*(tails)tales into the air while hurling heavy beer glasses at angry, bewildered men "dressed" as the NYPD (blue) force. Thus was set in permanent, forward motion on a sweltering summer night the historical liberation of gay people, by gay people, for gay people. And yes, undoubtedly, some of those gorgeously dressed fairies running out into the street were real kosher chicks—Jews, that is—*feygelehs* shrieking at the top of their very *yidish* lungs.

Thirty-four years later we have a repeat performance—of sorts—in the Broadway musical re*vamped* for the live stage by maestro Brooks himself. Only this time, Zero Mostel, "the authentic" Jew who plays himself, a.k.a. Max Bialystock, in the movie is now replaced. In 2001 he is now played by Nathan Lane who performs "the Jew" but in real life is not a Jew, but is, however, a real live "authentic" homosexual. And Gene Wilder, a.k.a. Leo Bloom, the goyishe *fey* sidekick, is replaced by Mathew Broderick, who performs faux Jew. Any way you read it, Jew*ish* has become virtual, while Queer*ish* has become virtuoso. The homosexual now literally (sur)passes the Jew. These guys transform Tony Kushner's end of the twentieth-century's assimilated, self-loathing homosexual (read Jew) into the twenty-first century's controlling national metaphor, newest cultural icon, queer. This is not surprising. This full-bodied reversal from Jewish assimilation to homosexual auto-emancipation was in rehearsal for decades.

The new millennium, then, begins with Broadway as the meeting/melding of queer and Jewish as the operative, contemporary, performance matrix. The Jew is now embodied and effortlessly performed by the very gay Nathan Lane (who in real life is almost always taken for Jewish but is not). Thus, Arthur Miller's, Paddy Chayefsky's, and Nathaniel West's twentieth-century Jew, who was always a proper noun, becomes, in the twenty-first century, a mere adjective, as in *jewish* (that's a lower case "j"), by virtually assimilating "himself" into the national American scene.

Meanwhile *queer*—replacing the "homosexual" or "gay-identified" person—now proudly claims center stage in language, theater, and politics. The act of passing for the Anglo-American heterosexual becomes thus elevated to such a high art that it is almost theatrically obsolete, not to mention in(di)visible from Jewish or queer, on or off the stage. (Once again, Jew is read as male as we enter the next century; it remains ambiguous and highly suspect whether queer really ever includes lesbian. But this is another, though perhaps not, story.)

And so, the biblical covenant is once again affirmed. *Mazel tov!* But this time, the covenant is affirmed by the character of Roger *de Bris*, the director of Bialystock's flop of a play that becomes a big hit, *Springtime for Hitler*. It's important to point out that the word "bris" in Hebrew refers to "circumcision," the slicing of the (Jewish) baby boy's foreskin, which is meant as a sign of the covenant with G-d. In *The Producers*, Mel Brooks continues to do again and again what he always has. He not so surreptitiously usurps Jewish identity for gay identity by making the director of the play about the man who hated Jews, a flaming fag, whose name represents that sacred, divinely Jewish bond between the One on High and all those old boys living in tents on the ground—Abraham, Isaac, and Jacob. Roger "The Circumcised" prances around the stage of *The Producers*, singing his *dick*tatorial philosophy:

> No matter what you do on the stage
> Keep it light, keep it bright
> Keep it gay!
> Whether it's murder, mayhem, or rage
> Don't complain, it's a pain
> Keep it gay!

In *The Producers*, we don't need to be reminded to Keep It Gay, for the play itself could not exist, and would not be the triumphant success that it is, if it were not so.

But in life and on stage, it is Nathan Lane who gives us "the queer performing Jew" who becomes "the queer Jew performing" who was always Mel Brooks's "the Jew performing queer." *Queer* then becomes a fluid signifier, connecting past generations of Jews with past generations of homosexuals. From *Angels in America* to the totally revamped *The Producers*, it is "the queer" who performs the poststructural patriotic metaphors of death, rebirth, and transformation in the new postmodern millennium.

OUTING THE ARCHIVES

FROM THE CELLULOID CLOSET

TO THE ISLE OF KLEZBOS

Eve Sicular

It is possible to feel nostalgia for a place one has never seen.
—GRETA GARBO IN *QUEEN CHRISTINA*, 1933

A yingl mit a yingl hot epes a tam?
(idiomatic: A boy with a boy, what kind of [taste/sense] is that?)
—MOLLY PICON IN *YIDL MITN FIDL*, 1936

ABOUT TEN YEARS ago, this activist secular Jew, dedicated lesbian, musician, and vintage film devotee opened up a celluloid closet in Yiddish cinema. In my exploration of film from the golden age of Yiddish film (from the mid-1920s to the very early years of World War II, particularly 1936 to 1940), of such classics as *Yidl mitn Fidl* and *Der Dibuk*, I unexpectedly discovered that quite a few of them contained sustained queer subtexts. And as I found in subsequent research, a deeper examination of these highly specific subtexts affords a detailed view of complex cultural tensions within the Yiddish-speaking world of that era. Eventually exploring the Yiddish celluloid closet became my primary intellectual activity. I wrote several articles and book chapters and toured widely with my video clips and lecture on this topic. I was intrigued first with finding any mention, however oblique or broad, of queerness embedded in such quintessentially Jewish popular culture, and then with the vibrant, intricate picture of that era's contemporary concerns and debates, which this lens of queerness has helped me see. These things seemed subtle, quaint, and often obscure at first, as do many retro cultural references, but with continued research, they read loud and clear.

Over the years, such discoveries from archival sources have not only become material for my film history projects but also for musical repertoire, which I share through my work as a klezmer bandleader and music producer. New hints turn up whether I'm working on theater, music, or film research. For instance, bilingual vaudeville lyrics by Molly Picon, one of the most beloved stars of Yiddish stage and screen, reveal her awareness of Greenwich Village as "the queerest place," where one can go for a drink and "feel inspired."[1] And then there were Molly's many drag personae documented in publicity pictures that kept turning up during my years as the photo and film curator at the YIVO Institute of Jewish Research.

As someone who grew up in what I call the land of presliced challah, I could never have guessed how a knowledge of Yiddish culture would tie together so many disparate parts of my life. The other passions and endeavors that have defined my personal and professional self—music, language, film history, coming out, and seeking commonality—have all become intertwined through a deepening awareness of Yiddish. *Yidishkayt* (a Yiddish expression meaning, literally, Jewishness) and queerness have both turned out for me to be elements of identity and community in themselves and also two distinct prisms; each allows the spectrum of the other's cultural possibilities to reveal itself more fully.

It was through my interest in klezmer that I first found the way to pursue my incipient interest in Yiddish. I had been playing drums since the age of eight, and was attracted to klezmer music since first hearing it in my senior year of college, but undertook the style much more seriously after finding the New York klezmer scene, in which lesbians and gay men were an integral part. I founded Metropolitan Klezmer with three [*het*] men in 1994 (we are all still members, along with one other man and three other women now). Then after a few years, the opportunity arose to form an all-female spin-off band, and the Isle of Klezbos was born. The creative dynamics of the two groups have led to new possibilities in repertoire, expanded performance opportunities for both bands, and have brought together audiences identifying as Jewish, queer, both, and neither. While in retrospect many aspects of these music and film projects have turned out to be deeply fulfilling and widely successful, none of it has been easy.

SEEING LAVENDER IN YIDDISH FILM

The ways in which *yidishkayt* spoke emotional, though not always pleasant, truths to me when I finally came to it were in some ways analogous to coming out. There were the little moments of discovery, which, in retrospect, signaled my latent attraction to certain types of culture, which would fully manifest later. There was my love of the old-style musical feel of chants (which I learned for my Bat Mitzvah from a cantor's 45rpm record) that so appealed to me, while Israeli folk dance (accompanied by other 45s) never had. There was my awe in realizing that a friend in high school could understand the lines from a 30-second commercial for soft ice cream, where Buddy Hackett's script was entirely in *mameloshn* (another Yiddish word for Yiddish, literally "mother tongue"). There was my high school choice to study Russian, not only for its beautiful sound, cryptic Cyrillic letters, and historic connections to a radical left, but also for the chance to find some more connection to my physician/pianist grandmother's side from Odessa, and to my father's difficult but brilliant relatives whom he seldom spoke of and I had barely known. Learning Yiddish eventually helped me interpret family dynamics I'd lived with all my life, especially the mixed all-Jewish marriage of Russian-rooted New Yorker and German-speaking Austro-Czech Holocaust refugee families into which I had been born. Yiddish helped me to find freeing truths, if not necessarily peace, about the historic frictions between these disparate Jewish groups.[2]

I couldn't have dreamt up a more meaningful research project: lesbian and gay subtexts in Yiddish-language movies. For some reason, though, many people's first response was that I must have dreamt it up; surely such things could not have existed among earlier Jewish generations. But after the first glimpses emerged from the "celluloid closet," my cinematic discoveries kept multiplying, broadening, deepening, and constantly teaching me about the complex attitudes toward queerness among Yiddish filmmakers and spectators throughout the twentieth century. Before long, my personal project became a ticket to festivals, conferences, colleges, and media arts centers, and publishing offers throughout North America and Europe.

As I presented my work around the country and abroad, I continued to learn from readers and audiences about which of their doubts I'd been able (or unable) to dispel, and, at the same time, to generate a forum for relating real-life stories seldom before spoken openly. One man told me about his proud lesbian aunt on the Lower East Side, whom they used to call an "independent woman" when he was growing up. The research director of a *shtetl* history project relayed recent interview accounts of two Jewish men living together in Libivne (today Luboml in the Ukraine) who, for reasons that may never be completely resolved, seem to have been referred to by all the other Yiddish-speaking inhabitants as *di meydlekh,* "the girls." A Yiddish teacher in New York explained that his teacher had remembered an old country term for male homosexual—*fraymayer*—a euphemism that literally means "freemason," perhaps indicating a supposed likeness to members of an exotic-sounding secret society (as to lesbians, the man apparently said he'd never heard of such people in Europe).

I've gotten to know a lot of other Jewish queers who share my curiosity about excavating representations of ourselves in our search for a place we fully belong. Maybe this is what makes the prospect of finding homosexual traces in Jewish popular culture so appealing to us, no matter how distorted, disparaging, or oblique the reference. Perhaps we will see a place we can feel at home onscreen or in literature, a long-obscured piece of ourselves projected from the past to affirm an existence we have been denied. Any evidence that people like ourselves were acknowledged within cultural works is validation, countering our apparent invisibility in Jewish heritage. While silence = death (a formulation popularized by the activists of ACT-UP!, and translated into Yiddish for the title of the popular and queer-influenced Klezmatics' debut klezmer music CD, *Shvaygn = toyt*), seeking reflections of ourselves is also part of any fully realized life.

Just what kind of reflections we may find is worth close examination. The distortions and refractions in the images we see of figures that somehow represent our own identities form a commentary on the period and the people who produced them, something equally true of homophobic, anti-Semitic, and racist depictions. They reflect a distinct awareness of the Other, and show the tensions that Otherness evokes, while not necessarily presenting any sort of genuine portrayal. In terms of these particular Yiddish films, a thorough inspection of the nature of their not-always-cryptic allusions to homosexuality reveals that each veiled reference is intertwined with any from a compendium of Jewish anxieties and concerns of the interwar period: racial degeneracy theory, conversion, intermarriage, assimilation, loss and denial of one's identity, stereotypes of the *goles yid* (diaspora Jew), and possible erotic overtones in same-sex religious institutions. Far from imaginary or unimaginable, queer subtexts are often defined by their relation to other "threats," which preoccupied contemporary Jewish psyches.

For instance, the topic of denial and "closet Jews" comes up amid triple entendre *feygeleh* (little bird/darling/fairy or faggot) jokes that emerge verbally, visually, and musically throughout the screwball comedy *Amerikaner Shadkhn* (*American Matchmaker*, 1940, USA). I only noticed these little gems after about five or six, or fifteen or sixteen, times rewinding to one scene that kept sticking in my mind. But after catching the first *feygelah* reference, suddenly I noticed telltale birdcages placed within carefully composed frames, and not-so-innocent song lyrics that originated in folk lullabies but here ever-so-archly reprised throughout the soundtrack and film credits, not to mention innumerable jokes about the bachelor protagonist and his *landsman* Friday (a.k.a. Morris the butler).[3] In addition to this male relationship, the filmmaker Edgar Ulmer includes Elvie, the irreverent butchy defiant sister of the dapper *fey* Nat Gold/Nat Silver character. I mention her, because it is one of the few lesbian subtexts I found in Yiddish film.[4]

In *Yidl mitn Fidl* (*Yiddle with The Fiddle*, 1937, Poland/USA), Molly Picon, whose career was launched in the more freewheeling years just after World War I with her male-impersonating stage role as Yankele, is cast as a girl who, in order not to ruin her reputation, has no choice but to wear boy's clothes while touring with an itinerant klezmer band. Her cross-dressed lead character is constantly accused of supposed effeminacy, an ironic case of drag employed to counter perceived degenerate "racial" tendencies and reinforce strict gender norms (by any means necessary, including homophobic sight gags). The film's director, Joseph Green, said in an interview conducted shortly after making the movie that he intended to make an allegory teaching viewers how to avoid [behaving like] the *goles yid*, that is, the old world Eastern European Jewish man stereotyped as weak, highstrung, and neurotic. For exemplary masculinity, the film also includes a tall, clean-shaven (in other words, "modern"), athletic character who is expressly not interested in Molly as a boy (he drops her in a lake when s/he tries to embrace him), but requites her love as soon as she resumes wearing a dress. Molly's heterosexual orientation is never in question in this movie; rather, queer subtext is employed in other characters' responses to her *fey* male appearance. Yidl is constructed as a foil in the then-current debate over dos and don'ts for the New Jewish Man.

The nineteenth-century narrative of *Der Vilner Shtot Khazn* (*Overture to Glory*, 1940, USA) includes strong overtones of both conversion and seduction in depicting a cantor's tormented double life. He is "recruited" by foppish condescending outsiders from the Warsaw opera, *goyim* who fit a stereotypical profile of predatory homosexuals. They have elitist mannerisms, and wear tophats and tails when they very nearly cruise his synagogue "performance." Later, they throw wolfish glances during furtive nightly rendezvous at which they tempt the pious *khazn* with The "Moonlight Sonata" and other forbidden fruits. Based on the true story of 1840s Vilna city cantor Yoel-Dovid Strashunsky and the Polish composer Moniuszko (composer of *Halka*, the first Polish-language opera), the script was written by Jewish war refugees in New York in 1940. The plot functions as a brooding allegory depicting the doomed fate of a Polish Jew attempting to embrace Gentile European culture. Strashunsky succumbs, ends his struggle to keep classical music in his own closet, and decides to join the alluring secular artistic milieu; the cantor is in effect seduced but then abandoned by the fickle *goyish* world once his Jewish identity resurfaces. Such is the commentary of the Jewish scriptwriters exiled from their own Polish homeland a century after their protagonist's earnest adventure.

In opening scenes of *Der Dibuk* (*The Dybbuk*, 1937, Poland), two former yeshiv partners are portrayed as a comically but passionately devoted pair, signalled most cinematically when one young man's rendition of Solomon's erotic psalm "Song of Songs" is intercut with close-ups of the other man's almost swooning response. A later scene in the film, including a sweaty, swaying male torso with well-lit nipples, seemed homoerotically charged, and these retrospective readings were supported after a later revelation regarding the sexuality of the film's director, Michal Waszynski.[5] The scene had such homoerotic overtones that, after seeing one of my lecture presentations, Sandi Dubowski included *Dybbuk* footage as part of an ultra-Orthodox coming out-scene in his documentary, *Trembling Before G-d*.

HOW I BROUGHT QUEER AND *YIDISHKAYT* TOGETHER

What first led me to perceive any of these covert meanings? Of course, growing up playing "spot the Jew" may sensitize one to pick up on other not-quitementionable subjects being hinted at, a process similar to developing gaydar. The thrill of getting an in-joke or catching a fleeting, even if pejorative, reference carries over from one marginalized experience to another. Also, as I knew from both cinema studies and my own production experience, every element and juxtaposition in a film is thoroughly intentional. Nothing onscreen is there by accident.

Some of my most valuable, enduring lessons came from reading Vito Russo's *The Celluloid Closet*, which proved to be a culturally liberating experience. This book came out of Vito's live lecture presentations with film clips, mainly from censorship-era Hollywood pictures, illustrating homosexual subtext in the movies (his work was posthumously made into a documentary feature of the same title). Vito's writing was hilarious, fiercely politicized, beautifully coherent, and well researched. I read it shortly after moving to Portland, Oregon, between filmmaking classes, restaurant shifts, R&B gigs, and working at the new lesbian/gay newsmagazine. A New York native with an alienated Ivy League past, I had just moved to the West Coast after graduating college. My formal studies had included film animation and a thesis on Soviet documentarian Esther Shub. In extracurricular life, I played drums with dozens of bands and theater productions, came out sophomore year, and first heard *klezmer* music as a senior. In Portland, I happily immersed myself in a women's film festival collective and lesbian/gay community band. My main connections with the Jewish dyke community were through a few musicians and film people I knew and potluck Seders with wonderful hand-Xeroxed cut-and-past haggadas.

I moved to Seattle after a few years, where I did get to start subbing as a drummer with the Mazeltones. Also, I heard from a friend that Vito Russo himself would be presenting his work live at the University of Oregon. I immediately agreed to drive down four hours or more for his show. Vito—soon to become one of the founders of ACT-UP—covered mainly Hollywood and mass-audience European cinema in his research, and even camped up his devout adherence to "Judyism" (meaning Liza Minelli's mother; Judy Garland was of course one of the first gay icons).[6] His vision and energy catalyzed my awareness of how, despite taboos and censorship, homosexuality had proven too intriguing to be left completely offscreen.

Around this time, the queer and *klezmer* threads of my identity started to get wound together too. I heard from the bandleader of the Mazeltones that in fact lots of out queers could be found in the Yiddish music and culture scene at the annual KlezCamp folk arts retreat in the Catskills. I had heard of

KlezCamp before, but learning that there was a place where being an out lesbian and a Jewish folk musician came together was even more of a revelation than Vito Russo's Judyism. The following June, I moved back to New York, pursuing my dreams of playing more *klezmer*, learning more Yiddish, and completing my own film history projects. Then, just after the November 1990 reelection of Senator Jesse Helms, a virulent homophobe and staunch opponent of AIDS causes, Vito Russo died.

I thought of Vito often, especially after I landed a job as curatorial assistant at one of his old haunts, The (initial caps always) Museum of Modern Art's film department, working on a film festival, "Yiddish Film: Between Two Worlds." Yiddish film study was still at that point a lonely and often seemingly irrelevant topic for me in the midst of the turbulent events of those late Bush Senior years. Despite my own ambivalence about immersing myself in what seemed at times to be escapist, obscure cultural artifacts, I found these movies fascinating, not as nostalgia but rather as some sort of key to understanding a vibrant culture, of an esoteric but important, not-so-distant past. I don't remember exactly what in Yiddish pictures beckoned me to look through the prism Vito Russo had unveiled, but I know I began to see glimmerings sometime during those six months at MoMA.

The MoMA series, coproduced by the National Center of Jewish Film, was the most extensive exhibition of Yiddish films ever produced. Various big stars and *makhers* from the glory days of Yiddish film attended, and for over three months, the audiences arrived daily, frequently in droves. Their old and young faces, their voices in the galleries outside the theaters (and sometimes, occasionally loudly, inside), their languages in the air, on the soundtracks, in their letters, and on my phoneline, all formed a hectic but welcome contrast to the decidedly un-heymish atmosphere found in the official museum. Watching from the projection booths or the darkened back aisles, I rarely had the chance to stay the length of any one screening, but certain moments and particular scenes must have caught my attention enough to invite further scrutiny.

Maybe it wasn't just what I saw or heard or read in the subtitles that prompted me. In retrospect, it seems more like atmospheric déja vu, that feeling when an aroma evokes a primal memory just out of conscious reach. The effect of these ineffable impressions was that, almost as an afterthought at the end of the Yiddish festival, I Xeroxed my own copies of the files of five or six particular films and packed them away for future reference.

Two years later, I had a more permanent position as curator of the film and photo archives at YIVO with my office in the garret of a Fifth Avenue mansion. One day, I overheard a researcher mention that he was editing a special media issue of some Jewish academic journal I'd never heard of. Since I knew and respected his work, and also knew that he was gay and politicized, I was emboldened enough to suggest my idea for an article based on these observations I'd made working on the MoMA show. Background research revealed more and fuller closets in Yiddish celluloid than I ever would have guessed. Somehow, even before I could have described them, queer subtexts emerged, nearly every one steeped in its own distinctive flavor of period Jewish angst.

The elements that drew me in even before I could articulate them came, I believe, from the subliminally attractive prospect of finding a refuge for my alienated queer identity. Influenced by the effect of opening Hollywood's celluloid closet, I had developed a homing instinct that, to my great surprise, took me back to these "other" roots, the *alter heym* [old country] of Yiddish film. Suddenly, gaydar seemed to reveal outposts in the regions once inhabited by my grandparents from Odessa and the Bronx. And the past seemed to acknowledge the existence of people like me, more than it ever had before.

As I launched into the project, I was deeply surprised and moved to find both knowledgeable support and severe skepticism in places where I least expected them. My initial research article and the first talks I gave applied caution in all my assertions, anticipating an onslaught by indignant *alte kakers* defending the hallowed legacy of Yiddish culture from supposedly baseless, slanderous revisionism. The fact that Yiddish films are often viewed today with a retrospective shadow of the Holocaust extending over their original contents imparts to them the air of sacred relics with an especially heavy emotional overlay.[7] Even before I finished my first draft, I had heard my work dismissed; one well-known film activist, a Jewish lesbian researcher herself, gave a curt assessment of my project-in-progress without reading any of it: "That'll be a short piece." Soon thereafter, though, two different retired (heterosexual) women volunteers at the YIVO Institute independently asked to read my manuscript. Then, encouraging me to continue this mode of inquiry, each told me her memories of homosexuality in a Jewish community between the World Wars—stories of an openly lesbian teenage friend in an Eastern European town, and of wild male escapades at Catskills hotels.

PRESENTING THE YIDDISH CELLULOID CLOSET

Being so often, and so publicly, at the crossroads of two such long-stigmatized yet exuberant cultures for the last few years, I have observed some fairly consistent dynamics in the venues where I have seen *yidishkayt* and queerness intersect. Sometimes, even the lip service of cosponsoring my presentation has turned out to be too controversial for Jewish festivals in cities where lesbian and gay cultural groups have hosted me. And at the lesbian and gay festivals where I generally receive an enthusiastic reception, there are still those whose response to Yiddish anything is automatic laughter at its supposed inherently campy nature. Such responses, even when tinged with sincere affection, reflect a narrow, condescending, and actually anti-Semitic sense of Yiddish culture, typical of people (usually Jews themselves) who want to distance themselves from things "too Jewish" that make them uncomfortable.

Ironically, the traditional Yiddish worldview of the dominant culture is analogous to one experienced now by queer communities. Yiddish historically has been used by people in insider/outsider positions, Jews who had to know the ways of the (sometimes hostile) dominant culture but also lived in a distinctive (sometimes separate) culture of their own, speaking a language and keeping customs that few non-Jews would bother to learn. For Jewish queers, an outsider role may be compounded, as we belong to a nondominant subculture whose language and traditions have not been generally shared, considered, or known by mainstream Jewish communities. Nevertheless, we are expected to be bilingual and understand "their" mindset. As members of both an ethnic and a sexual minority, we are attuned to "get" both queer and Jewish cues; straight Jews have the privilege of not paying attention to, or not even realizing the existence of, the lavender wavelength.

I believe this is why it often takes more effort to present my lecture to straight Jews than to non-Jewish queers. People of both these backgrounds may be uninitiated into cultural codes outside their own, yet while the need to translate Jewish linguistic and cultural content for non-Jews is taken for granted, heterosexuals are often unaware of the kinds of decoding required to illuminate lesbian or gay nuance. Of course there is also the resistance factor, the fact that homophobia prevents some Jews from wanting to take in what I am showing. Usually the skeletons they fear finding turn out to be only specters of fear itself, since the contents of this Yiddish celluloid closet often reveal more about Jewish attitudes and issues from a given period than anything actually approximating homosexuality. Then again, there's the *Dybbuk*, with its voyeuristic scene of a glistening, passion-crazed man in a mikve. This eroticism was always clear to at least some gay male viewers, and this film, with the least deprecatory and most tolerant depictions of same-sex bonding of any of the moving pictures discussed here, was made in the most anxious time and place among them, Warsaw in 1937.

It's been a few years now since I last booked my Celluloid Closet of Yiddish Film clips and talk. Traveling, meeting interesting people, and working in a retro culture medium I love inspired me and challenged or illuminated my listeners and readers. But as time went on, it became predictable that most queer venues would welcome this presentation as a novelty or niche item, while most Jewish venues would treat it skittishly if at all. The lesbigay or LGBT festivals all had their own idiosyncracies as far as where Yiddish culture fit into programming, demographics, or fetishization, including Hamburg's, where a woman with a microphone asked confessionally, "Is it true that you are Jewish?" But for the most part, the remarkable thing about my audiences at queer festivals was the number of straight people brought along by queer family members; many that spoke to me after the shows were quite engaged and sympathetic. Yet "straight" Jewish venues and straight Jewish audience members, without the benefit of some queer mediator or experience, tended to avoid or resist many of the deeper lessons of my presentations.

There were exceptions of course: independent media centers in Seattle, Portland, and Vancouver, BC, that had very mixed audiences, mainly progressive media makers with their focus on the history of the moving image and an open curiosity toward both Jewish and queer manifestations onscreen; Chicago's Spertus Institute of Jewish Studies and the Gerber-Hart (queer) Cultural Center, which organized and cosponsored a program; the Berkeley Jewish Film Festival, whose director was the first to encourage me to take this topic off the page and onto the theater screen for the public (though in the end not for the Berkeley festival audiences either, but that's another story); and that bastion of mainstream Jewish feminism, *Lilith* magazine, which featured the butch Molly photo on their cover but cutesily likened it to Victor/ Victoria. Various alternative/progressive Yiddishist Jewish cultural gatherings welcomed the talk as provocative and lively, including KlezCamp, Mameloshn, and the Women & Yiddish conference (again focusing on mainly Molly).

The Jewish establishment, other than journalists looking for an interview, was generally not interested in airing the topic I proposed. Most Jewish festivals were programmed by committee, and I often found that any supporters of my project lost out in the politics of programming; sometimes when I tried to find out what had been decided, it turned out my contact or advocate was no longer working on the festival. Then there was the charged atmosphere in the packed hotel hall for the Association for Jewish Studies first-ever panel discussion on queer studies in 1994, organized by Ph.D. candidate (now professor) Naomi Seidman; a comic institutional melodrama unfolded when AJS apparently could not bring itself to designate a panel chairperson. And the National Center for Jewish Film (the main clearinghouse, restorer, and distributor of Yiddish movie prints to Jewish film festivals) denied the validity of my research, dismissing it out of hand when prospective "mainstream" Jewish festival bookers inquired.

This sort of treatment has tended to make me want to take my cultural contributions elsewhere. The question is, where else? A certain solidarity may be found among righteous pariahs, but that satisfaction can wear thin pretty quickly, especially for an independent scholar like myself without the academic career points system to make publishing and lecture tours more than intrinsically rewarding. (Though it's been great to see more of the world on festival travel budget lines, honoraria alone don't pay the New York rent.) Occasionally I hear about a new possible venue and inquire to see if it's time to take the video clips reel off the shelf again, but mainly I've gone on to focus on other things. I wonder if the success of such queer Jewish films as *Treyf* and *Trembling Before G-d* has changed the cultural landscape, or if generational shifts are opening things up in this world of queer studies departments, *The Ellen Show*, and an out gay real-life hero rising up against hijackers.

These days, my professional involvement in the Jewish cultural scene is mainly with my two music groups, Metropolitan Klezmer and the Isle of Klezbos. We play everywhere from traditional suburban weddings to lesbian commitment ceremonies, from the concert halls of the 92nd Street Y and the Knitting Factory to—for our all-female group—the Night Stage at Michigan Womyn's Music Festival. We were even hired for the ordination party of a then-closeted lesbian rabbinical student which was (now famously) called off lest she be denied her diploma from the Conservative-affiliated Jewish Theological Seminary. On the brighter side, just getting Isle of Klezbos mentioned by name on CNN as we played to a worldwide audience last fall did my heart proud. The politics of Cable News Network are one thing, but the strategy of dyke visibility agreed with my Lesbian Avenger marching band roots. It's not all so ideologically pure though.[8]

The music people choose for any event, especially a wedding, has layers of meaning for them beyond its beauty, spirit, technique, or danceability. In looking for an authentic expression of themselves, or a talisman of their espoused worldview, or a means to bridge cultural dissonance, people may find our music a convenient way to project a positive/united progressive image that glosses over their own fragmented/conflicted identities or movements. I am happy for the income, and genuinely glad to bring pleasure to any celebration of love. Yet I am also ambivalent about being used to perpetuate the institution of heterosexual marriage, not only through working with my "traditional" band, Metropolitan Klezmer, but even more so with Isle of Klezbos.

I notice that self-congratulatory or radical-chic clients may be interested in hiring an all-female *klezmer* band, especially one called Isle of Klezbos, as a token of their own nonconformity. Sometimes it's more complex, and more comforting to me, as when a bride-to-be searching klezmer websites finds Metropolitan Klezmer and then happens to scroll down to the Isle of Klezbos section. Clients may not want Klezbos over Metropolitan for their own event, but the element of irreverent respect they see in the name seems to reassure likeminded people that they will not be swallowed up by the norms implied in traditional matrimony. Of course, if they didn't love our sound, they wouldn't book either band, but it helps to also be a vehicle for articulating their own ambivalence and need for self-expression.

Another paradox comes up around klezmer generally. Certainly klezmer culture demonstrably plays a role in helping disaffected Jews like my former self to rediscover a connection to the tribe (a point used by artist Frank London of the Klezmatics to attract "Jewish continuity" funding streams). But around the New York wedding scene anyway, I notice our musical services are sought after as the crowd-pleasing entertainment at many a mixed marriage. Perhaps because our repertoire for private parties also includes everything from swing to Balkan to Zydeco, my groups may be employed this way more than the average klezmer ensemble. It's not always a problem; for instance, we recently came up with a "Son of a Preacher Man" impromptu as a request at the wedding of a rabbinical student (a rabbi's daughter) whose groom was . . . well, like the song says. That was a very moving and beautiful meeting of two deeply spiritual families. On the other hand, a friend of a friend had been invited by the bride to a wedding we were performing at, only to be seated at a table full of anti-Semitic relatives of the groom. We were oblivious of these tensions in the room even though apparently part of the reason for having us there had been to ease them. I'm glad to have charms to soothe a savage breast, but don't wish to be pushed into the role of entertainment fig leaf. And then also there's the trap of chic becoming cliché ("queer Jewish documentaries with *klezmer* soundtracks, that's so early 90s"—very close to verbatim, as uttered by a lesbian filmmaker I know in Manhattan).

One of the things I've most enjoyed over the years is the rare moment when it's all come together: queer culture, film history, *yidishkayt*, and my own music. Jeffrey Shandler, the editor of my first journal article on the Yiddish celluloid closet, had recommended a book that was newly published at the time, George Chauncey's *Gay New York: Gender, Urban Culture, and the Making of the Gay Male World, 1890–1940*. For my work, it was most relevant in helping me examine the arch in-jokes and double-edged asides of that most urbane self-parody, *Amerikaner Shadkhn*. Six years after uncovering many other bits of nuanced language and visual in-jokes, I went to find a tango melody and found much more than I was looking for.

Vaguely remembering a tune sung in a nightclub setting, I had fast-forwarded the VCR to the film's cabaret scene. The dialogue and lyrics suddenly jumped out at me as I realized this was all a covert epiphany, a doubly musical coming out. It was like I was listening to simultaneous translation from two marginalized languages I'd waited all my life to learn. I recalled George Chauncey's explanation of the coded use of terms such as *musical* and *artistic* in describing people who were "that way." The Yiddish lyrics of the tango described the matchmaker/closet case singing his story as a way of letting down his worldly client who was enamored of him as easily as possible. When he finishes, the woman exclaims, *"Ir zent muzikalish!"* ("You're musical!") "Yes," he replies in Yiddish. "It's something I inherited from my *feter Shya*," the "funny uncle" Shya around whom so much of the film's running-in-the-family gay subtext revolves.

The Metropolitan Klezmer/Isle of Klezbos version of this tune appears on our latest release, *Mosaic Persuasion*, as track seven: "Muzikalisher Tango." Between our annotated CD liner notes and live presentation of material at concerts, this queer Yiddish in-joke gets a lot of play lo these many years after its onscreen debut.

Isle of Klezbos plans to perform this tune again as part of our show at Cafe Makor, a self-styled hip cultural enclave and well-funded Jewish nonprofit on New York's Upper West Side. I chose the date for this gig months before, when offered a selection of various Thursdays in the fall. My choice was clear, since National Coming Out Day fell on a Thursday that year, and also happened to be the day before my birthday and a day after our trumpet player's. Suddenly, because of what happened a month earlier, the date, October 11, 2001, had a whole new level of meaning and urgency as a remembrance of lives and a celebration of diversity. Earlier that week when we played for *Simkhes Torah* at Congregation Beth Simchat Torah, New York's queer synagogue,

Rabbi Sharon Kleinbaum told us, "People are afraid to come into Manhattan now [due to more terrorist threats since bombing raids began on Afghanistan]." Like Jewish congregants throughout NYC, Rabbi Kleinbaum's CBST worshippers were told by police this year not to take their *Simkhes Torah* holiday dancing onto the streets, to avoid an added security burden on the city. Despite having to forego the traditional outdoor revelry, they were some of the most spirited Jewish queers I've ever played for.

NOTES

1. From "Busy, Busy" a.k.a. "Heaven Help the Woiking Goil." Typescript in YIVO archives.

2. Though my father's side were hardly Yiddishists, there was certainly a queer element to explore. My Uncle Paul is a self-described "happy homo," as I have recently learned. And I discovered years after her death that my grandmother's psychiatric practice had been largely with gay men. My father's father was a card-carrying Communist and physician, while Dr. Adele Sicular, my father's mother, was a Socialist, a polished classical pianist, and a proponent of women's rights who advocated sexual liberation. Many clients apparently adored her; one male client close to my father's age, who had been a practicing homosexual, became her lover after my grandfather died in 1954. I remember grandma's younger companion well, and we are happily reacquainted in recent years. A retired public school administrator, he remembers his relationship with my grandma as a high point of his life. Today he is involved in social activities at the Lesbian and Gay Center. But he still avoids discussion of my grandmother's closest female friend, an irascible woman closer to grandma's own age who seems to have been a kind of rival to him.

3. I made another discovery about *Amerikaner Shadkhn* when it was booked to play at Berkeley's Jewish Film Festival, just one month after I'd given a detailed description of its rather evident queer subtext as part of my lecture across the bay at San Francisco's Frameline lesbigay film festival. When the film's leading man, Leo Fuchs, was unavailable to speak opening night, Shirley Ulmer, the director's widow and scriptwriter of the film, was flown in to do the honors. A sizeable contingent of the audience at my San Francisco talk made their way to the screening, and Shirley obligingly fielded a number of questions about the *feygelah* theme from these particularly interested fans. While I knew that the film's director, Edgar G. Ulmer, had been a protégé of the openly homosexual German Expressionist filmmaker, F.W. Murnau, I was astonished to learn from a friend who was in that Berkeley audience that the movie character of bachelor Uncle Shya, as well as many of the film's other *fey* innuendoes, was based on a real-life cousin of Ulmer's, Gustav Heimo, known to the family affectionately as "Uncle Gus." As I subsequently confirmed in interviews with Shirley and her daughter in Los Angeles, he is even given a screen credit that reads ambiguously: STORY, G. HEIMO. If not for the serendipitous coincidences at these two festivals, I wonder whether this tale would ever have been divulged. (Leo Fuchs had already turned me down for an interview after I sent his son a copy of my research.)

4. Tough-talking, good-hearted Elvie wears tailored jodhpurs, refers glibly to Orthodox "cowboys with black hats," spouts near-verbatim Bette Davis, and dismisses marriage in fluent, flippant Yinglish: *"Nadn iz* alright, *ober dem khosn shtel arayn seyf"* [Dowry's fine but keep the groom in a vault]. Elvie's dialogue reflects her worldly iconoclastic outlook, as well as the in-jokes which abound in this critique of anxious, sophisticated crossover culture. One line in a conversation between Elvie and a pregnant friend is lifted from another Ulmer movie (1934 syphilis pic *Damaged Lives*), quoted here with Yiddish accent and nudgy affect. Anna Guskin, who plays Elvie, was earlier cast by Ulmer as shtetl upstart Gitl in his 1939 *Di Klyatshe* [The Light Ahead]. Gitl instigates village girls to defy taboos against swimming on Shabbes, then during their forbidden dip tells her best friend how beautiful she looks in moonlit water.

5. J. Hoberman, the *Village Voice* film critic who was one of the curators of the MoMA show and author of *Bridge of Light: Yiddish Film Between Two Worlds*, read a draft of my first research article before its publication. He then disclosed to me that, although he had omitted it from his encyclopedic book, his own research on *The Dybbuk* had included an interview account of Waszynski in which a postwar acquaintance of the filmmaker matter of factly remarked that Waszynski was well known to be homosexual (and rather flamboyant, it seems).

6. The gay cult of Judy Garland began during her flamboyant, fabulous, and turbulent lifetime. The decades-old coded term for queer, "friend of Dorothy," is an in-reference to Garland's role in *The Wizard of Oz*. And in her death, Judy's symbolic presence/absence gave new fury to the burgeoning gay rights movement. The Stonewall riots of June 1969 famously began the night of Judy's funeral. I was seven at the time, and while I was nowhere near Greenwich Village, I do remember my mother pointing out the long lines of people waiting outside the Frank E. Campbell Funeral Home to pay her their respects. While Judy herself, née Frances Gumm, was far from Judaism, one apocryphal, Jewish showbiz legend has it that in her audition for Louis B. Mayer of MGM, the young Judy-to-be sang "Eili, Eili" after being tipped off about Mayer's musical taste by his secretary.

7. Filmmaker Gregg Bordowitz, a Jewish PWA whose autobiographical experimental documentary *Fast Trip, Long Drop* includes home movie clips filmed in *shtetls* during the years before World War II, once said that film audiences inevitably asked him where he'd found this "Holocaust" footage.

8. Like me, many of the queer *klezmer* professionals in New York have also at some time played in the designated sidelines set aside at the Israeli Day Parade for the "Two Peoples, Two States" group's annual appearance. *Klezmer* here is an attempt to make this contingent a less confrontational atmosphere, and among the many faces I see participating over the years are members of Jews for Racial and Economic Justice and the earlier political group, New Jewish Agenda, both of which have been headed by lesbians through much of their history. Sometimes we actually hear support from other parade goers and marchers, but those who are hostile to this contingent often resort to gay-baiting as well as making provocative suggestions about who is really Jewish and who is not.

TREMBLING ON THE ROAD

A SIMCHA DIARY

Sandi Simcha Dubowski

SIX YEARS IN the making, my baby had a gestation period longer than a sperm whale and an elephant combined. Now when people ask me, "So what are you doing next?" I answer, "The Talmud says that when one is nursing, one shouldn't get pregnant . . . and I feel like I have twins!" I am developing other projects, but one cannot just toss a feature documentary about Hasidic and Orthodox Jews who are gay or lesbian into the wind, and not expect a wild ride. There is an outpouring of intense emotion wherever I take the film. *Trembling Before G-d*, my baby, even in its as-yet short life, has kick-started a movement across the globe. Here are stories from the world premiere at Sundance and beyond.

JANUARY 2001, UTAH

You can say the word "Sundance," and my father starts to cry. He has a bad case of *shepping naches* (feeling proud) for his son. I believe I am descended from that weeper gene in my family, so my festival tour sometimes feels like a trail of tears. Sundance began with a near-death experience and ended with Tilda Swinton and I hugging, crying, and holding each other after my final screening. She and 60 others came to the first-ever Shabbat at Sundance that Rabbi Steve Greenberg, the first openly gay Orthodox rabbi, and I hosted. On the Friday night previous, I walked from a theater to the condo, where my family and friends of the film were awaiting a private Shabbat dinner. Sandi's 20-minute shortcut wound up being a 45-minute hike—on a deer trail next to a highway—in the snow, in the dark. A truck lost control and was skidding toward me. It swerved to avoid me at the last minute. Only by the grace of G-d did I survive to attend the festival!

After a screening, a man came up and said, "I am from Pakistan. I am Muslim. I'm straight. Give me a hug," and he didn't let go. He said, "This film is about my life."

Even my prom date from high school came to see the film. I think she is quite happy we did not get married.

We held a Mormon-Jewish gay dialogue. We thought maybe 20 or 25 people would come. Instead, the room was packed. People had driven from all over Utah. Many people spoke of their excommunication from the LDS church for "conduct unbecoming a member." Millie Watts, the head of Family Fellowship, the Mormon PFLAG, was a mother of a gay son and lesbian daughter. She was like a rock and personally keeps in contact with 1,500 Mormon families who have gay children. Given that in five years of making *Trembling Before G-d* I could find no Orthodox parents of gay and lesbian children who would come forward to be interviewed, I was amazed by Millie's courage. In the room too was a Mormon family with two babies. No one could understand why they were there. An hour into the conversation, the husband says, "I had a boyfriend before I got married. I became a devout Mormon and the Church told me this would go away. I met my future wife. We kissed but did not have premartial sex. Now, five years later, with two babies, these feelings for men are not going away, and we do not know what to do." All of us were blown away. While he spoke, his three-year-old son was pulling his pants down in the middle of the room, and he was being such a sweet father, helping his son fasten his buckle while he talked. He and his wife were facing the dilemma of his sexuality with such honesty and openness.

He later wrote, "When the whole thing was over, I was amazed at the outpouring of love and comments we received. We had numerous people come up to talk to us, several with tears in their eyes. We received contact information from several people and gave ours out in return. It is kind of overwhelming to think about what happened to me today. . . . I have known for a while that I wanted to come out publicly sometime this year, but I had never dreamed it would be in quite this way . . . especially in a way that could end up getting a national audience! But even though I feel nervous about the implication of all this, I feel good inside to know that I am becoming what I want to become, a beacon of light to shine in the darkness of ignorance. I want to help make this world a better place for people like us. I want to help others see that we are not the biological errors Dr. Laura has claimed we are, nor that God hates us as Pastor Fred Phelps has preached. I want to help replace myths and ignorance with truth and understanding. I am excited to live in this day and age when I actually get to help form the foundation of a better society that future generations will benefit from. I feel like I have direction and purpose in my life. And it feels good."

I found out later he and his wife divorced. I have yet to find him since.

FEBRUARY 2001, BERLIN

On Friday night, we took over a Jewish restaurant in Eastern Berlin (yes) during The Berlin Film Festival, where we koshered the kitchen (yes). We did a Shabbat dinner with 50 people—German, Dutch, American, British, Israeli, Australian, Jews, non-Jews, gay, straight. Having Rabbi Steve lead us in a rousing *niggun* of "Chiri biri bam" was extraordinary. One felt that such song was not heard in the neighborhood for a long time. Next door, we prayed in a synagogue that had survived the war, and where the *chazzan* or cantor had presided for 35 years before the Wall fell. We then walked across the city that night back to the Western part, a two-hour trek past war memorials and museums, parks, and commerce. One of the members of the gay Jewish community in Germany accompanied us and told us that he had discovered he was Jewish just 12 years ago. His grandparents had committed suicide in 1933 on the day after Hitler's rise to power. His mother was then raised by a non-Jewish family, and he was born in East Germany.

He lived as a Christian until he discovered that she hid the truth of his Jewish identity.

He became deeply identified as a Jew, but unfortunately she destroyed any papers proving they were Jewish (not surprising) and the Jewish gay community had split between those gay Jews who had papers to prove they were Jewish and those who did not and whose identity could not be trusted. A few Berlin Jews refused to come to our open Shabbat, because they did not want to be "Jewish theater," exoticized by philo-Semitic Germans. Ironically, German police guard every Jewish institution with metal detectors and guns.

And to top it off, we won the Teddy Award for Best Documentary in Berlin. Imagine carrying a stone with a strange bear on top through customs.

APRIL, NEWPORT, RHODE ISLAND

I include here the words of Rabbi Shmuel Herzfeld, of Hebrew Institute of Riverdale, an Orthodox synagogue:

> This past week I had the very meaningful experience, which I am deeply grateful for, of being on a rabbinic retreat sponsored by CLAL [a national organization for Jewish learning]. The retreat brought together rabbis from different denominations in Judaism, and we spent a week studying together in Newport, Rhode Island. And there was one moment in particular that happened on that retreat that will stick with me for a very long time. On Thursday night, we saw the film *Trembling before G-d.* . . . As powerful as this film was, what will make the moment unforgettable was what happened after the film, when I found myself in front of 35 other rabbis, some of whom were openly gay, and I felt a need on some level to explain how I, as an Orthodox rabbi, could advocate living in a society whose laws can at times be used as a vehicle that inflicts pain on individuals who by all other standards that we know of today are entirely innocent and noble. And so I sat there and openly wept for the pain of these individuals and their families. These people are in many ways real heroes. They are engaged in an extremely serious struggle. The concepts of *kedushah* and *Torah* are ideas that inhabit their lives daily. And I cried for the tragedy that they faced such a terrible conflict in their spiritual lives . . .
>
> It becomes our responsibility to rise as a community to a level that this film showed that our wider community is not yet at—to be able to say, your actions violate our laws, and yet we will not ostracize you, we will love you the same we love all of our brothers and sisters.
>
> . . . And so my response to the film *Trembling before G-d* is that we as a community have to formulate a better response to someone who appreciates the beauty of *Torah* and *halachah* and yet lives as a homosexual.

Rabbi Herzfeld has invited us to present the film at Hebrew Institute of Riverdale. It will be our first screening at an Orthodox synagogue.

MAY, BERLIN TO KRAKOW

After a screening at the Berlin Film Festival, a small old man rose and said in a thick accent, "I am a survivor of the Shoah. I remember when I was a child in Poland and there were men without *tallises* (unmarried) who used to come to the shul for Rosh Hashanah and Yom Kippur. And they would pray and cry in the back. I asked my mother, 'Who were these men?' And she said they were the *rashas* (the evil ones). Now, after seeing this film, I know who these men are, and I want to tell you that we are all G-d's children." . . .

In May, I took the film to Poland, and I met the one gay Jew in Krakow. He was struggling with coming out and like many Jews in Poland, only discovered he was Jewish later in life. He had a nervous breakdown a year ago. With the help of two Israeli filmmakers, we had him laughing and smiling by the end, and he later wrote that the film and this experience changed his life. I decided to stay in Krakow for Shavuot and spent two hours printing out the story of Ruth from the Internet in the cramped and crazy festival office. Our little *mishpacha* stayed up learning about Ruth, a woman who gleaned from the edges of fields side by side with the other poor. In the end, Ruth spawned the Davidic line. It reminds me of a line from The Book of Psalms, "The stone the builders forgot has become the cornerstone."

MAY, MEXICO CITY

Banned in Mexico! In May, The MIX Festival screened *Trembling Before G-d/ Temblando Ante Dios* at El Cinoteca. But a special screening we had also set up at the Mexico City Jewish Community Center (the $20 million nerve center of this tight-knit 40,000 strong mainly Orthodox community) was stopped. The five Jewish communities (Ashkenazi, Sephardic, Balkan, Syrian, and Conservative) that make up the Mexico Jewish Federation had pressured the community center to cancel the screening. It was probably the first time the communities actually ever agreed (and I was grateful for at least causing Jewish unity). In a city afraid of kidnapping and robbery, where even eyewear stores are guarded by security officers with machine guns, I was reminded of the story of Sodom. Sodom was not a story of homosexuality; it was a story of sexual violence. The city of Sodom was a perfect walled city, and anyone caught giving money to the poor or being hospitable to visitors was punished. One woman was even covered with honey and fed to the bees. If you slept in a Sodomite bed and were too tall, your legs would be chopped off. If too short, you would be stretched. This was a city fortified out of fear in ways that were excessive. As I and two other gay men stood in the walled and armed community center/city the Jews had built to protect themselves against the poverty and desperation of Mexico's masses, I could not help but feel that Sodom was playing a cruel historical trick.

How many observant Mexican gay people were there, and was the community complete without them? Within all of the stones of the Mexican Jewish community, there was a rock. Luis, head of the gay Jewish group Shalom Amigos (love that) was the hero in this story. "I have been waiting for this film for 25 years!" he told us. This fearless comrade turned his El Armario bookstore into a cinema by wiring it with closed circuit TVs, and we held a fantastic series of screenings, dialogues, Torah teaching, media conferences, and meetings with Rabbi Steve and myself. Luis made one of the most dynamic experiences I have had with the film possible. Troops of Jews and others piqued by the enormous publicity continue to go to the bookstore for special screenings, and we are pursuing Mexican TV. Luis is now director of Latin American education for *Trembling Before G-d.*

JUNE, NEW YORK, ARCHAEOLOGICAL DIG

My preschool and kindergarten teacher, Rachel, came to the New York premiere, which was held on the closing night of the Human Rights Watch Film Festival. I had gone to Hebrew day school in Brighton Beach, Brooklyn, for those first formative years. No doubt it was the *brachas* (blessings) over grape juice in mini Dixie cups that set me on a path to greater observance. My parents had old Super-8 movies of me then—upside-down bowl haircut, golfer shoes, loud plaid matching pantsuit—doing the Purim play and Chanukah party. I watched them like an archaeological dig, trying to decode my little gay self and the little Orthodox Jew in bloom. All I saw was a sensitive boy who shyly watched (very telling) and by no surprise I am a filmmaker now. Of course, being parents, they transferred these precious moments to video and threw the celluloid out, causing a near heart attack on my part.

EARLY JULY, JERUSALEM

We had a major feature published in the weekend magazine of *Yediot Achronot*, the most widely read publication in Israel (75 percent of the country). The Jerusalem screening was not volatile, as we feared, but was surprisingly full of love and tears. One-third of the audience was Orthodox. Rabbis, teachers, rebbetzins, and scholars all came, and the intensity in the room was palpable. Many were turned away as the show sold out. The film was the buzz across the country. The deputy mayor of Safed, one of the four holy cities, where the Kabbalah was born, called the festival director to say that he has seven yeshiva students who wanted to see the film and how could he arrange a screening. A married gay ultra-Orthodox friend of mine (yes, married to a woman) told me that when he was praying on Shabbat afternoon in his *shtibl* (synagogue), he heard men arguing and the word "homosexuality" being tossed around. The news of the *Yediot* article spread fast, and this group could not believe that there were such things as *haredi* (ultra-Orthodox) homosexuals. My friend secretly smiled.

After the screening, we had a lively panel with Rabbi Steve and David, one of the people in the film, and then a cocktail celebration with friends, film colleagues, and supporters outside the Cinematheque, which is perched on a stunning hillside beneath Mt. Zion. It was one of those rare Israeli moments in which gay and straight, secular and religious, old and young, Tel Aviv and Jerusalem, Jew and non-Jew all mixed together in the cradle of history (over kosher food). When a group of men gathered toward sunset, and faced the walls of the Old City to pray *Mincha* (the afternoon prayer), it felt like we truly gave thanks for the day.

An Orthodox woman approached me in front of the Cinematheque a few days later. She studied me and questioned, "I know your face. Why? Oh yes, you were in the paper." Then she leaned in closer away from her religious friends, "Can you help me cure my gay son?" I took her number.

She emailed this letter later:

> B"SD
>
> Dear Simcha,
>
> I hope that you still remember me. We met at the Cinemateque in Jerusalem last week, when, following a spontaneous impulse, I approached you with my son's problem. As I told you, I am at a stage where I conduct what I call "a crusade to rescue my son" from homosexuality. I feel that it is my duty and responsibility as a mother to try everything, everybody, and every way to save him.
>
> I know that you may not be the right person to turn to, because you might be biased—but somehow I felt G-d's hand in guiding me to that place at that specific time to meet you. Speaking to you, you made such

a positive impression on me, of being such a sensitive and understanding person, who honestly does care about other's sorrow. Therefore I trust that you will try to be objective and will try to help me to help my son. . . .

There are two issues that I am very much concerned with:

1. Could you recommend to me a person/persons (rabbis, therapists, or anybody charismatic) who might be suitable to try to save my son?

2. I would be very interested to know how other religious parents did cope with this painful matter?

I did not have, yet, the chance to see your film, but I have already visited your website, and I was very impressed by the good critics and the wonderful feedback you have gotten.

    I appreciate very much your readiness to help, and I thank you from the bottom of my heart.
With warm regards,
(–)

An hour before, I met with a rebbetzin (rabbi's wife) in Jerusalem who has a lesbian daughter. I have known this wonderful family for years. Now, having seen the film, she said, "It is time. If any religious parent needs to talk with someone about their gay child, I am ready to be of help." I tried linking the letter writer and the rebbetzin up, but the first mother was too afraid to call. I just received an email that she finally mustered up the courage, they spoke, and, for the first time, she felt truly understood.

LATE JULY, SAN FRANCISCO

"Two Jews and a Baptist Will Do Anything for Tickets!" read a sign spotted outside the Castro Theater for the sold-out premiere of *Trembling* at the closing night of the San Francisco Jewish Film Festival when hundreds were turned away.

    In San Francisco, the closing night of the San Francisco Jewish Film Festival was one of the most memorable highlights of showing *Trembling*. 1,450 people packed the Castro Theater, one of the most beautiful movie palaces in the world. The firecracker Frisco audience sure lets you know through their cheering and hissing if they agree or disagree with parts of a film. *Trembling* was punctuated by plenty of cheers—the audience even clapped when Malka got the gold medal for fastest Challah braiding recorded by an Orthodox lesbian!

Some of the most memorable moments occurred after the screening when Rabbi Langer—the Lubavich rabbi of San Francisco, who 20 years earlier directed David in the film to conversion therapy to change to straight—reunited with David onstage for a tense dialogue. I give Rabbi Langer tremendous props for having the courage and willingness to face such an audience while trying to tow the line on the Torah's prohibitions on homosexuality. When he apologized to David for not having stuck with him over these years, David was shocked, and one felt their conversation in the film inched a step further. It was powerful and painful to watch Rabbi Langer struggle to comfort David while not being able to offer the total acceptance that David craved. An article in the *Jewish Bulletin of Northern California* followed, "Gay man, Chabad rabbi heal wounds."

Rabbi Langer offered to host "Friday Night Live in the Castro!"—an all-inclusive Shabbat for everyone—when I come back to San Francisco for the theatrical release.

You are all invited.

www.tremblingbeforeg-d.com

ISRAELI GAYS AND LESBIANS ENCOUNTER ZIONISM

Ruti Kadish

"IT'S NOT ENOUGH that Clinton is making the Israelis give back land to the Palestinians; now two Berkeley lesbians are destroying the moral fiber of Israel!" a friend reported hearing after sheepishly admitting that she listened to right-wing radio. I, being one of those two Berkeley lesbians, was at once comforted and disturbed by the caller's opinion.

The occasion for the radio caller's comments was the May 29, 2000, decision by the Israeli Supreme Court to recognize a second-parent adoption[1] granted by the State of California. The ostensibly precedent–setting decision generated considerable media attention in Israel, and in the international mainstream and Jewish presses. One headline, playing on the idiomatic Hebrew saying, "mother, there is only one" (*"ima yesh rak achat"*), stated that it is no longer possible to make that claim. In Israeli society where families and family life play a central role, and women are still primarily seen as mothers, the idiom carries a tremendous amount of weight and meaning. There is no equivalent idiom regarding fathers. The Supreme Court decision seemed to have an effect on, if not produce a shift in, the Israeli public consciousness of motherhood.

Now it seems that the notion of two mothers has already entered the public discourse. The morning following the decision the political cartoon in the daily *Ha'aretz* featured a young boy looking up at a soldier and holding up a card (perchance his identity card)[2] that reads, "I have two mothers." The soldier is looking down at the boy and his card reads, "I have four mothers."[3]

On Israel's version of "Who Wants to Be a Millionaire," a contestant in the hot seat wished to use his "human" lifeline. The host asked who that would be. When the contestant replied that it was his mother, the host responded, "Mother, there is only one." He immediately corrected himself: "Actually, that is not true anymore."

Interestingly, while the Supreme Court's ruling was a very narrow legal decision,[4] it was widely perceived as pertaining to and as a victory for the entire lesbian community in particular and the gay community in general.[5] Friends in the community told us that they received calls of congratulations and that their friends throughout the country received similar good wishes. The public response speaks both to the malleability and adaptability of the Israeli public, and its general willingness and desire to consider itself in step with or even spearheading social change in Western culture. Israelis seem to perceive the West in general, and the United States in particular, as more progressive than Israel. With respect to gay and lesbian issues, Israelis assume that the United States is more progressive than Israel and is, generally, more progressive than it actually is. For example, after we mentioned in interviews that we were married in California by a Conservative rabbi, the Israeli media described us as a married couple, assuming that we were indeed married and that it was possible for us to get married under California law. Israelis were generally surprised that this was not the case in California and that it was not, in fact, possible for us to marry anywhere in the United States. In some sense, then, Israelis wish to model themselves after an American model that does not (yet) exist. Thus, when presented with a concrete example of their image of Western progressivism, such as Israeli recognition of a California adoption, the public is quick to adapt.

Israeli culture is a continuous interplay between Western liberal ideals and ideologies and Zionist culture. Israeli GLBTs, as products primarily of secular Israeli culture, are very much part of this interplay. Israeli lesbians and gay men come out of the closet and live their lives against the backdrop of the gendered and masculinist history of Zionism. The concern for egalitarianism, which was a central tenet of early Zionism, was superseded by a concern with a lack of Jewish pride, which yielded a masculine nationalist ideology. The primary concern, then, of this early Zionist ideology was to produce the "new Jew." The new Jew was invariably gendered male and masculine.

In this essay, I will discuss how Israeli identity is usually presented in the gay and lesbian communities. Let me also say that Israeli lesbian and gay communities are not as homogeneous as could be understood by the following. Nevertheless, I see the behaviors I will discuss as dominant particularly in terms of popular and political representation.

"NEW LESBIAN AND GAY JEWS"

Lesbians and gay men began organizing in the mid 1970s when 11 men and one woman founded *Ha'agudah lezkhuyot haprat* (The Society for the Protection of Personal Rights), known as the Agudah.[6] Lesbians had a second outlet for their political organizing—the feminist movement. In 1986, a group of lesbian feminists founded CLaF,[7] an acronym for *Kehilah lesbit feministit*, the main lesbian organization in Israel today. The first breakthrough for the community was the decriminalization of homosexuality in 1988.[8] Since 1992, the community has made significant strides on the legislative and judicial levels, including equal protection in the workplace and the equation (in limited ways) of gay and lesbian relationships with common law marriages. In 1993, the Israeli Parliament established a subcommittee on lesbian and gay issues that brought the issue of homophobia in the military to the Knesset floor, and passed nondiscrimination regulations. In the United States, similar pro-gay legislation would likely yield a deluge of lesbians and gay men filing suit, looking to benefit from the legislation and at the same time make a political point. In Israel, in a telling fashion, these precedent-setting legislative decisions and judicial rulings have been followed by little, if any, additional litigation.[9] This phenomenon illuminates the great discrepancy between legislative and political gains achieved by a few "out" activists and the closetedness of the vast majority of the community. At numerous events, whether widely publicized or small gatherings in private homes, it is common to see participants duck at the sight of a video camera and request not to be included in pictures. Use of only first names and/or initials is common practice in gay and lesbian publications. This condition of closetedness is frequently discussed and lamented, particularly by those who are generally out. I should also say that while I find the degree of closetedness politically debilitating, I can also empathize with the fear of the very "yellow" and voyeuristic Israeli media, if less so with the fear of one's family's reaction.

Given the high level of closetedness, legal and political progressivism, however, did not translate into queer visibility in the early and mid 1990s. By all accounts, 1998 constituted the true watershed for Israeli gay and lesbian visibility, and simultaneously queer visibility also. In May 1998, Dana International, a MTF (male-to-female transgender) pop singer of Yemeni background, represented Israel in the Annual Eurovision Song Contest and won first place. Her victory ignited a celebration of queer pride in Rabin Square in Tel Aviv, the site of the Tel Aviv municipality, many demonstrations, and Rabin's assassination. Interestingly the celebration also drew numerous secular straight Israelis. In the aftermath of several cultural confrontations between religious Israelis bound by tradition and secular Israelis bound (albeit differently and with different affects) by liberalism, International's victory signified for many secular Israelis a victory for liberalism in terms of both sexual and religious freedom. It highlighted the points of intersection between the struggle for gay rights and that against religious coercion. Her victory also occasioned a reexamination (if limited) of Israeli queer identity and politics, and the relation of the mainstream gay and lesbian community to its own "others." In the edition of the *CLaF* magazine following International's victory, an editorial explained why lesbians should take personal pride in her victory. The editorial did not assume that lesbians would or should necessarily feel affinity with International or take lesbian pride in her success.

Only days later, at Wigstock, a drag-show benefit for AIDS organizations, the somewhat newly found Israeli queer community put its also newly found pride and visibility into action when the crowd physically refused to accept police attempts to end the event slightly prematurely because the Sabbath approached, in a show of physical force likened to a mini version of Stonewall.[10] The gay pride celebrations that followed these events, in June 1998, included the first-ever Israeli pride parade through the streets of Tel Aviv in which, according to police estimates, over three thousand marchers participated. Since then the numbers have increased every year.

WHAT IS ISRAELI IN ISRAELI GAY AND LESBIAN CULTURE?

Before launching into their first number at Gay Pride 1995, a member of *Bnot Pesia*, a drag group, apologized that the group was not fully present for the occasion because Eti (an unmistakably female and somewhat old-fashioned name) was on reserve duty—*anahnu beherkev haser ki Eti bemilu'im.* His announcement was received with considerable laughter. On some level there is nothing that connotes Israeli (male) identity more than reserve duty. The picture of Eti, a drag queen, on reserve duty evoked numerous associations.

The image of the Israeli man as soldier plays a central role in the Israeli cultural imagination. There is a way in which quintessential Israeli identity is representable (at least in the public sphere) only as male. The recollection of such images is almost automatic, such as that of the bareheaded, fair-haired young soldier gazing up at the Western Wall secured by the Israeli forces only moments before,[11] or those of Yitzhak Rabin as politician/soldier. These pictures became ubiquitous following Rabin's assassination.

These images epitomize the "just warrior" to use Jean Bethke Elshtain's phrase.[12] The "just warrior," unlike its counterpart the "beautiful soul," stands on its own right, yet it acquires the depth of its meaning and its very raison d'être in juxtaposition to its counterpart in the binary construction—the "beautiful soul," in other words, women. War and military action draw on "excessive masculinity." It is necessary to maintain the distinction between the (female) "beautiful souls"—wives and mothers—and the (male and utterly masculine) "just warriors," fighting inescapable wars (*milhemet ein-breira*) and upholding the "purity of arms," going to war to protect the home and the hearth, or to borrow Nira Yuval-Davis's descriptive term, protecting "womenandchildren." As Yuval-Davis and others have argued persuasively, while the military is a citizenship-certifying institution for Israeli men, citizenship is conferred differently on Israeli women. Israeli women effectively become citizens through marriage and motherhood.[13]

The paradigm I have just described certainly does not coincide with the egalitarian mythology surrounding early Zionism, wherein divisions still existed between men and women but presumably there was an effort or a desire to make the distinctions less sharp and allow some overlap between the categories. Yet, according to feminist research, it indeed describes the reality. Moreover, even despite the breakdown in Israel's national consensus and changes in Israeli culture, the binary paradigm of just warriors and beautiful souls continues to carry purchase.[14]

What is interesting to me is the extent to which gays and lesbians today as individuals and as communities have chosen to position and represent themselves vis à vis this Zionist model. The fact that these models are still those with which to identify, or against which to react, is evident in much of gay and lesbian Israeli discourse. It is striking that even the harshest critiques begin at this point. For example, in an opinion piece arguing against gay and lesbian assimilation into the Israeli mainstream the author facetiously writes, "Let's prove that we too can serve in Golani (a macho infantry/combat unit) and shoot Arabs between the eyes, and if that will not suffice, we'll show them that we are also able to contribute our share and produce a few more offspring for the next war."[15] Ultimately, then, whether one argues in favor of the assimilationist model or against it, Israeli gay men can redeem themselves on some level by being soldiers and Israeli lesbians can do so by procreating. For first, foremost, and most importantly, no matter one's sexual orientation, men are soldiers and women are mothers.

JUST (GAY MALE) WARRIORS

During the spring and summer of 1997 an often-acrimonious debate regarding community representation and community goals took place in the pages of *Hazman Havarod*. The debate over representation came mostly as a response to the perception that the Agudah appealed only to mainstream gays, those who look and see themselves as no different than straight people—other than in their choice of same-sex partners—in the hope of gaining acceptance on the basis of their "sameness." The opposition to this assimilationist position was vociferous and contiguous, but relatively limited.[16] Despite loud voices of protest, the predominant public representation of the gay and lesbian community continues to reflect the "mainstreaming" school of thought and action. As a 19-year-old Israeli gay man told *Hazman Havarod*, "I prefer that our role model be a professor or a high ranking officer, because when a son comes out to his mother, better that she imagine in her mind's eye a respected professor who she's read about in the paper rather than Dana International."[17]

In early 1993, Knesset member Yael Dayan, head of the subcommittee on lesbian, gay, and bisexual issues,[18] initiated what was to be the first annual "Pride Day at the Knesset." The community chose two representatives to speak at this landmark event, Uzi Even, a middle-aged gay chemistry professor at Tel Aviv University and high-ranking officer in the IDF reserves, and Sharon Gershoni, a young lesbian university student. Even's national coming out created shock waves in the queer community and in the general public. Even, as an upstanding citizen and a decorated soldier, challenged stereotypes about gay men. Even's commanding presence, his deep voice, and his dignity were still commented on six years later, at the 1999 Gay Day at the Knesset. Several speakers pointed to Even's coming out as a watershed in their own identity as Israeli gays and the identity of the entire community.

Thus both the selection of Even, and the politics he represents, are illustrative of the way in which gay men and some lesbians wish to be seen and the politics they wish to advance. Even embodies the union between Zionist masculinity and gay male visibility. The attention paid to Even's status as a soldier both by the gay community and the media also points to the way in which gay men share in the common perception of, and weight given to, "Israeli man as soldier." While on some level there is a certain breakdown in this collective perception of Israeli (male) identity (indeed there are those who say that the very proliferation of gay images and gay visibility in Israeli culture is made feasible by that breakdown), the soldier is still never far from the surface.

BEAUTIFUL (LESBIAN) SOULS

In the summer 1998 issue of *CLaF Hazak* (the lesbian quarterly), the cover page depicts "lesbian pioneers"—a group of women dressed in farming clothing, gathered on a tractor. Bales of hay, a rainbow flag, and an Israeli flag serve as a backdrop. The caption reads, "Idioms such as 'salt of the earth,' 'builders of the State,' refer usually to men and not to the women fighters, to the women who dried the swamps, to the women pioneers and new immigrants that built this country with their blood and sweat." The editorial board then explained that the cover was designed to coincide with Israel's fiftieth anniversary and to express gratitude for and appreciation of 50 years of women's work in building the State. The cover and caption proudly asserted the position of Israeli lesbians, as women, within the Zionist pantheon. The editorial board of *ClaF Hazak* asserted a nationalist stance that may be viewed as in conflict with the feminist ideology of the organization. The policies of the journal state that the editorial board rejects themes that are offensive to members of oppressed groups, and statements that reinforce negative stereotypes. Despite *CLaF*'s egalitarian, feminist mission statement, in my research I found no negative response raised before or after publication of this issue of the magazine. The nationalist statement certainly comes in conflict with feminist activity in the women's peace movement undertaken by many of *CLaF*'s founders and the anti-nationalist political positions held by many of them.

Feminist lesbians involved in the larger feminist movement founded

CLaF. Most of these women were also involved in leftist politics and took part in, if not spearheaded, much of the work of the Israeli women's movement in the 1980s and early 1990s.[19] Many of the lesbian activists, as lesbian feminists, saw themselves as situated outside the mainstream, working against the system, as it were. As peace activists, nationalist claims were invoked only insofar as they lent credence to the call for peace, in other words, "as Israeli citizens we demand that the government listen to our opinion." This is far different than priding oneself in one's role in the Zionist project. Indeed, many of those women involved in the feminist movement and the burgeoning lesbian community saw the relationship between the two as not only "natural," but also necessary. In *Lesbiot*, a volume of oral histories of Israeli lesbians, many of the interviewees expressed an ambivalent relationship with their identity as Israeli nationals.[20] In a number of interviews, the women saw their work in leftist politics as integral to their identity as lesbians. Several women noted the disproportionately high representation of lesbians in peace activism. Several of the interviewees expressed awareness that being lesbian in Israel is on some level being "other" but, fundamentally, it is not *the other*—that position is occupied by Palestinians. Being one step removed or not the ultimate other has allowed lesbians both maneuverability and a certain degree of acceptability.[21]

The link, however, between leftist politics and feminist lesbianism is by no means a given. Indeed with the growth of the lesbian feminist community, and perhaps also with its increased acceptance in the general population, the connection is all but disappearing, which partially explains why the aforementioned *CLaF Hazak* did not illicit any negative public response. *CLaF* became a different organization, and while its mission statement remained as before, its direction changed. *CLaF* activities were more directed at personal and individual needs. The focus of *CLaF*'s activities on relationships, motherhood and becoming mothers, and families was an expression of the changing needs of *CLaF*'s members. These issues reflected the daily reality of many Israeli lesbians.

While during the late 1980s and early 1990s many lesbians accepted and internalized the belief that lesbian identity negated the possibility of family life with children, in the late 1990s the lesbian community began experiencing a full-fledged baby boom. Thus, whether deliberately or not (or at times both), as an organization, *CLaF* moved in a significant way into the mainstream, as part of the Zionist pantheon, rather than in opposition to it. *CLaF*'s political efforts toward securing recognition for lesbian relationships and families, and guaranteeing lesbians equal access to reproductive technologies, were effectively guaranteeing lesbians the same rights as heterosexual women to participate, in Lesley Hazelton's telling phrase, in "the cult of fertility,"[22] or in Yuval-Davis's terms, lesbians too can be "bearers of the collective."[23]

"STRAIGHT" LESBIANS AND GAY MEN

Dana International not withstanding, what the community offered the public, as coined in the local gay press, was *homoim straitim*, or straight gays.[24] As the family unit and "being coupled" maintain their revered status in heterosexual Israeli society, so too are they revered and aspired to among Israeli gays and lesbians. In this sense, Israeli gays and lesbians correspond with the national ethos. "[I]n Israel," writes Bat-Ami Bar On, "the Jewish-Israeli family has been among the material and ideological cornerstones of the Zionist nation-building project."[25]

Within the community there has been criticism of the assumptions regarding "coupleness" (*zugiyut*) and families. For example, at a *CLaF* panel discussion on the topic of relationships (spring 1999), three of four panelists assumed the centrality of relationships in lesbian lives. The fourth panelist, a woman in her early twenties, questioned both that assumption and the emphasis placed in the community on the topic in general. She asked the participants to consider why it was assumed that monogamous and long-term relationships were desirable. She charged that these assumptions excluded and delegitimated any and all alternatives, and silenced those who lived differently. She argued that lesbian identity was by definition outside the normative construction of gender, and seen as "other" by the general population. Lesbians, then, have the option to refuse to participate in the overdetermined construction and centrality of the family in the national imagination.

I suggest, therefore, that the current expectation and desire to "wed" and bear children (which is present in differing ways and degrees in the gay male community) stems from the internalization, even in the lesbian community, that becoming a mother is constitutive of the role and identity of an Israeli woman. Thus, even Israeli lesbian desires are socially mediated and nationally constructed. Considering again the aforementioned panel, I would venture to say that the panelist's critique is not about any individual desire to create a lesbian family, nor is it a critique of the efforts of the lesbian community to enable the possibility in terms of accessibility, legal protection, and recognition. The critique attends to the unreflective focus on these issues, almost to the exclusion of all else. In its political efforts, the community has emphasized its "sameness" or "likeness" to heterosexual Israelis. It has put forth its "best face," the "showcase" as one panelist phrased it—the perfect family: professional, middle class, mostly Ashkenazi. In short, but crucially, gays and lesbians present families that could "pass." And what of those who do not pass? What of those who choose not to pass? In articulating and defining a collective lesbian (and gay) identity, who has been othered?

At this point, it would behoove me to situate myself vis à vis this discussion. I could and have been charged with creating and perpetuating such a passing paradigm. I married a nice Jewish lawyer to whom I sometimes refer as my wife. My partner and I have two children, a dog and a cat, and I drive a minivan. We have been called suburban dykes and white-picket-fence lesbians. We have been reassured, only half jokingly, that it is only our lesbianism that saves us from our blandness and conservatism. I am always already conscious of the ways in which I am implicated in the mainstream lesbian politics I describe here and how I benefit from them and have come to depend on their achievements. No doubt we have benefited personally from the achievements of those who have come before us in securing legal protections such as second-parent adoption, for which I am tremendously grateful. I am not suggesting here that we abandon these causes. I am calling here for an assessment of what it is we are presenting when we present ourselves, and who is the "we" that is presented and represented. We cannot afford to forego the more radical politics. At the same time, I would not argue that all need to engage in all forms of political activity. Rather we need to recognize the benefit in, and encourage, the pursuit of multiple agendas in variegated ways. There is room and necessity for lesbian and gay liberal politics and for Queer Nation and everything in between and at either end.

PROVISIONAL CONCLUSION

In conclusion, these last questions occupy an important place in Israeli gay and lesbian discourse. While the mainstream models I have laid out here are, in my mind, still the dominant models of Israeli gay and lesbian public representation, a significant portion of the community is aware of the limitations of and dangers present in advancing solely positions that argue for and depend on "sameness."

But, on the other hand, we are made acutely aware of the extent to which even our so-called mainstream and palatable representations are abhorrent to some, and in the face of sometimes vicious homophobia, our assimilatory acts acquire a radical edge. As Oren Kenner has written, "For the religious authorities in Israel, for example, there is no difference between a masculine and a feminine gay man, or between a gay man who lives with his long-term partner and a gay man who sleeps with a different man every night." When Knesset member Avraham Ravitz distributes an article to all Knesset members in which he describes gays as "perverts, sick, weak of character, social failures, and disseminators of AIDS," then our ostensibly mainstream and liberal politics serve a radical function. And finally, on a personal note, at the moments when I feel I have sold out to mainstream middle-class respectability, I am partially and curiously vindicated by the words of the caller with which I opened this essay. At the risk of overstating the case, I would be proud to consider our political efforts in the area of GLBT rights as integral to the project of *tikkun olam*, repairing the world, of which I consider giving back territories to the Palestinians, among other things, to be a part.[26]

NOTES

1. Adoption of the biological or nonbiological children of a lesbian by her lesbian partner is termed *second-parent adoption*. This applies also to adoption by two gay men. This type of adoption, available in some of the United States, does not replace the mother with the adoptive mother. Rather, it gives both women the legal status of parent with all the attendant rights and responsibilities. In Israel, this is not yet possible.

2. The case revolved around the issue of the Ministry of Interior's authority to not register the second-parent adoption in the identity card of the adoptive mother and the child. In Israel, every citizen is issued an identity number at birth or upon being granted citizenship. One's identity card and computer file lists all personal information including parents, children, nationality, and religion.

3. Four Mothers was a women's political organization that pressured the government to withdraw from Lebanon. For cartoon, see *Ha'aretz*, May 30, 2000, op-ed page.

4. The legal issue at hand was whether the State of Israel would recognize an adoption granted abroad. Effectively, then, it was a Full Faith and Credit Issue rather than a challenge to Israel's adoption codes. In other words, the legal question was comparable to the recognition of Reform, Conservative, or nonreligious weddings marriages performed abroad and recognized by the State even though such marriages are not available in Israel.

5. The use of the term *Israeli gay and lesbian community* requires explanation. I use the term because it is representative of some form of community, even if this so-called community is ever changing with multiple and overlapping segments and fuzzy boundaries. Moreover, the term *the community* is used by Israeli lesbians and gay men to refer to a body that they do or do not relate to in different ways. In this study, I

speak to and of those who fall into this category. In June 1997, *Ha-zman ha-varod* (*The Pink Times*), the second-ever Israeli queer monthly, published since fall 1996, published a list of "65 Things Every Gay Man and Lesbian Need to Know." They described the community as follows: "A random term. Assessments on the size of the community range from 10% to 1% of the State's population. In reality we are talking about a collection of sub-communities (those who are active, the partiers, the closeted, CLaF [lesbian feminist organization], autonomous and unknown groups, geographical groups, trannies) who share a similar sexual orientation, but have diverse and different definitions of their identity" (*Ha-zman ha-varod*, no. 9, June 1997, 5).

6. Until 1988, homosexual sodomy was a criminal act under Israeli law. When the initial members sought to register their group, whose name included the word homosexual, with the office charged with registering nonprofit associations, they were informed that, because homosexuality itself was illegal, they could not register a group with the term *homosexual* in its name. The ostensible, coerced closetedness was in fact embraced by a significant number of the members for many years. Only in 1997, nine years after the decriminalization of homosexuality, did the organization change its name to The Association of Gay Men, Lesbians, and Bisexuals. In 1998, transgender was added.

7. I use the English spelling used by *CLaF*.

8. On the decriminalization process, see Yuval Yonai, "The Law Regarding Homosexuality—Between History and Sociology," [Hebrew] *Misphat u-mimshal— Law and Government in Israel*, no 4. (1998).

9. The Danilovitch case, where Danilovitch, a gay EL AL flight attendant, sued the airline for spousal benefits given to heterosexual couples is an important exception to this statement and also proves the rule. On the Danilovitch case, see Aeyal Gross, "Challenges to Compulsory Heterosexuality: Recognition and Non-Recognition of Same-Sex Couples in Israeli Law," forthcoming. On gay rights in Israel in general, see Lee Walzer, *Between Sodom and Eden: A Gay Journey through Today's Changing Israel* (New York: Columbia UP, 2000), pp 13–57.

10. For a detailed description of the events, see "The Israeli Stonewall," *Ha-zman ha-varod*, no. 21 (June 1998): 7–15.

11. To my surprise and delight, this famous photo of the soldier and his comrade, arm slung over his soldier, gazing up at the Wall, is used in the logo of several sections in *Ha-zman ha-varod*. See, for example, *Ha-zman ha-varod*, no. 32 (May 1999): 3, 16.

12. Jean Bethke Elshtain, *Women in War* (New York: Basic Books, 1987).

13. For a fascinating discussion, see Nitza Berkovitch, "Woman of Valor, Who Will Find?: Women and Citizenship in Israel," [Hebrew] forthcoming in Yoav Peled and Adi Ophir, eds., *Israel: From an Enlisted Society to a Civilian Society*. In addition, two recent books exhaustively demonstrate the centrality of motherhood to Israeli female identity, and the ways in which politics, culture, and religion all intersect in producing the centrality of motherhood, maintaining it, and reifying motherhood as the very meaning of Israeli citizenship for women. See Susan Sered, *What Makes Women Sick? Maternity, Modesty, and Militarism in Israeli Society* (Hanover and London: Brandeis UP, 2000); Susan Martha Kahn, *Reproducing Jews: A Cultural Account of Assisted*

Conception in Israel (Durham and London: Duke UP, 2000).

14. On women in the Israeli military, see Nira Yuval-Davis, "Front and Rear: The Sexual Division of Labor in the Israeli Army," *Feminist Studies*, vol. 11, no. 3 (Fall 1985): 649–676. On the construction of gender identity in Israel, see Barbara Swirski and Marilyn P. Safir, eds., *Calling the Equality Bluff: Women in Israel* (New York: Pergamon Press, 1991).

15. Oren Kenner, "Ahad Ha'am, Corner of the Community," in *Ha-zman ha-varod*, no. 12 (September 1997): 4.

16. Oren Kenner, quoted earlier, is arguably the most consistent and eloquent critic of the assimilationist model.

17. Lital Weinbaum, "The Next Generation," *Ha-zman ha-varod*, no. 14 (November 1997): 7.

18. The subcommittee operates under the Committee for the Advancement of the Status of Women.

19. An unofficial assessment suggested that lesbians account for at least 40 percent of the Jewish women involved in Women in Black, a weekly vigil against the occupation, begun in early 1988, two months after the beginning of the Intifada.

20. Tracy Moore, ed., *Lesbiot: Israeli Lesbians Talk about Sexuality, Feminism, Judaism and Their Lives* (London: New York: Cassell, 1995).

21. It should also be noted, however, that acceptability is always contingent and liminal. At Women in Black vigils, for example, some of the common epithets hurled at the participants by passersby were alternately "lesbians!" or "You sleep with Arafat." The link between the two is that in both cases the inference is that Women in Black do not sleep in the collective (heterosexual) Zionist bed. By being politically active, the participants effectively reject their national role as mothers and wives in need of protection. Their opposition to national policy in fact unsettles and calls into question the foundational paradigm of "just warriors" and "beautiful souls," and threatens its legitimacy. National identity is thereby linked with respectable and acceptable sexual (or desexualized) identity. Interestingly, similar sentiments were directed at Women at the Wall after the Israeli Supreme Court decision in the spring of 2000 allowing a women's prayer service at the Wall.

22. Lesley Hazleton, *Israeli Women: The Reality Behind the Myths* (New York: Simon and Schuster, 1977), chapter 2.

23. Nira Yuval-Davis, "The Bearers of the Collective: Women and Religious Legislation in Israel," *Feminist Studies*, 11 (1985): 15–27.

24. *Ha-zman ha-varod* recorded this debate. For example, after Israeli president Ezer Weizman made homophobic comments during a speech to high school students, and the political flurry that ensued, the community debated the nature of its response. There were those who charged the representatives of the community with being too apologetic and mainstream in their approach to the heterosexual public, attempting to sell themselves and the community as straight gays.

25. Bat-Ami Bar On, "Sexuality, the Family and Nationalism," in *Feminism and Families*, Hilde Lindemann Nelson, ed., (New York: Routledge, 1997), 221–234. Bar On

argues that liberalizing trends in the Jewish-Israeli family are what enable gays and lesbians to forge their way within this rubric. To some extent I agree with Bar On. I would also add, however, that the breakdown of the national consensus regarding just wars, and the changing political realties in the region, have also chipped away at Zionist ideology and mythology, thereby facilitating the surfacing of alternatives, sexual and otherwise, which previously posed a threat to that very mythology.

26. The Israel lesbian and gay community has generally associated itself with the political left, albeit the mainstream left (labor/Meretz). Nevertheless, the community as a community has not been outspoken regarding the peace process and Palestinian/ Israeli relations. Aeyal Gross, responding to the escalation of violence between Israelis and Palestinians in the fall of 2000, writes about the relation between the gay and lesbian community and the situation. "The identification of gays and lesbians," he writes, "with the struggle of all oppressed groups, demands that the community now stand for the human rights of Palestinians within Israel and in the territories. Our interest in an Israel that has room for all the colors of the rainbow demands that we put ourselves in the forefront of the struggle for a true and honest peace." *Ha-zman ha-varod*, no. 47 (December 2000): 6.

ALL POINTS BULLETIN

JEWISH DYKES ADOPTING CHILDREN

Marla Brettschneider

WE ARE JEWS living in Maine. We are also dykes and we were living in New Hampshire. We had to move. Until recently, New Hampshire would not let people adopt children if there was a person thought to be gay living in their household. You could be as straight as an arrow, but if you had taken in your Great Aunt Tilly, a raging bisexual in the 1930s, someone could cause trouble and the state could deny you that kid. We didn't have a Great Aunt Tilly. We were out and rather public, politically active queers. It would be difficult for a rabbi and a professor in a small New England town to be in the closet even if they wanted to (which we didn't and which we weren't), so adopting children was simply not an option as long as we lived in New Hampshire. We picked up and moved a mile, over the border into Maine. That's how we made it possible to have Paris (Peretz is her Hebrew name) in our lives.

In 1997, New Hampshire finally passed a law including sexual orientation in its civil rights code. Around the same time, Maine passed a similar law, but the Christian Right organized like mad and succeeded in overturning it. The difference between the Maine and New Hampshire cases is that although

Maine repealed its gay civil rights law, it never had a specific ban on homosexuals adopting children. Despite New Hampshire's newly passed "gay" civil rights code, the ban on queers adopting was not originally overturned.[1] Basically, we had to give up our newly won general civil rights in order to have the specific right to adopt kids. Admittedly, it is a complicated story. A Jewish lesbian couple that wants to raise children will usually have a complicated story.

I am a professor at the University of New Hampshire, an activist, and writer. My partner is, among other things, the rabbi in the university town. We're Euro-American Jewish dykes living in rural Maine with an adopted child of African heritage. I have been asked often to write about my experience in the adoption world. Thus far, however, I have only been able to think in response: where could I possibly begin? Folks often assume we faced "interesting" challenges being lesbians. What most do not seem to realize is that we faced as much resistance to our adoption plans because we are Jewish. Most people in the United States simply don't want their biological kids to be raised by Jews. Because adoption is a big business, agencies in many states are therefore not going to waste their time taking on Jewish clients.[2]

Queers generally seem to know that they might face obstacles creating families through adoption. I've tried to understand why most Jews don't know the situation for other Jews. After all, Jews are doing a somewhat disproportionate amount of the adopting in the United States relative to our small percentage of the population.[3] I think the reason has to do with the fact that most Jews who want to adopt children either utilize the services of Jewish agencies and/or live in cities or other places with large Jewish populations. The agencies they use generally know that Jews can't adopt in most places, and the adoption workers therefore know to focus on the organizations that will work with Jews. Prospective parents are rarely informed of all the details involved in creating an adoption placement. Jewish prospective parents must also, therefore, not know the politics of anti-Semitism that frames their opportunities negotiated at the agency level.

With our "highly normative" profile as Jewish queers in a state with very few Jews, we were largely left to our own devices. I had to do the research to find the services and the available children out there, tasks that most Jews in cities can delegate to their adoption agencies. With a lot of research, I found a number of agencies and brokers happy to work with queers, Jews, older people, those without tons of money, folks who had been arrested protesting at the Pentagon in the 1960s and were thus shut out of most of the adoption world for having a criminal record, and individuals with some aspect of their health histories that sparked irrational biases of many state-paid social workers. Occasionally I found the kindness of a stranger along the way. These random moments of kindness significantly helped me to stay on course. I needed those moments badly because most of what I found in my foray into the adoption world was ugly. I'll say it again: ugly.

We moved over the state border into Maine, a state where a gay person can legally adopt children, in late November 1988. I called the Department of Human Services adoption office right away to get the process rolling. I wanted to be up front from the start that we were gay in order to help avoid homophobic surprises later. A senior state employee then told me all the reasons that, although Maine does not discriminate, they would likely have trouble placing children with us. Every sentence she uttered began with the phrase, and I quote, "Although the state of Maine does not discriminate on the basis of sexual orientation," and then proceeded with examples of why we would not be considered as fit parents for hypothetical little Janie, Dexter, Matilda, and Lewis.

I got concerned. It occurred to me that I might as well come out about being a Jew too. Same response. "Although the state of Maine does not discriminate on the basis of religion," we would not be considered fit parents for Mary, Chris, John, and Kathy. The woman further explained that it was her job to determine what was in the best interest of the child. Because there are no children in the Maine state system born to Jewish parents,[4] her office would be left to determine what was a good fit. Since every child in the state system would have been, more or less, raised Christian, it was up to her to evaluate just how important Christianity had become to the child. Although (U.S.) Americans pride themselves on, in Thomas Jefferson's words, "putting a wall of separation between 'church' [need I say more] and state," U.S. institutions are de facto Christian institutions. Any child in the state's care will most likely have attended state-sponsored Christmas parties, been sent an Easter basket, been blessed by a Christian clergy member, been brought to church on Sundays, or received any manner of Christian instruction and influence. This meant that she could potentially claim we were "unfit" parents for any child in the system.

Our chances looked bleak. I began to do some research. In 1988, the Child Welfare League of America issued a policy statement saying, "Gay/lesbian adoptive applicants should be assessed the same as any other adoptive applicants. It should be recognized that sexual orientation and the capacity to nurture a child are separate issues." Despite this, innumerable instances of discrimination occur against queers trying to adopt. I learned that queers sometimes waited for years to have children placed with them. In states where it is not expressly illegal for homosexuals to adopt children, there are likely to exist numerous homophobic practices foreclosing placement options for queer clients. Individual social workers and/or local adoption bureaus might accept funds and applications to do homestudies from queers wanting to adopt children, but be either unwilling or unable to negotiate placements on their behalf. Although not expressly or legally prohibited outside the state of Florida anymore, many other states *practice* discrimination and will reject applications from those whose homestudies state or suggest that they are queer. The politics of anti-Semitism may work similarly, though often operates within a specific field of prejudices and practices.

Queers find it difficult to adopt children due to a set of intermingling homophobic assumptions about who queers are, what they believe, and most especially how they live. Queers are still too often thought to be, for example, unstable, anti-"family," predators of children, poor role models for the young, and without morals or religion. On this score, stereotypes about Jews often come together in a "pro-family" cluster. Some of the stereotypes of Jews in the United States are that we have strong families and "good" family values. We are presumed to be smart, education minded, emotionally stable, economically successful, drug and abuse free, and tradition and family oriented. When it comes down to it, however, many Christians still would not want Christian children sucked into one of those "good" Jewish families. It's like the straight people who give a lot of money to the AIDS walk but freak out if their kid comes home with a rainbow sticker on their car. Not for my daughter. Not for our children.

Yes, there are hundreds of thousands of children drowning in foster care.[5] There are tens of thousands of children yearning to belong to new healthy families.[6] Yes, the state works very hard to find adults willing to adopt the overload of kids in their dockets. We, like many Jews and queers, were happy to take kids in all sorts of the categories the states deem "hard to place" and "special needs." Unfortunately, we probably would not have any kids placed with us. I realized we would have to find a private agency and pay sizable sums.[7] So much for my desire to be a good citizen, to work with the state, and also receive the medical benefits and other support offered to children placed in adoptive families by state agencies. I suppose that I shouldn't have found it surprising: minorities too often wind up with extra financial, and other resource-draining, burdens. Due to discrimination, we would not be working through the state and would be required to employ numerous levels of inter- mediaries and brokers, and to hire costly lawyers specially trained in discrim- ination and adoption law instead of using our resources on our hoped-for child. When we had a child, we would be ineligible for an array of free or sub- sidized health care, special needs, and childcare programs, financial allowances, and free placement follow-up services made available through state agencies.

I make my living writing about and working against injustice including especially racism, sexism, homophobia, anti-Semitism, and classism. But if anyone had tried to explain to me the depths of the hierarchies of human worth at work in the adoption world, I admit even I might have found it dif- ficult to believe. Some of the ugliest aspects of U.S. versions of discrimination and dehumanization are crystalized in the trading in human beings that all too frequently occur in the adoption world. There are clear hierarchies of human worth in this country, and the adoption world has done the market research, assessed the situation, organized a filing system, and very neatly attached price tags to services and humans according to their appropriate rank. I was constantly surprised by the intensity of the biases in play, and shocked by the unabashed and "matter of fact" manner in which agencies marketed the biases. What follows are some examples from my personal experience and research.

We, as the prospective adoptive parents, faced these forms of privilege and discrimination in complex ways. As Jews and queers, we were effectively dis- qualified from consideration in large portions of the country. We also very much benefited from a stratified and hierarchical social system in other ways. We are both highly educated, with seven (and soon to be eight) advanced academic degrees between the two of us. Despite being Jewish, we are also both Euro heritage, often enough enabling us to engage in the great "American" pastime of passing. "White" in the U.S. means "white-Christian." My partner and I are both "white enough looking" so that average (U.S.) Americans can sometimes forget the fact of our Jewishness, which they find so inexplicably disturbing. We appear somewhat healthy and young enough. Finally and significantly, we were able to pretend we had a sufficient amount of money to support ourselves and the bundles of joy we hoped to raise.[8] Discrimination operates in multiple imbricating ways. We faced negative bias just as we also tapped into aspects of privilege that are denied other likely "perfectly fit" and loving people who want to adopt children.

Our being a presumably monogamous couple also contributed to our "privilege." "Family" in U.S. ideology largely means a *set* of parents, so that even if we are queer and Jewish there are at least still two of us. This plays out in specific ways for Jewish queers. Often queers seeking to adopt children as singles, not as part of long-term couples, may "benefit" by presenting themselves as "just" single, leaving heterosexuality presumed and therefore avoiding being targeted as queer. This is usually of more assistance for women, as women are assumed to "naturally" want/need to be mothers. Surely, women's single status may call into question their ability to provide a proper (read: with a male) home. Even so, they can still rely on social institutions and ideas that seek to fulfill the natural destiny of women: to be mothers. Single women are at times even favored as it is assumed that they will have more of a capacity to focus on the well being of their children. The assumption is that these women will not be harried by the divided loyalties heterosexually married women have between their demanding children and their demanding husbands. For a number of years, for instance, single women were looked upon favorably for these reasons in adopting children (girls) from China. With all this, however, single women are still stigmatized for being so in family building, particularly where the state plays as large a role as in adoption. Men face a different set of biases. Single men are presumed to be potentially dangerous to children. They are seen as a threat to the physical safety of children as single men are presumed to be gay . . . and therefore child molesters. Single people generally may also be seen as a potential threat to the moral development of children because it is assumed that they will expose their children to "inappropriate" sexual behaviors otherwise safely hidden within the legal arrangement of single-partner marriage.[9]

There is a further consideration regarding the benefits for and biases against singles adopting. The multiple factors of discrimination make it difficult for many people to fit the mold sufficiently on their own. Single people who want to adopt children, therefore, may have fewer chances than couples do to arrange the details of their life stories to make the grade. As a couple, my partner and I could pool our resources of privilege, and work to deflect our individual "deficiencies" as categorized in society by highlighting the other's socially constructed "proficiencies."

In our case, my partner has the dubious advantage of having been raised Christian. This means that anti-Semitic Christians can sometimes excuse her self-identification as a Jew because they can classify her as not "racially" Jewish. They think of her Jewishness as "a religious thing." In fact, to many

Christians, she's just an interesting *kind* of Christian. Not having been born (here race retains its biological base) Jewish, they don't project all of those "problematic" Jewish racial characteristics on to her. Those they reserve for me. Christians presume that she can "understand" them more than other Jews can, they may feel "more comfortable" with her when they find out she is a convert to Judaism. Further, they do not necessarily interpret her strength and intelligence as superior, overbearing, rude, devious, and untrustworthy. They do not necessarily equate the financial stability they demand with trickery, usury, or miserliness. There are likely many contributing factors to this aspect of her acceptance, though that she avoids biologically based racial stereotypes of Jews figures largely. Also, my partner is a member of the clergy, a rabbi, and (although people don't always know what to make of women religious leaders) this scores points. But that Jew thing often still gets in the way. For example, many people in "America" don't know what a rabbi is, so she often misses out on the clergy perk.

Despite my partner's many publications, high-profile and prestigious positions, and despite the fact that she has always supported her needs just fine, she was concerned about her financial credibility. This is a situation common to many women, especially those working as professional Jewish feminist dykes. Women rabbis generally earn less money than their male counterparts for the same work, when they can get it. Despite the large institutional apparatus of U.S. Jewry, full-time or adequately paid positions with any benefits are a rarity for women Jewish professionals, and even more so for out lesbian and bisexual women. As a full-time tenured professor, I'm the one with the more normative financial profile and I happen to have a health history that looks "nicer" on paper. I'm the one within the requisite age spread agencies deem acceptable between adoptive children and parents. (Though the fact that Dawn "looks" younger than she "is" explicitly helped us when our agency showed our photographs to birth parents.) Is it any wonder that I'm the one the homestudy names as "parent-to-be," while my partner is given the shifting labels "other adult who resides in abode," "partner," or " legal guardian." Once we entered into the maze of adoption laws and markets, "family planning" in its conservative manifestations designed through instances of state structures, ideologies, and practices, forced society's power hierarchies further into our home and relationships than they had been before.

The standards by which adults are measured, however, barely compare to the intensity of the racism, in its many forms, which charts the life course of children and prospective children in the adoption world. After all, if no one picks them, prospective parents still have their homes, lives, and autonomy. There are services to help cope with disappointment and depressive responses to "childlessness." A kid who doesn't get chosen is likely destined to a living hell. These are children who end up being bounced around foster homes and state institutions.[10] What makes certain children "undesirables?" Children who are considered "special needs." This designation may be limited to children with health "issues" or physical "deformities." The classification of children as "special needs" or "hard to place" also usually includes young people older than infant age,[11] who are not white,[12] and/or who are to be placed with their biological siblings. Children are considered "undesirable" if the system labels their birth parents "riffraff." As will be discussed further below, this means that children may be deemed "undesirable" if their birth mothers were the victims of violence and poverty. These designations apply but are not only related to battery and sexual assault, drug use, IQ, education level, job/welfare status, truancy, prison record, mental and physical health, as well as the racial makeup, legal status, and "coherence" of the biological mother and her birth family. Occasionally such information is gathered and disclosed about fathers (biological or legal).[13] Generally, the state and other adoption workers do not attend to the status of fathers the ways they do birth mothers.[14]

In the state system, there are thick books (usually three-ring binders so they can be updated easily) with page after page of information on individual waiting children. Each page has a photo of a child and some facts about race, history, and health status. Each page is dated with the month and year the child officially entered the system and became a waiting child. Each state has a book and large cities often have thick binders separate from those of their state. The stats are like war records. Private little wars. Children scarred from abuse, neglect, violence, and poverty. Children suffering unending physical, psychic, and emotional syndromes as a result. But four-year-old Stanley has improved greatly since his placement in foster care three months ago. Ten-year-old Shanika likes to help with the housework. You will find pages of older black kids with comparably few war stories. They are still in the system simply because being black makes you a "special needs" child and hard to place. As I said, there is much that is ugly, and exposed, in the adoption world.

In the private adoption world, there are a number of agencies that specialize in African-American or Latina/o infants. This can be helpful for those who want to adopt minority children. It is also necessary because many more agencies will only trade in white kids, based on so-called market demand.

Due to the lack of domestic supply of white children compared to the demand, international adoption is a special favorite of white folks.[15] These people may take incredible risks to adopt children from Bulgaria, Romania, and the former Soviet Union. They want a newborn but will compromise on a two year old. The information they are given is too frequently unreliable, the orphanages are often in terrible condition, and the adoptions are extremely expensive.[16] For some Ashkenazi Jews, adopting a child from these parts of Europe feels like a connection to their past. The prevailing logic in the United States is, however (inscribed within the class bias regarding the distinct class positions of the parties in an adoption): who wouldn't pay up to $50,000 for a white kid? Many agencies play up the idea that the domestic pool is too small for the white demand. Why wait? Go to Eastern Europe. There are thousands of kids waiting to be adopted domestically; they just aren't white.

Certainly many people who choose to adopt Latina/o children are doing so as a result of much self-conscious and race-critical research. However, some white folks get involved in very questionable deals trying to adopt children from Latin and Central/South America. I have heard many people who identify as white say (either explicitly or implicitly), "Well, they look almost white and if they are raised by us, they won't even have those accents." Some prospective parents specify "white looking" or "light skinned" when they agree to pursue adoption options from Central and South America. On a related note, stealing children and trafficking in babies from the south is a terrible reality for many poor women from the southern western hemisphere. I know many people who have adopted children from Latin America who have made certain that the birth families of the children offered to them actually did put these kids up for adoption. Many people, however, do not undertake such investigations.

Another favorite for white folks is to get kids from Asia. Chinese girls, kids from Vietnam, Korea, and Cambodia are some current favorites. Many white adults in the United States who adopt children from Asia do so out of a sincere commitment to social justice and love that crosses constructed racial difference. However, given the fact of so much racism, particularly in adoption, I was interested to learn about this option more broadly. As with other "racial" preferences, I questioned many individuals and adoption workers in an effort to understand this practice. The prevailing logic in the adoption world appears to be that, whether domestically or internationally, Asian kids come in only one rung lower on the ladder of racial worth than Latina/o children who can pass as white. U.S. racial classifications categorize "Asians" as a distinct group with presumed distinct phenotypes. Despite the presumption that racism is about excluding those with nonnormative (in the U.S. case, a cluster of characteristics grouped as relating to the peoples of Europe) observable features, racist stereotypes operate on many levels. In this example, discrimination against Asian children for the fact that they will "stand out in white society" is occasionally offset by other stereotypes. The primary factor here is that (U.S.) Americans think Asians are smart.

Related to the partial desirability of those from Asian countries is the phenomena that Native Americans are also somewhat desirable. Prompting cultural genocidal policies for centuries, European/white people in the United States often think that Native Americans can be made to "look white." Children born to Native American parents are commodified as "almost white" in the adoption world by the ideological fiat that given the "proper" cultural upbringing, Native Americans can be just as white as the biological children of white parents.[17] Further, in current practices, propaganda as advertising is used to enhance the desirability of Native American children by suggesting that one can basically raise these children to be white, but retain certain commercially advantageous public claims to their Native American bloodlines. These advertising strategies in the adoption world rely on and reinforce the growing tendency for U.S. whites to appropriate and commodify Native American history and customs.

Sometimes racial classifications in the adoption world separate and categorize children into two groups: white and nonwhite. In these instances, all children of color are put into a common set of files distinct from white children. Other times a different classification is utilized. Many agencies have three sets of dockets: white, colored, and black.[18] Whether brought together officially with other nonwhite children or distinguished as a class unto themselves, African, African-American, and African-Carribean children have a problem. Their problem is the racism of others. In the adoption world as in many other realms, black often signifies race itself. Many scholars and activists have discussed this notion. Let two examples from the adoption world suffice here to demonstrate this tendency. First, when children are classified as "biracial," this does not generally mean that they are biracial in any way. In "adoption speak," this term usually does not refer to a child who may be any combination of white, Latina/o, indigenous, or Asian. The term is generally used to refer to a child who is any part African heritage. In these situations, it is not only significant that black is the signifier of naming race as a matter of import, but the issues of power at stake. Naming a child biracial to call attention to blackness alerts consumers in adoptions (in other words, prospective parents) of the "quality" of the goods in a system of racial hierarchy. To be part *black* means that one's adoption costs less than that of most other children. To be *part* black can also be cause for an agency to raise the price of the adoption above that for "all black" children because nonblackness is a desired commodity.

Transracial adoptions domestically are another example wherein blackness signifies race.[19] For sure, many white people adopt nonwhite children.[20] However, when domestic transracial adoption is treated as something to be problematized, it is almost always regarding the adoption of black children. As with the case of mixed race children, it is not only the blackness that is significant but the power relations involved in a system of racist discrimination. Basically, what are referred to domestically as "transracial" adoptions involve white adults adopting nonwhite, and usually black, children. The notion of a minority family being eligible for a white child is almost a joke in the adoption world.[21]

All minority children are devalued in the U.S. adoption world. However, as blackness still most likely defines race itself, children of African heritage, whether domestically or internationally, are treated as a (extra with regard to other minority children) special case. Agencies commonly charge less to adopt black children, because they say "people will not pay as high rates for black children as for other children." Sometimes adoptive parents are actually paid to adopt black children, this in a huge money making industry. Thus, although black women give their children up for adoption at the same or lower rates than women of other racial groups,[22] black children are overwhelmingly disproportionately represented among those the state makes eligible for adoption, they will usually wait longer to be adopted, and are less likely to ever get adopted than children of other races.

Race is a central matter of concern in adoption, though as I said above, there are hierarch*ies* of human worth at work in the adoption world. For example, along with race in the private system, there are gradations of health risk. Health risks and other factors are determined largely with reference to health and status issues for the child's birth mother—for example, drug, alcohol, and tobacco use during pregnancy. There are gradations related to class locations, the birth mother's amount of schooling, and/or her "intelligence." Adoption workers also prepare bizarre calibrations presented as tradeoffs: birth mother used alcohol at times during pregnancy but is college educated;

birth mother is schizophrenic but is white and from a "good" (meaning middle-class) family. There are gradations and then there are price tags to fit.

Technically it is illegal to pay for a child. One can pay the expenses of a birth mother: her rent, medical expenses, maternity clothes, counseling, sundries. It does not take a Ph.D. in math to realize that the sums do not add up to the thousands of dollars prospective parents are often required to pay. When you hear of people paying $20,000 to $50,000 for an adoption, that money is mostly not going to the women who bear the children. For example, in cases I have seen, in a $20,000 adoption, approximately $1,500 may go to the birth mother. The majority of the money billed to prospective parents in an adoption generally pays fees of agencies and lawyers. While supposedly working to enforce an ethic that humans cannot be bought and sold, the government ignores the large fees paid to agencies. In U.S. law and custom, the money paid to birth mothers is seen as buying humans. However, money paid to agencies is protected as free market capitalism. Most women give their children up for adoption due to poverty and an assessment that their class/life circumstances will not improve. There are agencies who will find jobs and homes for women once they sign over their legal parental rights. Our culture does not sufficiently support women before they reach the point of considering adoption.

These birth mothers lack the resources to live their lives independently and to support the children they are trying to raise or are pregnant with. It is the agencies, however, that make the money. There are a very few organizations that provide care, housing, counseling, and other services to pregnant women in need that might be thinking about surrendering their parental rights. They work with women to help ensure that adoption is the best solution, while giving women concrete support to see if they can redirect their lives and possibly care for children. These efforts are woefully understaffed, underfunded, and too infrequently available and advertised to the women in need. Sexism, racism, violence, poverty and classism, our cultural inadequacy to educate and deal with sexuality, gender power differentials, and reproductive choice all contribute to self-fulfilling doomsday predictions of unwanted pregnancies. Anti-abortion policies, negative attitudes regarding and obstacles to safe and affordable contraception directly complicate women's capacities to make choices about conceiving, birthing, and raising their biological children.

Among other factors, race also fundamentally affects the manner in which birth mothers are treated. In general, to be sure, women who choose to give their children up for adoption or whose children are forcibly removed from their care by the state face social stigmatization. Society tends to view and treat all these women badly as they challenge the notion that women *are* mothers naturally and that mothers represent all that is good and wholesome. As class plays a large role in women's "choice" to put their children up for adoption and in the state's assessment of which women are "fit" to parent, poor women across race suffer with regard to adoption practices in particular ways. Poor (and/or uneducated) women across racial groupings will have less access to adequate care (medical and psychological) and material support than wealthier women in adoption bureaucracies. They are less likely to be treated with respect and have their rights and dignities honored. Having said this, race continues to make a significant difference among birth mothers in adoption bureaucracies regardless of class. Women from racial minorities are generally likely to face the circumstances I mention of poor women and more. Beyond stigma and racist assumptions about their status (as illicit sexually, irresponsible, and so on) minority women are likely to receive less medical attention and be treated worse by health care professionals. They tend to receive less attention from agency social workers, and be given less information about their rights and about prospective adopting parents. Minority women as birth mothers are more likely to be treated in a paternalistic manner and their participation less solicited in choosing adoptive families and the circumstances of the adoptions. They are also likely to receive smaller portions of the funds paid by prospective parents than are white birth mothers.

So what happened with us? In August, we got a call: you are mothers. Our agency in Maine was contacted by a southern agency with two girls, sisters, available for adoption. Jews and queers cannot usually adopt children from the South. As the self-proclaimed Bible Belt, the U.S. South is generally written off as practicing conservative, ideologically based discrimination. But here we were being offered children from the South. We were overjoyed. As siblings, as "older children," as Creole/African Americans, the girls were considered "too hard to place" and with these unusual circumstances, we were contacted. We went into full swing to make this adoption happen, working with Scott, the head of the southern agency, who prepared us to talk with the birth mother. She knew we were a lesbian couple. She had had some concerns, but Scott had talked to her and smoothed things out. I asked if she knew we were Jewish. I had been briefed that in meetings with birth mothers you are usually expected to talk about your religious beliefs and how you plan to raise the children. No, Scott replied, the birth mother did not know that we were Jews. We were surprised and inquired as to why. The head of her agency told us that he thought it would jeopardize the placement. This was a problem and also probably illegal as law requires disclosure of all relevant information to both birth parents and to prospective adoptive parents. Religious affiliation is a standard piece of information that disclosure laws require. If particular state laws are vague on the details, the general ethic in the industry is that religion is considered "relevant" information.[23] We reminded the agency director of this, but he said that he had put too much time into arranging this placement already and he could not afford for it to fall through. He would stand to lose too much money and would have to start looking for another placement all over again. He found this particularly problematic as his family and that of his coworker were about to go on vacation for a few days together and he did not want to disrupt their plans. He continued to refuse to tell the birth mother that we were Jewish because he "knew" that she would then refuse us. Despite the hard-sell approach, there were further complications. We lost the girls.

The next fall we received a call from social services (the state agency that was so concerned about protecting the interests of Christian children). In Maine, prospective adoptive parents have to register formally to be foster parents in order to adopt children. We were asked if we would take in a little boy who was coming into their custody. Nathaniel did not fit the profile we had signed up for at all (as we were forced to make many choices over time, we eventually were slotted for older, African-American girl siblings). We said yes anyway. They said they might bring him over that night or the next morning. We said, "Great!" So they told us more about him. One of his birth parents was from a Native American tribe in our region. I inquired how they had worked through the process of offering him to non–Native American prospective parents so quickly. According to federal law, the state must protect "Indian" "children who are members of or are eligible for membership in an Indian [sic] tribe" by working to place them in Native American tribes. The federal government passed this law in the direct interest of the children and the tribes. The law states clearly that "an alarmingly high percentage of Indian [sic] families are broken up by the removal, often unwarranted, of their children from them by nontribal public and private agencies and that an alarmingly high percentage of such children are placed in non-Indian [sic] foster and adoptive homes and institutions." The worker on the other end of the phone said that they did not bother to try to place Nathaniel within his or any other tribe. She reminded me that it is within her purview to determine what was best for the child. It would take "too long" to try to find a Native

American family to adopt him, in her estimation being bad for the child. The law notwithstanding, his lifetime interests and identity concerns notwithstanding, the rights of his kin and the tribe not withstanding, they were offering him to non–Native American families. I said we would be happy to take him (assuming that if he was offered to us as foster parents, at least *we* could try to work something out), but how could they ignore this constellation of needs, let alone the law? Needless to say, the foster care worker placed Nathaniel with a different (nontribal) family.

We had a number of other possibilities that all fell through. Word got around in our region about the Jewish dykes in Maine trying to adopt kids. I received a call from GLAD, the Gay and Lesbian Advocates and Defenders, which had begun researching discrimination in adoption for people who faced multiple barriers in adoption. The GLAD lawyer explained that they wanted to be able to work on GLBTQ concerns, where they also overlapped with other aspects of discrimination. Would I help? I told her that we still had not been able to adopt children and that I did not want to jeopardize our prospects. I had decided while still in New Hampshire that I would help fight discrimination in adoption, but not put our own process on trial as a test case. The GLAD lawyer told me that it was enough now to write up a report on being lesbian and Jewish for their records only. I told her I would do it. (And I did.)

We got another call from our caseworker. This time she had waited until further along in the process before she contacted us. The family knew we were queer. They knew we were Jewish. They had picked us. Increasingly, domestic private adoptions work by the birth parents choosing the adoptive parents, and then the prospective parents get to choose back. We chose back. On the last night of Chanukah 5760, December 10, 1999, Paris Mayan Brettschneider/Rose was born. She's beautiful and happy. She comes with me to the meetings of the UNH Presidential Task Force on GLTB issues, which I chair. She takes naps during the meetings of the Jewish queer thinktank I coordinate. She comes with us to services at Dawn's *shul* (synagogue). Paris goes with Dawn to the rabbinical seminary, where Dawn is on faculty. Paris traveled all over Israel with us last summer, where we went to give lectures for Bat Kol, a feminist yeshiva run by a lesbian couple who are both rabbis. Basically, Paris comes with us everywhere . . . everywhere her out, loud, political Jewish lesbian moms go in the course of their wanderings. People can't help falling in love with her, even total strangers. She's great, and we are truly blessed to have her in our lives. We have already begun the paperwork to try it all again. We think Paris will love having a little sister.

This is some of our story adopting Paris. I also want to note that over the years of our involvement in the adoption world laws, practices and attitudes have continued to shift (though not always in clearly laudable ways).[24] With all the problematic aspects, there are also so many wonderful ones. I find many practices in the adoption world awful, but still think that adoption is a beautiful blessing. There are many caring and informed people seeking to challenge the hierarchies operating in adoption processes. Specifically with respect to the Jewish and queer communities and how they engage also with issues of race, class, and health bias, there are numerous efforts to change social norms.[25] These people, agencies, and organizations need to be supported. I hope that, in some small way, telling aspects of my experiences will help enable more work to challenge the system and provide better care for children, birth mothers and families, and prospective and adoptive families.

NOTES

This article is dedicated to Dawn Rose and Paris Mayan Brettschneider/Rose. I want to thank my family, the editors of this volume, my fall 2000 graduate assistant in the University of New Hampshire Political Science Department, Shiju Cui, Mary Bonauto from GLAD, our adoption agency MAPS (Maine Adoption Placement Services), and our caseworker Gayle Merlin Knee. This is the first in a series of articles the author is writing on adoption.

1. With the change in the New Hampshire law, Florida remains the only state with a formal prohibition against homosexuals adopting. Adults wanting to adopt children in the state of Florida must sign an affidavit declaring that they are not homosexual.

2. As of 1992, 127,441 children were adopted in the United States. The National Adoption Information Clearinghouse 1996 reports that the largest group are adopted by stepparent or other relatives (nearly half). Approximately 37 percent were handled by private agencies or independent practitioners such as lawyers. 5 percent were children adopted from other countries. In the following discussion, I am generally referring to what is commonly called "stranger adoption," or the approximately 42 percent of adoptions not done within the children's existing families (either by blood or marriage).

3. The Evan B. Donaldson Adoption Institute estimates that between two and four percent of families in the United States have adopted children. The 1990 National Jewish Population Study estimates that more than three percent of the children in Jewish homes had been adopted.

4. There are very few children of Jewish parents eligible for adoption in the nation as a whole. Many of these have special needs. The Jewish Children's Adoption Network (JCAN) places about a hundred children born to Jewish mothers in Jewish homes. About 85 percent of those placed have special needs, or have been abused, neglected, or abandoned. (As reported in *Star Tracks*, the newsletter of Stars of David, Vol. 16, No. 1, (2000): 5.)

5. According to the data collected by Adoption and Foster Care Analysis Reporting Systems (AFCARS) released by the Children's Bureau of the U.S. Department of Health and Human Services, as of January 2000, there are approximately 520,000 children currently in foster care.

6. According to the AFCARS data, 117,000 of the children in foster care are eligible for adoption. The data on both the number of children in foster care and those available for adoption represent increases.

7. Jews and queers are often disqualified from denominational/Christian agencies, though adoptions through them tend to be less costly than other private means. Nondenominational private agencies and "independent" (such as through lawyers) are the most expensive methods of adoption. Adoptions, particularly of white newborns, can cost up to $50,000. Adoptive Families of America estimates that nondenominational and other private adoptions tend to cost on average $15,000. Whereas working with public agencies is usually free, or requires minimal fees, or adoptive parents may be eligible to receive subsidies.

8. Adopting children is a competitive enterprise. In 1997, the National Center for Health Statistics reported that there are approximately five adoption seekers for every actual adoption. Perhaps not surprisingly, those most likely to adopt are white women with higher than average levels of income and education.

9. The "structure" of families adopting children as collected by AFCARS is revealing: married couples 66 percent, unmarried couples 2 percent, single females 30 percent, single males 2 percent. These figures obscure the numbers of gay and lesbian singles and couples adopting as the majority adopt as "singles" to avoid naming a gendered partner.

10. AFCARS reports in 2000 that the mean length of time children spend in foster care is 46 months.

11. AFCARS 2000 reports that the average mean age of children waiting to be adopted is eight years, and over a quarter of the children are over ten years of age. This bodes ill for the children as the Voluntary Cooperative Information System reports that the younger the child, the more likely he or she will be adopted from foster care. For example, over half of finalized adoptions were of children between new born and five years old. The numbers go down to 7.7 percent of the children between 13 and 18.

12. The average racial breakdown of children in foster care is 43 percent African American; 36 percent white; 15 percent Hispanic; 2 percent American Indian/Alaskan Native, and Asian/Pacific Islander; 4 percent unknown. The average racial breakdown of those in foster care needing adoptive families is 51 percent African American; 32 percent white; 11 percent Hispanic, 2 percent American Indian/Alaskan Native, and Asian/Pacific Islander; 5 percent unknown. (Notice that Jews are not a category.) Compare these percentages to the population at large. In the year 2000, the U.S. government census estimates that non-Hispanic whites comprise 74 percent of the population, non-Hispanic blacks 12 percent, Hispanics 10 percent, non-Hispanic American Indian/Eskimo/Aluet 0.7 percent; and non-Hispanic Asian/Pacific Islanders 3.3 percent. The U.S. census gathers no data on the percentage of the population that is Jewish.

13. In *Reproducing the State* (Princeton University Press, 1999), Stevens discusses the multiple designations of fatherhood, mostly biological and legal (through marriage to a child's biological mother). Her research demonstrates that the state privileges legal fathers over biological ones. This can make information on waiting children's "fathers" more complicated to obtain.

14. Martha Morse Rawlings has done excellent research on and analysis regarding the mutual construction of race, class, and gender in the ideological construction of focusing on mothers. She looks at African-American teen women's choices of who to impregnate them according to skin tone and asks whether such choices are adaptions or resistances to caste, classism, and racism. ("Reconstructing Identities: The Utility of Adolescent Pregnancy," Race, Gender, and Class Conference, October 28–30, 1999, New Orleans.)

15. The United States is the largest receiving country of adoptees from other countries, actually more than all other nations combined and nearly double the amount from a decade ago. (*Boston Globe* 9/21/00.) The numbers of children adopted to U.S. adults from other countries in 1999 was 16,396 (as reported by the U.S. Immigration and Naturalization Services and the U.S. Department of State). The logic of the national distribution will be discussed below. The countries most frequently adopted from are Russia, Romania, then Guatemala, China, and Korea. International Concerns for Children reported in 1996 that on average, adoptions from Eastern European countries such as Russia and Romania are most expensive, then "Hispanic" countries such as Guatemala and Columbia, then Asian countries such as China, Korea, and Vietnam. U.S. adoptions from countries with black populations such as Haiti, Ethiopia, or other African states cost on average one-half to one-third of those from other regions.

16. In 2000, the United States ratified a new international law for international adoption called the Hague Convention on Intercountry Adoption. (See *Boston Globe* 9/21/2000, "Senate Ratifies Treaty Setting Global Adoption Standards".) The treaty "establishes the first global standards intended to protect children from being sold and mandates cuts in bureaucratic red tape for finding them homes." The *Globe* reported that the treaty had "the support of an unusually broad coalition of groups." However, U.S. ratification of this international treaty was held up, for example, in the House by Christopher Smith (a Republican from New Jersey) because he wanted the legislation to explicitly "preclude adoptions by homosexuals, unmarried Americans, and people with 'promiscuous lifestyles.'"

17. This logic has contributed to the lucrative black market in stolen Native American babies being passed off as "white" to white U.S. prospective parents. A personal account of the involvement of Jews as consumers in this market is told from the perspective of a stolen child in Yvette Melanson's *Looking for Lost Bird: A Jewish Woman Discovers Her Navajo Roots* (New York: Bard, 1999).

18. Whites adopting children who could not be passed off as white is a relatively new situation in adoption reflecting a slight shift in racism among the white majority in the United States. Since the civil rights movement, however, there also have been intense debates about whether transracial adoptions (to be discussed below) are good or bad.

Minority communities wanted an end to discrimination, but at various times publically opposed transracial adoptions. For example, since the early 1970s, the National Association of Black Social Workers (NABSW) has put forth the view that it is not in the best interests of the children and the black community for black children to be adopted by white people. Many states do not do transracial adoptions—based not on the logic of the NABSW but on the logic of white supremacy. There have been laws passed (and some repealed) attempting to address racial discrimination in adoption. However, many agencies nevertheless practice discrimination as a matter of course. (As will be discussed below, adoptions involving Native American children are treated under separate laws than those aimed at ending discrimination against other racial minorities.)

19. I specify U.S. domestic adoptions purposely. Although many international adoptions are also "transracial," these are usually referred to by the euphemism "international." Note that the word race is not invoked. International transracial adoptions usually involve white adults adopting Latina/o or Asian children. As international adoptions rarely involve black children, the term *transracial* is used less frequently.

20. Different studies report various percentages of transracial adoptions. To give readers an idea of the range, in 1995, The Child Welfare League of America reported a slightly higher level than other studies at 4 percent, though states such as New York may have yet higher rates of transracial adoptions.

21. According to the latest National Surveys of Family Growth data (from 1995) in the comparison between white and black women's preferences, fewer white women seeking to adopt would accept black children than black women who would accept white children, and almost none (1.8 percent) of the white women prefer black children. Thus, the joke is not that minority adults would not prefer or accept children of other races, but that the system deems absurd having a white child raised by nonwhite parents, while it considers white people as potentially fit parents for minority children.

22. According to the National Center for Health Statistics in 1999, there has been a decline in the numbers of women giving their children up for adoption. This is largely due to the dramatic drop in white women relinquishing their children (from 19 percent in 1965–1972, to 1.7 percent today). Relinquishment rates for Black and Hispanic women have remained basically constant. The rate for Latinas has been consistently at or under 2 percent. The current figures for black women relinquishing their infants for adoption is less than 1 percent, meaning that African-American women actually relinquish their children for adoption less frequently than white women and Latinas.

23. For example see the Maine statute (8205) on collection and disclosure of information in adoption cases.

24. For example, between our search for Paris and our search for her sibling, we learned that many adoption agencies had abandoned their policies offering black children at cut rates, believing that such practices reinforced racism. Some have argued, however, that certain agencies have done so more for financial gain. As transracial adoptions becomes less stigmatized, agencies find they might be able to charge more money for minority children. At the same time as the "formal policies" might be changing in

some areas, many of the same agencies still end up charging half or otherwise lower prices for black children, suggesting the disingenuousness of "looking good" formally, but still responding to a market in which they assess "people (meaning whites) won't pay full price for black kids."

25. Although I cannot vouch for all of their practices and individual workers, organizations such as Jewish Family Services, which also has an Alliance for Adoption division, or other Jewish family and children services with adoption resources offices, Stars of David (a national organization with local chapters, which makes available many resources on the Web, on paper, and in their newsletter *Star Tracks*) and the Jewish Social Service Agency (JSSA) are all helping Jewish families adopt and are increasingly open to queers and multiculturalism. The Jewish Multiracial Families Network is doing important work helping multiracial Jewish families, many created through adoption, build community and address bias. GLAD, other queer and ally groups, many local activists and legislators are working to end discrimination against queers in adoption and foster care and seeking to connect these struggles with anti-racist ones.

"NEXT YEAR IN FREEDOM!"

TAKING OUR SEDER TO THE STREETS

Jo Hirschmann and Elizabeth Wilson

And the more one dwells on the Exodus from Egypt, the more one is to be praised.
RABBI NATHAN GOLDBERG, *THE PASSOVER HAGGADAH*

PASSOVER, IN THE words of the Seder in the Streets Haggadah,

> is the Jewish holiday that celebrates resistance and the struggle for liberation. Each year, Jews gather in our homes to re-tell the story of Exodus—the story of the Jewish peoples' deliverance from slavery in Egypt. Passover is the holiday of remembrance, the holiday of asking questions, the holiday of re-committing to the struggle for the liberation of all oppressed people. We know that freedom comes only through struggle. Although the Jews are no longer slaves in Egypt, we live in a world where liberation struggles are as important as when Moses parted the waters of the Red Sea.[1]

This Haggadah was written for a 1999 outdoor Seder that was organized by a dozen radical young Jews in the San Francisco Bay Area. The Seder in the Streets formed part of the international effort to free Mumia Abu-Jamal, an African-American journalist, former member of the Black Panther Party, and political prisoner who is on death row in Pennsylvania. The two of us were part of this organizing committee. Our group hoped to add a Jewish voice to the campaign for Mumia's life and freedom; to invoke the Passover liberation story in the service of the campaign to free Mumia; and to retell the story of Ethel and Julius Rosenberg, radical Jews and the last political prisoners to be executed in the United States. We have written this essay to document the Seder in the Streets, and to explore our commitments as politically active and religiously observant queer Jews. It is not intended to represent the beliefs of the entire organizing committee. Rather, it presents our reflections on the Seder in the Streets, our relationship to Judaism, and the ways in which our queerness and Jewishness fuel our political work.

Four important themes undergird our experiences and commitments as queers, Jews, and leftists. First, we understand the connections between multiple forms of oppression, and we are committed to pursuing a broad-based agenda for freedom and liberation. We are inspired by people who look beyond the narrow confines of single-issue and identity politics, and who have the courage to create political programs based on the premise that no one is free until everyone is free. We especially encourage Jews and queers to regard tackling anti-Semitism and homophobia as parts of a broader agenda for liberation. We see the connections between the racism that fueled Mumia's arrest, incarceration, and death sentence, and the anti-Semitism and vicious persecution of Communists that propelled the state-sanctioned murder of the Rosenbergs. As queers, we do not forget the rampant homophobia that was part of McCarthyism's toxic mix.[2] And as Jews, we will not forget slavery in Egypt, the pogroms, or the Holocaust.

Second, we regard our queerness as a call to political action. We are committed to participating in the work of ending the exclusion, hatred, and violence that lesbian, gay, bisexual, and transgender people face in almost every corner of society. Tackling homophobia and transphobia requires that we use every available tool to further personal and political transformation. We call on queer and transgender people to use our words, minds, hearts, and bodies in the service of our liberation—and the liberation of all oppressed communities. Freedom and justice for queer and transgender people is intimately connected to freedom and justice for people of color, working-class people,

women, immigrants, disabled people, and youth, not least because many people's lives cross multiple communities. The liberation of all oppressed communities is dependent on our ability to forge unlikely alliances, and we expect
queer and transgender people to rise willingly to this challenge.

Third, we are committed to raising difficult issues in Jewish communities
in the United States. We call on all Jews to engage in examination of the
Torah and our liturgy and to take responsibility for the problematic aspects of
our tradition. In our own practice and congregation, we welcome a religious
observance that is feminist and queer positive; and we place women, lesbian,
gay, bisexual, and transgender people at the center, not the margins, of our
liturgy and practice. We are committed to nurturing Jewish communities that
welcome queers and queer families—people who are at best made invisible
in, at worst outright excluded from, mainstream Jewish life. We encourage
Jews to wrestle with the parts of the Torah (including Exodus) that justify
oppressing other communities in order to make our home in the Promised
Land. We are committed to anti-racist and anti-imperialist politics in the
United States, in Israel/Palestine, and around the world. We cannot support
the displacement, persecution, and outright murder of Palestinians that mas-
querades as "freedom" for Israeli Jews. With regard to race politics in this
country, we recognize that somewhere between 85 percent and 97 percent of
all Jews in the United States are Ashkenazi,[3] which means that the majority
of Jews in this country are of European descent, have white-skin privilege,
and benefit from the class privilege that often accompanies it. We take a
stand against the complacency that often follows white-skin privilege and
middle-class values. We also recognize that not all Jews are white. Indeed, as
Melanie Kaye/Kantrowitz writes, "Jews are often defined as white, though
this wipes out the many Jews who are by anyone's definition people of color,
and neglects the role of context: many Jews who look white in New York City
look quite the opposite in the South and Midwest."[4] As Ashkenazi Jews, we
stand in solidarity with our Mizrachi, Sephardi, and mixed-race Jewish sisters
and brothers.

Fourth, we are inspired by the challenge of creating a political practice that
is grounded in faith. We do not think that belief in G-d or observance of religious practices alone will solve all of our planet's problems, and we know that
social, economic, and political understandings of the world are also required.
But we regard Judaism as a guide for compassionate living, vigorous questioning of the world, and serious political struggle. We are especially moved
by the Exodus story: its annual recitation at Seders, its relevance as an alle-

gory for contemporary liberation struggles, and its basic teaching that G-d sides with oppressed and exploited people.

The two of us brought these four political and religious principles to our participation in the Seder in the Streets organizing committee. This predominantly queer group was composed of young Jewish labor and community organizers, teachers, popular educators, cultural workers, and students. The organizing committee was predominantly white and, for all of us, our Jewish heritage is Ashkenazi. About half of the members of the organizing committee had met regularly over the previous year to study and discuss Zionism, the creation of the state of Israel, and the Palestinian liberation struggle to further our development as politically conscious, anti-Zionist Jews. Many of us in the organizing committee come from families with radical histories: parents, grandparents, or great-grandparents who were Communists in the United States or Europe. We talked about our experiences of meeting large numbers of left Jewish activists in our political work. We discussed our impression that many of these activists are secular Jews who have a strong affinity to Jewish culture but not to Judaism as a religion.

For the two of us, as observant Jews, helping to organize the Seder in the Streets was an opportunity to bring our political activism and our religious lives together. We were especially excited by the opportunity to combine religious ritual and political action against a contemporary injustice. Although the two of us followed very different paths of religious and political development, we were both embarking on the life-long process of exploring the intersections of faith and politics. Elizabeth grew up in Manhattan, the daughter of an assimilated, third-generation German-American Jew, and of a refugee from the Holocaust. She inherited her parents' progressive politics and her father's desire to hold onto the familiar rituals of European Jewry. She attended an Orthodox *shul*, excelled at Hebrew school, and was not allowed to chant from the Torah at her Bat Mitzvah. She came out as queer at 21, while at college, and gradually found her way into campus and community activism. After coming out, she returned to the *shul* of her childhood for Rosh Hashanah services one year, only to find the rabbi condemning homosexuality from the *bimah*. After moving to San Francisco (the obvious destination, she thought, for a 22-year-old gender-deviant dyke), she became more deeply involved in political activism, especially with a group of radical teachers working for educational equity. Meanwhile, Congregation Sha'ar Zahav, San Francisco's queer synagogue, presented opportunities to deepen her connection to Judaism and to recapture the religious fervor of her childhood *shul*.

Jo grew up in the United Kingdom. Her father is a British Jew and her mother an Irish-American Catholic. Both her parents are committed atheists, and Jo was not religiously educated in either tradition. She grew up with few Jewish role models, and her main connection to Jewishness and Judaism was via the shadow of the Holocaust. Among many of her school peers, the word "Jew" was a term of abuse that meant parsimonious. As an obviously "Jewish-looking" child, she was aware of gradations and hierarchies of "whiteness," and it was clear that the few children of color in her predominantly white, Christian environment faced pervasive and blatant racism. She became an activist—fueled in part by her knowledge of her own queerness— at age 14 and spent her teenage years exploring the Labour Party and antinuclear, environmental, feminist, and queer politics. She started coming out to herself at 14, to other people at 16, and fell in love with the San Francisco Bay Area at 19. She moved to San Francisco in her early twenties to do antipoverty and human rights work. She joined Congregation Sha'ar Zahav and started to find ways to live Jewishly and think about how a Jewish theology of liberation could enhance and support her political work. By the time the Seder in the Streets organizing committee started meeting, both of us were beginning to find ways to build internal bridges between the disparate parts of ourselves.

Among the members of the organizing committee, the level of Jewish religious practice ranged from observant to secular. We hoped to create common ground between the secular Jews who have a strong presence in social movements, and religious Jews who participate in traditional Seders. Traditional Seders often exclude any political content, instead focusing on gratitude for the miracle G-d performed for the Jews, and the vengeance wreaked upon the Egyptians. We hoped to help traditional Jews understand modern liberation movements, such as Mumia's struggle against the racist criminal justice system.

By organizing the Seder in the Streets, we also hoped to build bridges between Jewish communities and communities of color (communities that are not mutually exclusive). We were especially struck by the centrality of the Exodus story to black liberation theology. Cornel West explains that black Christianity developed in the United States in the context of brutal slavery. He writes, "The African slaves' search for collective identity could find historical purpose in the exodus of Israel out of slavery."[5] Indeed, Harriet Tubman was called "the Moses of her time" in recognition of her courage and bravery in operating the Underground Railroad. She traveled back and forth on the Underground Railroad 19 times and brought more than 300 slaves to freedom.[6]

Unfortunately, we underestimated the challenges of organizing in faith communities—both our own and others. We didn't realize how difficult it would be to organize congregants of synagogues and churches of which we are not members. As a result, we were not as successful as we had hoped to be in meeting our goals of building bridges between different sectors of the Jewish community and between Jews and people of color. With hindsight, we can see that the Seder was no more and no less than a useful building block in the generations-long process of overcoming the distance between communities that are taught to distrust each other.

Our group joined a long Jewish tradition by creating a Haggadah, the Passover prayerbook of stories and blessings that accompanies the Seder, for the Seder in the Streets. According to Alfred Kolatch, more than 3,500 versions of the Haggadah have been published since the thirteenth century, when the first one appeared in book form.[7] Each contains alterations to the text, to make the Haggadah meaningful to a particular community. We used several existing progressive Haggadot, as well as our own writings, to compose a Haggadah that stresses the liberatory aspects of the Passover story.[8] We interspersed traditional blessings and songs with the retelling of three stories: the biblical Exodus from Egypt, the fight of Mumia Abu-Jamal, and the struggle and execution of the Rosenbergs. We explained the symbolism of the ritual foods in ways relevant to those involved in political struggle. For example, we introduced the blessing over the parsley with these words:

> We now pass out the Karpas, the parsley, that represents the spring,
> renewal of life, and with it, the renewal of our commitment to struggle
> against oppression. Please take a piece of parsley that has been dipped
> in salt water. The salt water represents the tears of oppressed and
> enslaved people everywhere. While we eat this combination, we
> remember that tears accompany change, rebirth and struggle.[9]

At the Seder, held outdoors in downtown San Francisco's United Nations Plaza, 200 Jewish and non-Jewish activists braved an unseasonal hailstorm and bitterly cold winds to attend. We spent the earlier part of the day preparing enormous amounts of Passover food. We passed out huge plates overflowing with sprigs of parsley, bitter herbs, and Hillel sandwiches (a sandwich of matzah, bitter herbs, and sweet charoset). We read the Haggadah and collectively blessed and ate the food. Two women acted as cantors, leading the assembled people in prayer and song. Mort Sobell, the Rosenbergs' codefendant, who was wrongfully imprisoned for over 18 years for his refusal to perjure himself and make up a story against the Rosenbergs, attended the Seder. Now in his eighties, Mort inspired us as a Jewish elder of the movement. He gave a moving speech about the McCarthyist witch hunts of the 1950s and his ongoing commitment to the struggle for liberation. At the end of the ritual, in the spirit of the Passover tradition of opening our doors to the hungry and needy, we served enormous vats of matzah ball soup to everyone in UN Plaza, including the large numbers of homeless people who make their home in downtown San Francisco.

We concluded the Seder with the words, "Next year in Freedom!" to express our hope for, and commitment to, the possibility of a better world. Progressive and radical Jews often say these words at the end of a Seder to remind us that although another year has gone by and the world still has not been redeemed, the coming year heralds infinite possibilities for change. As part of this commitment to a better world, we chose to organize our Seder in Mumia's name. In 1999, Mumia had been on death row for 17 years and his case was—and still is—at a critical juncture. We knew that the weight of public opinion would be a key factor in whether Mumia wins in court. We were also struck by the disturbing similarities between Mumia's case and that of Ethel and Julius Rosenberg. We wanted to call on the Jewish community to defend Mumia as one of our own. Using biblical imagery, we told Mumia's story in our Haggadah:

> [Mumia Abu-Jamal] moonlighted driving cabs in downtown Philadelphia. . . . One night in 1981, he drove by an all-too-familiar scene: [A] young black man was being harassed and beaten by a white police officer. Upon closer inspection, Abu-Jamal realized that the young black man was, in fact, his brother. He ran from his cab to find out what was going on. Ten minutes later, ambulances arrived as Abu-Jamal and the police officer, Daniel Faulkner, lay bleeding in the street.

> Officer Faulkner died. Abu-Jamal was shot in the stomach, and survived after surgery. He was immediately charged with first-degree murder of a police officer. . . . The case against Abu-Jamal was riddled with inconsistencies, blatant violations of due process, and, perhaps most disturbingly, a concerted effort on the part of the district attorney to use Abu-Jamal's political beliefs to build a murder case against him. . . . Abu-Jamal was convicted and sentenced to die by a jury that was over 90 percent white.

> For 17 years, Mumia Abu-Jamal has continued to write and speak out
> from death row. . . . [He] has continued to raise his voice from behind
> steel and concrete, telling the system not only to free him, but to let all
> of his people go.[10]

There are disturbing parallels between Mumia's story and that of the
Rosenbergs. Because of this, we felt strongly that Jews have a special imperative to raise our voices in defense of Mumia. It often seems that Jews easily
forget, or never learn of, the lives and deaths of Ethel and Julius Rosenberg—
despite the Passover teaching that we should hold onto our memories of
oppression. We wanted to use the Seder in the Streets to highlight the U.S.
government's deadly commitment to silencing dissent, and to remind the
Jewish community about the murder of the Rosenbergs. Our Haggadah
reads:

> This Passover, as we eat matzah and remember the struggles of our
> ancestors for freedom, we bring particular attention to the memory of
> Ethel and Julius Rosenberg. The Rosenbergs, both of whom were
> members of the Communist Party, were executed by the U.S. govern-
> ment at Sing Sing Prison on June 19, 1953. They had been convicted in
> the Rosenberg-Sobell Atom Spy Case for supposedly spreading the
> secret of the atom bomb to the Soviet Union.
>
> Tremendous evidence has been published in volumes of books pointing
> to the innocence of the Rosenbergs. Looking back through history, it is
> clear that the Rosenbergs were in fact framed and scapegoated in one of
> the most brutal extensions of McCarthy Era anti-Communist hysteria.
> The execution of the Rosenbergs was part of a psychological warfare
> campaign being waged against Communists, particularly in the Jewish
> community. They were put to death because of the depth of their
> courage, integrity, and commitment to social, political, and economic
> justice.[11]

The thread that binds together the stories of Mumia, the Rosenbergs, and
the Exodus from Egypt is that they all teach us about the weight of oppression
and the righteousness of struggling for justice. As we have noted, many
Haggadot expand the liberatory message of Passover to be of relevance to
other communities and struggles. These Haggadot, however, form only part of
the picture. The origin of Passover is in the Torah itself, the basis of our faith.

We believe that it is important to engage with this text, and especially necessary because so few politically radical Jews engage in Torah study. The two of us have been studying Torah, and have found many aspects of it that inspire our commitment to political struggle, as well as some aspects that trouble us.

Our reading of Exodus teaches us that the redemption of the Jews could not have happened without acts of resistance on the part of the people. At the beginning of the Exodus story, Pharaoh gives the order to kill all male Jewish babies, which rabbinical commentary interprets as declaring war against the Jews. When Shifrah and Puah, the two midwives, refuse to follow Pharaoh's orders, their civil disobedience is the first step in the liberation process. Later, the text relates another step in this process. The portion reads, "When they [the Jews] cried out because of their slavery, their pleas went up before G-d. G-d heard their cries and [G-d] remembered [G-d's] covenant with Abraham, Isaac, and Jacob" (Exodus 2:23–24). This reminds us that for G-d to join our side, we must make noise and protest in the face of oppression.

We know that we do not act alone when we fight for justice. We are reminded that Moses finds the strength to act righteously because of G-d's presence. When Moses expresses doubts about his ability to confront Pharaoh and lead the Jews out of Egypt, G-d answers him that Moses does have the strength, "Because I will be with you" (Exodus 3:12). Moses continues to express doubts about his ability to speak to Pharaoh, and G-d tells him, "I will be with your mouth and teach you what to say" (Exodus 4:12). As Moses and the Jewish slaves did, we take courage from the presence of the Divine in our lives and our struggles.

However, even before G-d speaks to him, Moses demonstrates that he will not tolerate injustice. Rabbi Nachshoni notes that the Torah presents three events in Moses' life that occur before G-d sends Moses to bring the Jews out of Egypt. First, Moses kills an Egyptian overseer who is beating a Jewish slave; second, he admonishes the wrongdoer in a quarrel between two Jews; and third, he comes to the aid of Jethro's daughters in Midian. Thus when G-d speaks to him at the burning bush, Moses already knows in his heart that he must return to Egypt to help the Jews fight for freedom. Moses becomes the redeemer of Israel because he already stands against injustice. We learn that we do not have to wait to be chosen by G-d; instead we must start action now, and then G-d will give us strength.

Even though G-d is on our side in our struggles for justice, G-d does not provide easy paths to freedom. At the first signs of trouble, when Aaron and Moses initially confront Pharaoh, Pharaoh punishes all the Jews by intensifying the exploitation of the slaves: "You will not be given any straw, but you must deliver your quota of bricks" (Exodus 5:18). This prompts Moses to question G-d: "O Lord, why do You mistreat Your people? Why did You send me? As soon as I came to Pharaoh to speak in Your name, he made things worse for these people. You have done nothing to help Your people" (Exodus 5:22–23). We learn from the Torah that G-d will not spare us the process of oppression and liberation; instead we must work hand in hand with G-d for justice.

Through engaging with the text of the Torah, we also found some troubling aspects that do not sit well with our political and theological beliefs. Although not a focus of most Seders, the Exodus story in the Torah is full of references to the Promised Land, a land waiting exclusively for the Jews. For example, Exodus 13:5 reads, "There will come a time when G-d will bring you to the land of the Canaanites, Hittites, Amorites, Hivites, and Yebusites. [G-d] swore to your ancestors that [G-d] would give it to you—a land flowing with milk and honey." The notion that the Jews historically deserve Eretz Yisrael for ourselves, even though other people are already living there, is repeated throughout the Torah, and echoed in the traditional Haggadot by the closing words, "Next year in Jerusalem!" Both before and since the creation of the state of Israel, many Zionists have clung tight to the words of the Torah, declaring that this land is promised to us, and only to us, by G-d.

There is no empty land, however, waiting for one group of people to settle. There is no "land of milk and honey" destined for one chosen community. We reject this logic of colonialism, the logic upon which this country and much of the world is built, and in the service of which G-d's name is often invoked. We believe that we must engage in the hard work of sharing land and power in a just manner. No group has the right to oppress other people in the name of G-d. As part of our commitment to anti-racist, anti-imperialist alliances, we stand in solidarity with the Palestinian people whose land is being occupied, and whose rights are taken away by the Israeli state. In this spirit, the Seder in the Streets ended with the words:

> In Hebrew, the literal translation of Israel is the vision of a peaceful
> land, but the Israel of today is a country embittered by racism, inequity,
> and violence. We stand in solidarity with the people of Palestine and
> call for peace and justice in Israel and Palestine. . . . This year we live in
> a world at war with itself, a world in agony; next year may we celebrate
> in a world at peace and a world made free.

The Exodus story is an inspirational tale, but also a complicated story that requires critical engagement. We must face our troubled histories and our present, and look honestly at the weight of racism and ethnocentrism in our communities. As Aurora Levins Morales, a mixed-heritage Puerto Rican Jew, writes:

> We were slaves in Egypt, say the words we are taught to remember, and we were exiles in Babylon, never to forget the days of our bondage, the years of weeping, but no one told us there was a choice about how to remember these facts, or that our survival would depend upon that choice. That we could use the memory of pain to sharpen our vision of freedom, to hold tight to that vision, trace with our fear and sorrow a map to show us exactly what total liberation would look like; or surrender the vision for the vengeance, hug to our chests the pain too heavy to let go, count and recount each blow, each bruise, each death and despoiling, reckon up what is due.[12]

The Seder in the Streets was an attempt to use our history "to sharpen our vision of freedom," rather than to search for vengeance. As Jews and queers who inherit histories of oppression and resistance, we take these words to heart, fighting for justice in times of slavery and in times of freedom. We continue to draw strength from these words in the Seder in the Streets Haggadah: "[I]n time of freedom we must not forget the bitterness of slavery; in time of oppression we must keep alive the hope of freedom, not only for ourselves, but for others as well.[13]

As observant Jews, we are committed to engaging with our biblical traditions and the teachings of the Torah with the conviction that G-d is on the side of the oppressed and dispossessed. As queer Jews, we embrace the opportunity to make religious practice relevant to those who have traditionally been excluded. As white Jews, we are committed to challenging racism in white communities, within the Jewish community, and in Israel/Palestine. As politically conscious Jews, we are committed to examining the Torah for inspiration and guidance, and also to wrestling and speaking out against the parts with which we do not agree. Most of all, in our daily lives, we are moved and guided by the belief that holiness and justice are intimately connected.

NOTES

This essay is dedicated, with love and respect, to everyone who organized the Seder in the Streets: Ilana Berger, Julie Browne, Maria Cordero, Amanda Enoch, Sara Flocks, Adam Gold, Harmony Goldberg, Margot Goldstein, Stefan Goldstone, Rachel Lanzerotti, Liza Oppenheim, Janel Stead, Rachel Timoner, and Risa Wallach.

1. *Let My People Go! Seder in the Streets Haggadah,* 1999, p. 1. Throughout this essay, we have made some minor edits to the original text of the Haggadah.

2. See John D'Emilio, *Sexual Politics, Sexual Communities: The Making of a Homosexual Minority in the United States, 1940-1970* (Chicago: University of Chicago Press, 1983), pp. 41–43, for a good description of the connections between anti-Communism and homophobia.

3. Melanie Kaye/Kantrowitz, "Jews in the US: The Rising Cost of Whiteness" in *Names We Call Home,* Becky Thompson and Sangeeta Tyagi, eds. (New York and London: Routledge, 1996), p. 122.

4. Ibid., p. 125.

5. Cornel West, *The Cornel West Reader* (New York: Basic Civitas Books, 1999), p. 436.

6. Howard Zinn, *A People's History of the United States* (New York: The New Press, 1997 [1980]), p. 132.

7. Alfred J. Kolatch, *The Jewish Book of Why* (Middle Village, NY: Jonathan David Publishers, Inc., 1995 [1981]), p. 198.

8. In particular, we drew from Arthur Waskow, et al., *The Shalom Seders* (New York: Adama Books, 1984) and *A Humanist Haggadah for Passover,* compiled by Machor, the Washington, D.C. Area Congregation for Humanistic Judaism, 1996 edition.

9. *Let My People Go,* op. cit., p. 2.

10. Ibid., pp. 8–9.

11. Ibid., p. 6.

12. Aurora Levins Morales and Rosario Morales, *Getting Home Alive* (Ithaca, NY: Firebrand Books, 1986), p. 204.

13. *Let My People Go,* op. cit., p. 9. Adapted from *The Shalom Seders,* op. cit., p. 65.

GLOSSARY

Adonai: masculine word for God.

aliyah: honor in which one is called up to the Torah to recite a blessing before a reading.

alte kakers: older people (Yiddish).

Amidah: Central prayer in Jewish services, consisting of 18 sections, which is always said while standing.

bachurim/bochers: boys or students, as in "yeshiva bochers" (Hebrew/Yiddish).

bashert: meant to be, soulmate (Yiddish).

Bat/Bar Mitzvah: ceremonial rite of passage for adolescents, in which they are welcomed into the Jewish community as adults with full obligations and responsibilities.

bimah: stage where the Torah is chanted.

brachah/brachot: blessing(s).

brit milah/bris: circumcision ceremony 8 days after a boy's birth (Hebrew/Yiddish).

bubbe: grandmother (Yiddish).

challah: bread eaten on the Sabbath and holidays.

Chassidism/Chassids: ultra-Orthodox sect that emphasizes an emotional relationship to God.

chevruta: Talmud study partners.

chuppa/huppa: wedding canopy.

daven: to pray (Yiddish).

feygeleh: little bird/darling/fairy or faggot (Yiddish).

galut: the diaspora.

Gemara: a section of the Talmud.

goyische: pejorative for Gentile or non-Jewish person (Yiddish).

Habonim: literally "the builders"; a socialist Zionist camping movement for children and adolescents.

haftarah: text chanted at every Sabbath morning service.

Haggadah: text read during Passover recounting the Exodus from Egypt.

halacha/halachic: the written law that governs Jewish observance.

hamantaschen/hammentaschen: three-cornered pastry eaten during Purim, the Feast of Lots (Hebrew/Yiddish).

heymish: Warm and comfortable, folksy, homey (Yiddish).

Kaddish: mourner's prayer.

kavannah: intention, concentration.

ketubah: written marriage contract.

kippa(h): yarmulke, head covering.

Kol Nidre: service that ushers in Yom Kippur.

Kotel: the Western Wall in Jerusalem.

kvell: to be filled with pride (Yiddish).

mechitzah: partition that separates women's from men's sections in Orthodox synagogues .

mensch: a good person (Yiddish).

meshugas: craziness (Hebrew/Yiddish).

midrash: an interpretation of a biblical story.

mikveh: ritual bath.

minyan: quorum of ten people required for public prayer.

Mi sheberach: blessing of healing for those who are ill.

Mishnah: a section of the Talmud.

mishpacha/mishpukha: family (Hebrew/Yiddish).

mitzvah/mitzvot: obligation, often confused with "good deeds."

mohel: person who performs circumcisions.

naches: joy or pride (Yiddish).

negiah: prohibition against touching between women and men.

Neilah: service that concludes Yom Kippur.

niddah: The laws of "family purity" that govern women's menstruation, immersion in the *mikveh*, and sexual contact between Orthodox women and men.

payos/payes: side curls, worn by some Orthodox men.

Pesach: Passover.

rebbetzin/rebbetsin: a person married to a rabbi.

Rosh Chodesh: the beginning of the month, often marked in Jewish feminist circles by a ritual or celebration for women.

Rosh Hashana: the Jewish new year.

ruach: spirit, wind, also a word for God.

schritzing: sweating (Yiddish).

Seder: ritual and meal conducted on the Passover holiday.

Shabbat/Shabbos/Shabbes: the Jewish Sabbath (Hebrew/Yiddish).

shamos: sexton, beadle of the synagogue; also, a policeman (slang).

Shechina: feminine expression for God.

Shehechiyanu: blessing to give thanks for reaching a particular milestone or holiday.

sheva brachot: the seven blessings recited at Jewish weddings.

shiksa: pejorative for non-Jewish woman (Yiddish).

shmata: rag, anything worthless (Yiddish).

shtetl: Jewish village.

shul: synagogue or temple (Yiddish).

simchas: celebrations.

streimel: fur hat, worn by men in some ultra-Orthodox sects.

tallit: prayer shawl.

Talmud: an encyclopaedic text of Jewish knowledge, compiled over several centuries, comprised of many volumes, including the Mishnah, the Gemara, and the Tosafot.

tefillin: phylacteries worn during morning prayers.

tikkun olam: literally, to repair the world, a central concept in Judaism obligating Jews to engage in social justice.

treif: unkosher.

tzedakah: charity or philathropy.

yahrzeit: memorial or anniversary of someone's death.

yeshiva: Jewish institution of higher learning.

yiddishkeit: Jewishness (Yiddish).

yontif: Jewish holiday (Yiddish).

CONTRIBUTORS

ABOUT THE EDITORS

Caryn Aviv currently directs the Program for Collaborative Care at the University of California, San Francisco Breast Care Center. Aviv's recently completed doctoral dissertation, *Home-making: Gender, Emotional Zionism, and American Immigration to Israel*, investigates the gendered and emotional dimensions of transnational migration and American diasporic communities in Israel. She has published articles on the politics of breast cancer and women's health, global immigration, feminist theory, Orthodox Jewish communities, gender and sexuality. She is collaborating with Lynn Davidman, associate professor of sociology at Brown University, on a new book examining Jewish identity, race, and multiculturalism.

David Shneer is assistant professor of history and Judaic studies at the University of Denver, and was the education director of Congregation Shaʼar Zahav in San Francisco. His forthcoming book, *Revolution in the Making: Yiddish and the Creation of Soviet Jewish Culture,* examines the relationship between language, identity, and political power in the creation of modern Jewish cultures. He and Aviv are currently at work on their next project titled "Rooted Cosmopolitans" which examines how Russian, North American, and Israeli Jews struggle with and resist the idea of diaspora. He has written several articles on modern Jewish culture, and was visiting lecturer at the

University of California, Davis, and the Graduate Theological Union in Berkeley. He lives in Denver, Colorado, with his husband, Gregg.

ABOUT THE CONTRIBUTORS

Anonymous is an advanced rabbinical student. He holds several advanced degrees in the humanities. He has worked with Jewish HIV and AIDS patients and looks forward to ordination and a chance to work to advance Jewish gay and lesbian causes.

Christie Balka is executive director of the Bread and Roses Community Fund and founding member of Congregation Mishkan Shalom, both of Philadelphia. She coedited, with Avi Rose, *Twice Blessed: On Being Lesbian or Gay and Jewish*, published by Beacon Press, in 1989.

Marla Brettschneider is a professor of Political Philosophy at the University of New Hampshire with a joint appointment in political science and women's studies. Her publications include *Democratic Theorizing from the Margins*, *Cornerstones of Peace: Jewish Identity Politics and Democratic Theory*, *The Narrow Bridge: Jewish Views on Multiculturalism* with a forward by Cornel West and winner of the Gustavus Meyers Human Rights Award, and *Race, Gender, and Class: American Jewish Perspectives*.

Ali Cannon, a transgender man who identified as a butch dyke for almost 20 years, is a writer of short stories, poetry, and theater pieces. He appeared in and is the assistant producer of the film *It's a Boy: Journeys from Female to Male*. His writing is published in the anthology *Secret Sisters: Stories of Being Lesbian and Bisexual in a College Sorority*. Most importantly, Ali celebrates his life as a newlywed; he is still *kvelling* over his marriage to his beautiful bisexual wife, Jessica, who has been an amazing supportive partner in his transition process.

Joanne Cohen studied sociology and philosophy at the University of Toronto and is now pursuing graduate studies in social and political thought at York University (Toronto). Her interests include theories of identity construction, ideology and social controls, power and resistance, moral regulation, and ethical community development. In 1996 to 1997, she served as list manager for Nice Jewish Girls, a vibrant international internet community of lesbian and bisexual Jewish women, which strengthened her personal, academic, and political queer Jewish identity and communal involvement. She has recently been appointed as the first gay representative to the Candian Jewish Congress. Her essay is dedicated to the memory of Johnny Abush, a passionate queer Jewish activist and colleague.

Sandi Simcha Dubowski is a filmmaker and writer based in New York. His current film, *Trembling Before G-d,* currently in a smash theatrical release in the U.S. with New Yorker Films, has been the recipient of over ten prizes including the Teddy Award for Best Documentary at the Berlin Film Festival and the Mayor's Prize for the Jewish Experience at the Jerusalem Film Festival. He is a recipient of the Rockefeller Foundation's 1999 Film/Video/ Multimedia Fellowship. He recently received a grant from Steven Spielberg's Righteous Persons Foundation to launch a *Trembling Before G-d* Orthodox community education and outreach project, and, with Working Films, is launching a tour of Christian theological seminaries in the American South.

Hadar Dubowsky is a Ph.D. student in educational thought and sociocultural studies at the University of New Mexico. She has taught middle school for the past six years, and currently teaches at the Solomon Schechter Day School of Albuquerque. She has published numerous articles in *Lilith* magazine and assorted feminist and queer journals and zines and is a mother to Rafael Ma'ayan.

Jyl Lynn Felman is assistant professor of women's studies at Brandeis University. Her one-woman show, *If Only I'd Been Born a Kosher Chicken*, has been aired on C-Span, and her previous books include *Hot Chicken Wings*, a Lambda Literary Award Finalist; *Cravings*, a memoir; and, most recently, *Never a Dull Moment: Teaching and the Art of Performance.*

Steven Greenberg is a rabbi and senior teaching fellow at CLAL, a national organization for Jewish learning. He received his B.A. in philosophy from Yeshiva University and his rabbinical ordination from Rabbi Isaac Elchanan Theological Seminary. He is a graduate of the Jerusalem Fellows program, a two-year fellowship for senior Jewish educators from all over the world sponsored by the Mandel Institute. Steve was on the curriculum development team of KOLOT, a new organization that empowers Israeli economic, political, educational, and cultural leaders to meet the challenges of contemporary Israeli society. Steve also serves as the educational advisor of the Jerusalem Open House, a cutting-edge organization advancing the cause of social tolerance in the Holy City. Steve has finished a book on the subject of Judaism and homosexuality to be published in 2002, titled *Wrestling with God and Men.*

Jo Hirschmann is a writer and long-time social justice activist who recently moved from the Bay Area to New York City.

Ruti Kadish is a postdoctoral Israel studies fellow at the Meyerhoff Center for Jewish Studies at the University of Maryland, College Park. Her recently completed dissertation is titled "Mothers and Soldiers: Israeli Lesbian and Gay Negotiations of Jewish, National, and Sexual Identity." She and her partner, Nicole Berner, and their sons, Mattan and Naveh, live in the Washington, D.C., lesbian mom outpost of Takoma Park, Maryland.

Jaron Kanegson lives in Berkeley, California, with her dogs, Hershey, Ruby, and Bear. Jaron is the founding executive director of Youth Gender Project in Berkeley, California, an organization by and for transgender, transsexual, intersex, genderqueer, and questioning (TGIQ) youth and young adults (*www.youthgenderproject.org*), and a second grade teacher at Congregation Sha'ar Zahav in San Francisco. Jaron also teaches classes in creative writing for youth, Jewish folktales, and other stuff at the Harvey Milk Institute in San Francisco and elsewhere, and has had work published in various anthologies and literary magazines including *On the Page* and *Spoonfed Amerika.* Jaron has an M.A. in English/creative writing from San Francisco State University, a B.A. in women's studies from U.C. Berkeley, and generally likes to avoid gendered pronouns.

Inbal Kashtan has a master's degree in Jewish Studies from the Graduate Theological Union. Her master's thesis, "Fissures, Hermeneutics, and Ideology: Reading Women in Rabbinic Midrash," explores texts about women from *Sifre Bamidbar.* She is also the Parenting Project coordinator at the Center for Nonviolent Communication (NVC) and leads public workshops as well as trainings in schools and organizations. Her work most recently appeared in *Mothering* magazine, and she is currently working on a book on parenting. She and her partner, Kathy Simon, are the mothers of a vibrant son, Yannai.

Jonathan Krasner is a doctoral candidate in American Jewish history at Brandeis University. He also chairs the history department at the New Jewish High School, in Waltham, Massachusetts. Jonathan lives with his partner, Frank Tipton, in Newton, Massachusetts, and is active at Temple Israel, a gay-friendly Reform synagogue in Boston.

Jane Rachel Litman has consulted with the National Council of Churches, the Metropolitan Community Church, and numerous Jewish institutions on religious education for alternative families including GLBT, interfaith, multiracial, and single-parent families. She is the rabbi educator at Congregation Beth El in Berkeley. Prior to that, she served gay outreach congregations Kol Simcha and Sha'ar Zahav for eight years. She has taught religious and women's studies at California State University Northridge and Loyola Marymount College. She is the coeditor of *Lifecycles 2*, and a regular columnist for Jewish and gender issues for *Beliefnet.com*.

TJ Michels is an editor and writer living in Washington, D.C., whose articles have appeared in both the Jewish and gay presses. In addition to teaching classes on transgender theory for the Harvey Milk Institute in San Francisco, she has presented academically on topics relating to dyke masculinity, feminism, and queer theory. TJ thinks her Bubby Tootsie's love and mondelbrodt inspired her to be the Jew she is today, and that her older sister Mindy's love and mentoring inspired her to be the queer she is today. God made it possible to be both.

Jill Nagle is a queer Jewish writer, speaker, and sex-positive activist. She has published widely on issues ranging from queer sex spaces and the feminist politics of sex work to white supremacy and white queer identity. She is a passionate and charismatic advocate for sexual freedoms like abortion rights, GLBT liberation, and S/M. Her editing credits include *The Female Fag*, an anthology of writings by women who identify with man-on-man sexual desires, practices, or presentations; *Male Lust: Obsessions, Transformations and Politics*; and *Whores and Other Feminists*, an anthology of writings by feminist sex workers, among other publications.

Joan Nestle was born in the Bronx, New York City, in 1940 to a widowed Jewish mother, and came out as a fem in the working-class bars of Greenwich Village in the late 1950s. She protested the HUAC [House Un-American

Activities Committee], and the Vietnam War; marched against nuclear war, segregation, apartheid, and U.S. involvement in Central America; and demonstrated for women's rights including abortion and gay liberation. In 1973, Joan became cofounder of the Lesbian Herstory Archives. In 1979, she started writing erotic stories and in 1982, ran afoul of the anti-pornography movement, thus becoming a fervent pro-sex activist in the "Sex Wars." In 1966, she started teaching writing in the SEEK Program at Queens College and did not stop until cancer forced her to retire in 1995. She is the author and editor of innumerable books, anthologies, articles, essays, short stories, and poems, including *A Fragile Union: New and Collected Writings* (1998), *A Restricted Country* (1988), *The Persistent Desire: A Femme-Butch Reader* (1992), *Sister and Brother: Lesbians and Gay Men Write about Their Lives Together* (coedited with John Preston, 1994), and *Best Lesbian Erotica* (coedited with Tristan Taormino, 1999).

Lesléa Newman has published 40 books for adults and children, many of which explore Jewish and lesbian themes. Her titles include the novel *In Every Laugh a Tear*; the short story collections *A Letter to Harvey Milk, Girls Will Be Girls*, and *She Loves Me, She Loves Me Not*; and the audiobook *Just Like a Woman*; the poetry collection *Still Life with Buddy* and *Signs of Love*. She has also published children's books, including *Matzo Ball Moon, Remember That, Too Far Away to Touch*, and *Heather Has Two Mommies*. Visit www.lesleanewman.com to learn more about her work.

Avi Rose is a longtime activist in the Jewish, GLBT, and HIV/AIDS communities. Avi coedited *Twice Blessed: On Being Lesbian or Gay and Jewish*, published by Beacon Press in 1989, and has been a frequent speaker on GLBT and HIV/AIDS issues for the past two decades. Avi holds a B.A. from Brandeis University and master's degrees from Hebrew Union College and the University of Southern California. He currently serves on the board of The Shefa Fund and is former cochair of New Jewish Agenda. Avi has worked as a social worker, psychotherapist, and nonprofit administrator and currently works as an organizational consultant. He lives with his partner and son in Oakland, California.

Eve Sicular is a drummer and bandleader of Metropolitan Klezmer and the all-female Isle of Klezbos sextet, and has produced their award-winning CDs *Mosaic Persuasion* and *Yiddish for Travelers*. A former curator of the film and photo archives at the YIVO Institute for Jewish Research, she wrote her thesis, "Ideology & Montage: The Early Works of Esfir' [Esther] Shub, Soviet Film Documentarian," for the Department of Russian History & Literature at Harvard. Her writings on the celluloid closet of Yiddish film have been published in *Davka, Mix* magazine (Toronto), *Lilith, Jewish Folklore & Ethnology Review,* and the British anthology *When Joseph Met Molly: A Reader of Yiddish Film* from Five Leaves Publications. A native Manhattanite, she lives ten F-train stops from her partner, clarinet/saxophonist Debra Kreisberg.

Elizabeth Wilson is an educator and youth worker in New York City. She is active with Jews Against the Occupation.

oscar wolfman is currently completing his Ph.D. in sociology at York University, Toronto, Canada. His work centers on sexuality and its intersections with institutional structures. Sometimes, oscar is a gay Jew; other times he is a Jewish gay. But he is al(l)ways both.

INDEX

288   INDEX

Lesbian and Gay Center, 213n
Lesbian Avengers, 210
Lesbian Rabbis: The First Generation
     (Rebecca Alpert, Sue Levi Elwell, and
     Shirley Idelson), 4
Lesbian Review of Books, 33
Liberation movement, 4, 6, 8, 17, 24,
     196, 258–259, 262, 264–268
Lilith *magazine*, *48, 209*
Lillith, 65
Los Angeles, 139
Luna Sea, *94*
Maariv, 43
Maine, 238–239, 250, 252, 256n
Marxism, 8
Marriage
     anti-, 10, 14n, 25
     aufrufs, 144
     birkat erusin, 150
     commitment ceremonies, 4, 19, 31,
          170n, 177, 210
     huppah, 31, 95, 112–113, 115, 150,
          154, 180
     institution of, 6–7, 38, 111, 150, 164,
          173, 191, 228, 233
     intermarriage, 203
     Jewish Weddings, 112, 148, 167
     ketubah, 96, 112–113, 117, 151–152,
          178
     legalizing same-sex, 10
     mixed gender weddings, 114–115, 181
     recognizing marriage across borders,
          234n
     same-sex weddings, 3, 14n, 111–114,
          116–118, 144, 149, 160, 172–173,
          178, 180–181
     transgender people and, 95–96, 117
Masculinity, 8, 56, 85, 94, 203, 225–226,
     228, 230, 234
Mechitzah, 91–92, 97, 167
Metropolitan Community Church, 118
Mexico, 219, 220
     Mexico City Jewish Community

Center, 219
Michigan Womyn's Music Festival, *see*
     Music
Midrash, 66, 152, 189, 266
Mintzer, Phyllis, 139
Monogamy, *see* Sex
Moore, Tracey, *Lesbiot*, 4, 231
Mormons, 189–190, 216
Mt. Holyoke College, 29
Museum of Modern Art (MoMA),
     206–207
Music, 210
     Eurovision Music Contest, 14n, 227
     Klezcamp, *205–206, 209*
     Klezmatics, 202
     Klezmer, 31, 200, 203, 205, 214n
     Michigan Womyn's Music Festival,
          111
     parade songs, 126
National Center for Jewish Film, *see* Film
National Coming Out Day, 212
Native Americans, 52
New Hampshire, 238–239, 252
New Israel Fund, 121
New Jewish Agenda, 214n
New Mexico, 46–47
New York, 4, 32, 37, 39, 139, 260
     Bronx, 58, 190, 207
     Brooklyn, 192, 220
     Catskills, 205, 207
     Greenwich Village, 6, 24, 131, 196,
          200, 214n
     Lower East Side, 202
     New York Times, 7, 26, 124
     Soho, 40
Newman Lesléa, 6, 17
Nice Jewish Girls: A Lesbian Anthology, 4,
     16, 19
Non-monogamy, *see* Sex; Marriage, anti-
North America, 3–4, 12, 183–184
Nostalgia, 199
Obscenity, 25
Oppression, 5, 9, 10, 12, 24, 93, 111, 146,

Lightning Source UK Ltd.
Milton Keynes UK
UKOW052006261112

202814UK00005B/97/P